LIFE IN THE LAW

SERVICE & INTEGRITY

EDITED BY
SCOTT W. CAMERON, GALEN L. FLETCHER,
and JANE H. WISE

J. REUBEN CLARK LAW SOCIETY
BRIGHAM YOUNG UNIVERSITY LAW SCHOOL
PROVO, UTAH

Photos courtesy of L. Tom Perry Special Collections, Harold B. Lee Library, Brigham Young University, Provo, Utah (MSS 303). Captions are as follows:

(1) Title Page: Joshua Reuben Clark Jr. (1871–1961) [JRC], second from left, as U.S. Ambassador to Mexico (1930–1933) presenting his credentials to President Ortiz Rubio, Mexico City, Nov. 28, 1930.
(2) Page 1 (Be Ethical): JRC on steamship S.S. *Ile de France,* Dec. 1935.
(3) Page 63 (Be Healers): JRC and his wife, Luacine S. Clark (1871–1944), at organization of Oahu Stake, Honolulu, July 12, 1935.
(4) Page 127 (Be Professional): JRC in New York City, early 1935; photo by Blackstone.
(5) Page 185 (Be Servants): JRC at ranch in Grantsville, Utah, 1942.
(6) Page 247 (J. Reuben Clark Law School): JRC in Salt Lake City, Jan. 19, 1960; photo by Ralph Clark for Lorin F. Wheelwright; this photo hangs in the Moot Court Room of the J. Reuben Clark Law School.

To contact the J. Reuben Clark Law School or the J. Reuben Clark Law Society, write to 341 JRCB, Brigham Young University, PO Box 28000, Provo, Utah 84602.

Library of Congress Cataloging-in-Publication Data
Life in the law : service & integrity / edited by Scott W. Cameron, Galen L. Fletcher, and Jane H. Wise.
   p. cm.
   Includes index.
     ISBN 978-0-8425-2738-5 (hard cover : alk. paper)
     ISBN 978-0-8425-2741-5 (paper back : alk. paper)
   1. Legal ethics. 2. Lawyers—Religious life. 3. Law—Moral and ethical aspects. 4. Religion and law. 5. Christian ethics—Mormon authors. 6. Church of Jesus Christ of Latter-day Saints—Doctrines. 7. J. Reuben Clark Law School—History. I. Cameron, Scott W. (Scott Wallace), 1946– II. Fletcher, Galen L. (Galen LeGrande), 1961– III. Wise, Jane H., 1951– IV. J. Reuben Clark Law Society.

K123.L545 2009
174'.3--dc22

                                   2009027883

Printed in the United States of America
10 9 8 7 6 5 4 3 2

Contents

Preface

An ethical life in the law is both a process *and* a product. This collection of talks is designed to assist law students and attorneys in their work to be moral healers, professionals, and servants in the law. Some of the speeches focus on the process of being ethical or competent. They speak to the practical and spiritual decisions that professionals make to become better. Other talks touch on the results of moral choices for Christian lawyers, holding them up as worthy goals.

The book's categories, "Be Ethical," "Be Healers," "Be Professional," and "Be Servants," address what lives of service and integrity in the law can look like. Each of these categories has aspects of both process and product. Our hope is that the readers will become ethical lawyers, constantly striving in the process and always improving themselves as the product. In addition, at the end of this volume are a set of materials specific to J. Reuben Clark Law School, an institution founded to leaven the loaf of the legal profession and society, a continual process and a never-ending product.

This volume seeks to perpetuate the memory and name of J. Reuben Clark Jr., a man of integrity, who constantly improved himself throughout his life by serving others. This book is *not* about him, although seven photos are included and he is profiled substantially in two chapters (see pages 225–38 and 287–89). Rather, this volume shows the legacy being created by good men and women associated with the two institutions that carry his name: J. Reuben Clark Law School and the J. Reuben Clark Law Society. Most of these chapters originally were talks given at BYU Law School, at Clark Society events, or at Brigham Young University and published in the *Clark Memorandum*. This book is a successor volume to an earlier compilation, *Life in the Law: Answering God's Interrogatories* (2002).

Many individuals assisted in the process of producing this book. For their enthusiastic support we thank the recent deans of BYU Law School (Kevin J Worthen, James D. Gordon III, and James R. Rasband) and the chairs of the J. Reuben Clark Law Society (Lew Cramer, Joseph Bentley, Brent Belnap, and Nancy VanSlooten). For their significant help in many ways, we thank: Kevin J. Abbott, Dave Eliason, Joyce Janetski, Tyler Lake, Doug Maxwell, Natalie Miles, Bjorn Pendleton (cover design), Adrian Selle, and Rebecca Wood. Finally, a special thank-you goes to Jeanette Befus and the Law School accounting staff for their tireless service with the prior, current, and future volumes of *Life in the Law*.

Scott W. Cameron
Galen L. Fletcher
Jane H. Wise

BE ETHICAL

How Do We Practice Our Religion While We Practice?

Thomas B. Griffith

I was asked to speak at a J. Reuben Clark Law Society event in Portland, Oregon, as a last-minute fill-in replacement for Senator Gordon Smith, who couldn't attend because he was participating in the Senate's debate over the Iraq War resolution. All agreed that his absence was excused. I knew that the audience would be bitterly disappointed to settle for me in the place of Senator Smith, and, wanting to lessen their disappointment to the extent that I could, I decided that I would take a stab at the topic he had chosen for the day, "How Do We Practice Our Religion While We Practice?" I found the exercise of addressing that topic to be helpful to me. I hope that you find it helpful to you.

Senator Smith's question is, I believe, an acknowledgment that certain endeavors in this life entail greater spiritual risks than do others. Now, I realize that there are spiritual risks in all human activities, including church work. No less an authority than Screwtape himself observed, "Nowhere do we tempt so successfully as on the very steps of the altar" (C. S. Lewis, "Screwtape Proposes a Toast," *The Screwtape Letters* [New York: Macmillan, 1961], 172). Remember the Lord's warning to us in D&C 121 about the unrighteous use of the priesthood: "We have learned by *sad experience* that it is the nature and disposition of *almost all men* . . . to exercise unrighteous dominion" (D&C 121:39, emphasis added). Why, you may be surprised to learn that there are even spiritual risks that come in working at BYU!

It doesn't seem to me to be a very controversial proposition that *some* professional activities expose our souls to *greater* risks than do others. I

3

believe the Savior was warning us of this fact of life when He said, "I tell you the truth, it is hard for a rich man to enter the kingdom of heaven. . . . [I]t is easier for a camel to go through the eye of a needle than for a rich man to enter the kingdom of God" (Matthew 19: 23–24 NIV). Thomas Jefferson was certain that farmers, by virtue of their unique economic activity, were better prepared than any of us here today to contribute in a positive way to a republican form of government. (See, e.g., Thomas Jefferson, *Notes on the State of Virginia,* "Query XIX" [1787]: "Those who labour in the earth are the chosen people of God, if ever he had a chosen people, whose breasts he has made his peculiar deposit for substantial and genuine virtue. . . . The mobs of great cities add just so much to the support of pure government, as sores do to the strength of the human body. It is the manners and spirit of a people which preserve a republic in vigour. A degeneracy in these is a canker which soon eats to the heart of its laws and constitution.")

Even our own church leaders have acknowledged that some careers lend themselves more easily to the religious life than do others. I remember attending the sessions of general conference at which James E. Faust and Grant Bangerter were first called to be General Authorities. Elder Faust noted that prior to his call, he had been a lawyer. He then remarked that since his call, he had been repenting of that (James E. Faust, "To Become One of the Fishers," *Ensign,* January 1973, 81). Elder Bangerter, by contrast, noted that prior to his call, he had been a carpenter. For some reason, he said, he had not felt quite the same need to repent (William Grant Bangerter, "The People Who Influence Us," *Ensign,* May 1975, 39).

In *A Man for All Seasons,* his play based on the life of St. Thomas More, the patron saint of lawyers and politicians, Robert Bolt contrasts the public life of Thomas More, a Christ-figure who is a lawyer (I know that must require a significant suspension of disbelief for many of you), with that of Richard Rich, a pathetic Judas-figure. At the opening of the play, we are allowed to overhear a spirited discussion at the house of More in Chelsea. More's house had become a center of the New Learning taking hold in 16th-century England. Rich is a hanger-on in this distinguished company, envious of the prominence of More, who is the most respected man in England and is soon to become Henry VIII's lord chancellor—the highest appointed office in the realm. Forgive my inadequate attempts at acting.

RICH: (*Enthusiastically pursuing an argument.*) But every man has his price.
MORE: No, no!
RICH: But, yes! In money, too.
MORE: (*With gentle impatience.*) No, no, no!
RICH: Or pleasure. Titles, women, bricks and mortar, there's always something.
MORE: Childish.
[Robert Bolt, *A Man for All Seasons* 4 (1962)]

Rich then complains that despite his friendship with More he has been unable to find a political position. He wants More's recommendation, which he is confident will be the key to unlocking the door that is blocking his ascent to power. More, knowing Rich to be a weak, self-centered man, refuses to recommend him to government office. Instead:

MORE: The Dean of St. Paul's offers you a post; with a house, a servant, and fifty pounds a year.
RICH: What? What post?
MORE: At the new school.
RICH: (*Bitterly disappointed.*) A teacher!
MORE: A man should go where he won't be tempted. . . . Why not be a teacher? You'd be a fine teacher. Perhaps—a great one.
RICH: And if I was who would know it?
MORE: You, your pupils, your friends. God—not a bad public, that. Oh, and a *quiet* life.
[*Id.* at 5, 6]

Rich rejects More's suggestion that he be a teacher, and by the end of the play he loses his soul. Rich yearns for worldly power and prestige. Because More will not aid that pursuit, Rich turns to More's enemy Thomas Cromwell, secretary to the king. Cromwell willingly appoints Rich to a series of government positions in exchange for Rich's undivided loyalty. As you know, More's refusal to support Henry's declaration of himself as head of the church in England—a stand born of his conviction that the Pope was the rightful successor to St. Peter as the head of the church—cost him his life. And it was the perjured testimony of Richard Rich, elicited by Cromwell at More's trial for treason, that led to his death.

Upon hearing Rich's perjury at that trial, a disheartened More knows that his fate has been sealed. Exercising his right to examine the witness, however, More responds:

MORE: I have one question to ask the witness. That's a chain of office you are wearing. (*Rich reluctantly faces More.*) May I see it? (*Norfolk, the presiding officer at the trial, motions Rich to approach. More examines the medallion.*) The red dragon. (*To Cromwell.*) What's this?
CROMWELL: Sir Richard is appointed Attorney General for Wales.
MORE: (*Looking into Rich's face; with pain and amusement.*) For Wales? Why, Richard, it profits a man nothing to give his soul for the whole world—but for Wales!
[*Id.* at 90, 91]

Now, for those of us who have rejected the advice of Thomas More and have gone places in our careers where we will be tempted, places worth far less than Wales (I'm of Welch ancestry, by the way), what are we to do to save our souls? I think that is a more blunt way to address the question posed by Senator Smith.

May I suggest that the answer to our dilemma—and by the way, I believe it is a dilemma—lies within a familiar passage of scripture describing an event from the last week of the mortal ministry of Christ, which may, by its very familiarity to us, have lost some power to guide our professional lives. Aptly, the answer to our dilemma comes in the Savior's response to a hostile question put to him by a lawyer:

> Then one of them, which was a lawyer, asked him a question, [testing] him, and saying,
>
> Master, which is the great commandment in the law?
>
> Jesus said unto him, Thou shalt love the Lord thy God with all thy heart, and with all thy soul, and with all thy mind.
>
> This is the first and great commandment.
>
> And the second is like unto it, Thou shalt love thy neighbour as thyself.
>
> On these two commandments hang all the law and the prophets. [Matthew 22: 35–40 KJV]

Love God. Love your neighbor as yourself. *These* are the templates by which we should measure our professional conduct. This is how we are to practice our religion while we practice our professions. Is that unrealistic? It is difficult, to be sure, but it is only unrealistic if we have bought into Satan's fictions about what is real and unreal. How does one go about living one's professional life out of a love of God and neighbor—something we are not only called to do but commanded to do?

First, we must reject the tendency to place our professional and religious lives in separate compartments. The "at-one-ment" of Christ is intended to bring unity and wholeness to our relationship with God, to our fellow beings, and within ourselves. Years ago, as I was about to graduate from BYU with a bachelor's degree, I attended a stake conference in the Provo Tabernacle. In a few months I would be entering law school at the University of Virginia, but I was by no means certain what I wanted to do for my life's work. I was ready to be taught. Elder Eyring teaches that the primary way God speaks to us is through speakers at church (Henry B. Eyring, "Ears to Hear," in *Conference Report,* April 7, 1985; or *Ensign,* May 1985, 76). Although we can each identify obvious limits to that principle, this was an occasion when I believe the Lord was speaking to me. Gene Dalton, who was on the faculty of BYU's business school, spoke as a member of our stake presidency. President Dalton told the story of an Italian immigrant to America who, when he passed through Ellis Island in the early 20th century, recorded on his papers under the box marked "Occupation": "I am a servant of God. I mend shoes."

That anecdote reminds me of what Dorothy Sayers, the Catholic apologist, translator of Dante, and mystery novelist, wrote:

> The church's approach to an intelligent carpenter is usually confined to exhorting him not to be drunk and disorderly in his leisure hours, and to

come to church on Sundays. What the church should be telling him is this: that the very first demand that his religion makes upon him is that he should make good tables.

Church by all means, and decent forms of amusement, certainly—but what use is all that if in the very center of his life and occupation he is insulting God with bad carpentry? No crooked table legs or ill-fitting drawers ever, I dare swear, came out of the carpenter's shop at Nazareth. Nor, if they did, could anyone believe that they were made by the same hand that made Heaven and earth. No piety in the worker will compensate for work that is not true to itself; for any work that is untrue to its own technique is a living lie. [Dorothy L. Sayers, *Creed or Chaos?* (New York: Harcourt, Brace, 1949), 56–57]

Now, that is a tall order, and it makes me feel about the same way that I feel whenever I hear the oft-used John Taylor quote about being accountable for those I might have helped had I been more diligent in my callings. Nevertheless, I believe that Sayers is correct when she recognizes that our professional work cannot be separated from our religious life. (By the way, I believe that President Taylor is also correct. Although I hope that the words of Mother Teresa quoted in general conference several years ago are also correct: "I know only two things about God's judgment. First, it will be absolutely fair. Second, it will be filled with wonderful surprises.") As Latter-day Saints, we understand that what Sayers is describing is part of the law of consecration. C. S. Lewis described that law this way:

Christ says "Give me All. I don't want so much of your time and so much of your money and so much of your work: I want You. I have not come to torment your natural self, but to kill it. No half-measures are any good. . . ."

. . . The terrible thing, the almost impossible thing, is to hand over your whole self—all your wishes and precautions—to Christ. But it is far easier than what we are all trying to do instead. For what we are trying to do is to remain what we call "ourselves," to keep personal happiness as our great aim in life, and yet at the same time be "good." We are all trying to let our mind and heart go their own way—cent[e]red on money or pleasure or ambition—and hoping, in spite of this, to behave honestly and chastely and humbly. And that is exactly what Christ warned us you could not do. [C. S. Lewis, *Mere Christianity* (New York: Macmillan, 1943), 167–68]

A modern day apostle of the Lord Jesus Christ, Elder Boyd K. Packer, described the commitment he made to the law of consecration early in his life:

I knew what agency was and knew how important it was to be independent, to be free. I somehow knew there was one thing the Lord would never take from me, and that was my free agency. I would not surrender my agency to any being but to Him! I determined that I would give Him the one thing

that He would never take—my agency. I decided, by myself, that from that
time on I would do things His way.

That was a great trial for me, for I thought I was giving away the most
precious thing I possessed. I was not wise enough in my youth to know that
because I exercised my agency and decided myself, I was not losing it. It was
strengthened! [Boyd K. Packer, "Spiritual Crocodiles," *New Era,* January–
February 1981, 29: emphasis in original]

Consecration is a lofty goal and I wish that I could tell you from my
own personal experience how it may be attained. But I cannot. Still, I am
convinced that unless we have that law firmly fixed in our mind as a principle by which we are *currently* bound, we will look short of the mark, *cf.*
Jacob 4:4, and our professional lives will work at cross-purposes with our
religious lives. In other words, we will not be practicing our religion while
we practice our vocations.

But how do we live the law of consecration here and now in this
world? Do you remember how Elder Maxwell has described the frustration of following celestial traffic signs in telestial traffic jams? (Neal A.
Maxwell, "Notwithstanding My Weakness," *Ensign,* November 1976, 12).
Aren't our careers the ultimate examples of telestial traffic jams? I believe
there is an important lesson to be learned from the life of Thomas More.
Now, as you have already recognized, I am of the view that there are many
lessons to be learned from More's life, and I would heartily recommend
to any of you to learn as much as you can about this man. In my estima-
tion, the best biography of More was published in 1999. The author is Peter
Ackroyd. His book is titled *The Life of Thomas More.* I own no stock in the
publisher; nor do I have any relationship with the author.

More is fascinating for our topic because, unlike his good friend and
fellow Christian humanist Erasmus, More rejected the life of the cleric and
the life of the scholar, both of which Erasmus estimated to be more suitable to More's deep spirituality. Instead, More, like most of us here, chose
the life of business, politics, and the law. (The educators among us have
chosen the better part, are immune from all weakness, and don't need a
lecture from me. Rather, I should be learning from them.) Yet More is,
in my view, only a shade behind King Benjamin as a role model for the
nonclerics and the nonscholars among us. More was a devout churchman whose piety was genuine. Each day he would spend much time in
prayer, devotion, and the contemplative study of the scriptures. (He wore a
hair shirt, too, but I wouldn't recommend that.) More was a devoted family man who held daily devotionals and taught his children (five daughters and a son) virtue and the liberal arts. By the way, the education of his
daughters was of equal priority with that of his son. His daughter Margaret
was known throughout England as the most erudite woman of her day.
More was widely respected as one of the finest lawyers of his time. Listen
to this description of More's approach to his profession, supplied by one

of his biographers. Although it is not the ultimate lesson from his life that will help answer Senator Smith's challenge to us, it is such a remarkable account that I couldn't resist including it in my remarks:

> To his clients [More] never failed to give advice that was wise and straight-forward, always looking to their interests rather than to his own. [Remember President Faust's conference address from the October 2002 general confer-ence, "What's in It for Me?"] In most cases he used his best endeavors to get the litigants to come to terms. If he was unsuccessful in this, he would then show them how to carry on the action at least expense. He was so honorable and painstaking that he never accepted any case until he had first examined the whole matter thoroughly and satisfied himself of its justice. It was all the same whether those who came to him were his friends or strangers . . . : his first warning was ever that they should not in a single detail turn aside from the truth. Then he would say: "If your case is as you have stated it, it seems to me that you will win." But if they had not justice on their side, he would tell them so plainly, and beg them to give up the case, saying that it was not right either for him or for them to go on with it. But if they refused to hear him, he would refer them to other lawyers, himself giving them no further assistance. [Quoted in Gerard B. Wegemer, *Thomas More: A Portrait of Courage*, at 51, 52 (1995)]

A prayer he composed for lawyers captures the essence of his spiritual approach to his vocation, a vocation that he knew had power to do great good and great evil. "Lord, grant that I may be able in argument, accurate in analysis, strict in study, candid with clients, and honest with adversaries. Sit with me at my desk and listen with me to my client's plaints, read with me in my library, and stand beside me in court, so that today I shall not, in order to win a point, lose my soul" (quoted in Ave Maria School of Law Applicant Information booklet, 2003).

In all these ways, we can and should emulate Thomas More, but there is one virtue in particular that made him the man for all seasons that he was. It is this virtue I believe is central to our effort to consecrate our pro-fessional lives to the Lord—to practice our religion while we practice our vocation. From his earliest days as an adult, Thomas More believed that the most effective way to put himself in a frame of mind where he could resist the temptations attendant to his profession was, in his own words, "to consider how Christ, the Lord of sovereign power, Humbled Himself for us unto the cross." "Christ's ineffable Passion," More wrote, is "a strong defense against all adversity" (id. 25 [quoting from one of the earliest of More's works, *The Life of John Picus*, in *English Works of Thomas More*, 360]).

In the film version of *A Man for All Seasons*, there is a poignant scene in which a physically spent Thomas More, dressed only in a tattered monk-like robe, is kneeling in prayer in an anteroom adjacent to the courtroom where he is about to be tried for treason. He has spent more than a year imprisoned in the Tower of London. If you turn up the sound on your TV set and listen very carefully, you can hear More utter a prayer that includes the phrase "Sweet Jesus." This private and soulful prayer before his public trial and execution reminds us of the Savior's private and soulful prayer in Gethsemane before His public trial and execution. That scene in the film is an artist's version of history. It is based, however, on good history, for in the final months of his life, during his imprisonment in the Tower, More was able to pay wholehearted attention to the topic that motivated him throughout his life, and it is the topic, I believe, that will help you and me most as we try to bring all areas of our lives—even our professions—under the Savior's charge to love God and love neighbor as self.

During his imprisonment in the Tower, Thomas More wrote *De Tristitia Christi*, "a . . . meditation upon the 'sadness' of Christ; it is a commentary" upon the New Testament account of Christ's suffering in Gethsemane (Ackroyd, 380). It was the premise of More's final work, based upon a lifetime of experience and reflection and a mortal life that had known enormous professional success but was now ending in the Tower of London, that "nothing can contribute more effectively . . . to the implantation of every sort of virtue in the Christian breast than pious and fervent meditation on the successive events of Christ's Passion" (Wegemer, 208–209).

What does this have to do with Latter-day Saint professionals in the 21st century? Can it possibly be that this Catholic saint from the 16th century has something profound to teach us about how we are to practice our religion while we practice our professions? I think so. To support my argument, I turn to a lesson from the life of the Prophet Joseph Smith I learned several years ago while teaching an early-morning seminary class in Church history in Leesburg, Virginia. We decided that we would look at Joseph Smith as an Everyman figure. In other words, we would look at the lessons Joseph learned as if they were lessons that each of us needs to learn as we improve our efforts to be disciples of Christ. As we followed the lessons Joseph learned under the tutelage of the Lord, we discovered something quite startling.

Joseph Smith learned a number of lessons that deepened his discipleship from the time of his first visions until he was prepared to organize anew Christ's church on the earth. The last canonized revelation he received almost immediately prior to organizing the Church in April 1830 is set forth in D&C 19. In verses 18 and 19 of that revelation, the Savior took Joseph Smith (and takes us) back in time to Gethsemane and Calvary—the scenes of the most awe-inspiring events since the Creation. Here the Lord narrates a personal account of the suffering He endured so that we could gain access to the transforming and redemptive power of His atoning sacrifice.

Which suffering caused myself, even God, the greatest of all, to tremble because of pain, and to bleed at every pore, and to suffer both body and spirit—and would that I might not drink the bitter cup, and shrink—

Nevertheless, glory be to the Father, and I partook and finished my preparations unto the children of men.

It occurred to our class that the Lord was telling the Prophet Joseph (and us) that we should do nothing in His church, or I would argue, in our lives, without bearing in mind what the Father and the Son did for us in Gethsemane and on Calvary. We should carry on our vocations in light of this sobering yet joyous reality.

One of the distinctive features of the Mormon experience, one that is widely noted, has been our emphasis on community building. It shouldn't surprise you then that one of the icons of our faith is the beehive. To be sure, Mormon communitarianism is, in part at least, a natural reaction to the persecution we have experienced and a predictable result of our exodus history. But our communitarianism, which was so threatening to 19th- and early-20th-century America, is also a reflection of our belief that although spirituality begins with allowing the effects of Christ's atoning sacrifice and His awe-inspiring grace to heal the wounds that sin has inflicted upon our broken hearts, its most profound manifestation comes when we work to make the effects of the Atonement of Christ radiate beyond ourselves and our families to unite our communities. There are in the canon of the Restoration powerful insights into the link between the Lord's Atonement and the imperative to build community. The work of community building is, I believe, the most important spiritual work to which Christians are called. It is a natural outgrowth of what Thomas More called "pious and fervent meditation on the successive events of Christ's Passion" (Wegemer, 208–209). All other spiritual work is preparatory to this and therefore incomplete without this.

Two stories from the Book of Mormon make this point. The first is the story of the prophet King Benjamin, who worked to unite his people, people deeply divided by culture, language, class, and race. He had tried, without a great measure of success, educational reform, political reform, and legal reform (see Mosiah 1–2). It was only when he taught his divided people of the great unifying power of the at-one-ment of Christ that he was able to help them create a community. It was only by teaching them of their fallen nature—which reveals itself in the very breaches Benjamin was seeking to heal—and the atoning power of Christ's suffering that Benjamin was able to achieve, for a season at least, unity among his people (see Mosiah 3–6).

The second story describes the post-resurrection ministry of the Risen Lord Jesus Christ to the Book of Mormon people. In that story the Risen Lord descends out of heaven in a foreshadowing of his Second Coming, and the people fall to the earth in worship. After teaching them about His suffering (3 Nephi 11:11), He commands each of the almost 3,000 people to come one by one and feel the wounds in his hands, feet, and side (3 Nephi 11: 14, 15). As one might imagine, this shocking and gruesome experience transformed them. In fact, those who were confronted by the physical emblems of his suffering form the core of a new Christ-centered society that for the ensuing 200 years is devoid of strife, malevolence, racism, and greed (see 4 Nephi 3, 15–17: "And they had all things common among them; therefore there were not rich and poor, bond and free, but they were all made free, and partakers of the heavenly gift. . . . And it came to pass that there was no contention in the land, because of the love of God which did dwell in the hearts of the people. And there were no envyings, nor strifes, nor tumults, nor whoredoms, nor lyings, nor murders, nor any manner of lasciviousness; and surely there could not be a happier people among all the people who had been created by the hand of God. . . . [T]hey were in one, the children of Christ, and heirs to the kingdom of God"). Significantly, we are asked to do the same each Sunday when we partake of the sacrament of the Lord's Supper. We are commanded to have physical contact with the emblems of His suffering. The response of the people in 3 Nephi ("they did cry out with one accord, saying: Hosanna! [Save us, now!] Blessed be the name of the Most High God! And they did fall down at the feet of Jesus, and did worship him" [3 Nephi 11:16–17]) becomes the mark by which we measure the depth of our appreciation for the Lord's sacrifice.

Now, what is so striking to me about these stories is that each highlights the idea that one cannot serve a God who has no personal needs in any other way than by working to unite His children. Each makes clear that it was the shared understanding of Christ's role as Savior and Redeemer that formed the basis for creating a community. We learn from the story of Adam and Eve that Satan's primary goal and his chief tactic are to divide God from humanity, Adam from Eve. The most cursory study of human history shows his relentless pursuit of that goal and his effective use of that tactic. Everywhere we see around us the carnage of his work. We are divided by sex, race, class, religion, and nationality, just to name a few. By contrast, the at-one-ment of Christ is a powerful force to overcome those divisions and create a bond of unity among humankind. To build a community that extends beyond family or congregation—and I believe we are compelled by our understanding of the Atonement of our Savior and especially those sources to which I just referred to do just that—involves law. Properly understood, then, the vocation of a lawyer is to help build communities founded on the rule of law. By doing so, lawyers are participating in the redeeming work of the atoning power of the Savior at its zenith. To be sure, the working out of the power of the Atonement occurs initially at the intimate level of a sinner realizing her individual need for God's grace.

But it must also ultimately include creating a community based on the rule of law. Near the close of his biography of Thomas More, Peter Ackroyd wrote, "He embodied law all his life, and he died for it" (Ackroyd, 400). That is a challenge worthy of each of us, especially those, like More, who have gained some awareness of the power of the Atonement of the Lord Jesus Christ. We should each, in the words of Thomas More, engage in "pious and fervent meditation on the successive events of Christ's Passion" (Wegemer, 208–209).

When we do, at least two things will happen. First, we will begin to develop a sense of gratitude to God for the "shock of eternal love" expressed in the Atonement, and that gratitude will humble us before God (Eugene England, "That They Might Not Suffer: The Gift of Atonement," *Dialogues with Myself*, 90). Second, we will begin to realize that Christ's Passion was not endured solely for us, but that He suffered what He did because He loved those we encounter everyday in our lives as much as He loves us. In the words of C. S. Lewis,

> It may be possible for each to think too much of his own potential glory here-after; it is hardly possible for him to think too often or too deeply about that of his neighbour. . . . There are no ordinary people. You have never talked to a mere mortal. . . . Next to the Blessed Sacrament itself, your neighbour is the holiest object presented to your senses. [C. S. Lewis, *The Weight of Glory*, 18–19]

In the name of Jesus Christ, amen.

This address was given to the Salt Lake Chapter of the J. Reuben Clark Law Society at the Joseph Smith Memorial Building in Salt Lake City on November 19, 2003. Reprinted from the Clark Memorandum, *fall 2004, 12–19.*

Thomas B. Griffith received his JD *from the University of Virginia in 1985, served as legal counsel of the United States Senate 1995–99, and assistant to the president and general counsel of Brigham Young University in Provo, Utah 2000–2005. He is currently a judge for the* U.S. *Court of Appeals for the District of Columbia Circuit.*

A Restatement of Contracts

Cree-L Kofford

Recently, I was visited by a young lawyer who wanted to discuss his decision to leave the law. He reviewed his reasons including the endless nights and weekends at the office, the pressure of balancing the demands of several matters at the same time, the frustration of satisfying the requirements of multiple clients, and the difficulty of pleasing his employer. He ended with this statement: "I'm tired of the rat race, and I want nothing more to do with the jealous mistress." When he finished we talked for a while. I hoped that my encouragement to rethink his decision would be of value. Among other things, I told him that I know of no other profession or occupation so grand and glorious as the law. It is as broad as the horizons of the world, and its depth is nearly endless. Within its majesty, there is a place for almost every kind of person—each with different interests, abilities, and desires. Where else can be found a profession or occupation that equally honors someone who thrives in a probate practice, hard-driving business litigation, or the nuances of the tax code, works as a general counsel, or fills the role of rainmaker? The list of differences could be compounded almost endlessly.

In addition, consider the variety of choices that the law affords in which to conduct a practice. From the biggest of the big to the smallest of the small, all are welcome and respected—from private law firm to government employment, with dozens of options along the way. Like the gospel, the law is unlimited in recognizing individual abilities and desires. Where else can be found a profession or occupation that affords the multiplicity of individual choices found in the law? Even as life changes, and needs and interests change with it, law provides the opportunity to change how one practices. From the courtroom to the boardroom or from the schoolroom to the office are only a few of the available choices. I told him that I believed he was wrong in blaming the law for his "rat race."

The law is an assortment of rules and regulations by which civilized societies govern their conduct. It is neither a jealous mistress nor a permissive one. Indeed, it is genderless. The difficulty is not with the law—it is with the way in which it is practiced. Practice may be a jealous mistress or a jealous master, and it indeed may be a rat race, but it is the individual practitioners who are responsible for those circumstances, not the law. Practitioners choose their way of conducting a legal practice, and they have the power to change it. That change is possible only when they fully understand the difference between the law and the practice of the law. How attorneys choose to engage in the magnificent profession of the law is fully within their control, crafting a practice of any dimension, any type, and any demand. Thus, it becomes axiomatic that with complaints about the demands of the law the subject is really a serious misunderstanding of where the difficulty resides. That misunderstanding may keep lawyers from ever resolving the issues unless they focus on the cause of those issues. That focus leads them to look at their practice—and as I have earlier said, only the individual practitioners can change that practice to meet their needs, abilities, desires, and circumstances.

The law, like the Lord, knows we are individuals unique among all individuals, and the law can provide for those individual differences. For some, the well-publicized route of law school, law review, court clerk, and corner office in the "best and biggest" firm, in the best and biggest city, may be exactly right. For others, an Atticus Finch–like practice in a rural community may be right. For some, more is better; for others, it comes down to what Sabrina said to Linus in the movie *Sabrina*: "More isn't always better. Sometimes it's just more."[1]

All of these opportunities are provided by the law. The law does not offer a "one size fits all" opportunity. Rather, it seeks to meet our abilities, our interests, our desires, and our circumstances, for only then are we able to contribute to its continued vibrancy. At one point in your life, under circumstances existing at that moment, you may find that a heavy commitment of time, attention, and energy is consistent with your desires. But add a husband or wife, and a child (especially one that is physically or emotionally challenged), and you may determine that a different commitment is needed. The law stands ready to accommodate all of these situations and embraces each with equal acceptance. Some would have you believe that the "best and brightest" all follow a particular course. That is simply not accurate. For some of the best and brightest, any one of the many alternative options is the best course. All choices are more a function of (1) what you are, (2) what your circumstances are, and, therefore, (3) what your desires are than of your (a) grade point average, (b) class standing, or (c) what someone else thinks you can or ought to do.

The simple fact is that you have the ability to design your own practice. All that is needed if you are to be successful is that your design is true to who and what you are and, as we will discuss next, what your circumstances require.

As lawyers who are members of The Church of Jesus Christ of Latter-day Saints, you have certain factors that you must consider before you design your practice. You, more than any other lawyers on earth, know what the purpose of this life is. You are well aware of the threshold doctrine announced in the Pearl of Great Price where we learn: "For behold, this is my work and my glory—to bring to pass the immortality and eternal life of man."[2] You also know that the New Testament establishes that to obtain eternal life you must know God and Jesus Christ, whom God has sent,[3] and that knowledge requires that you obey the commandments.[4] The Prophet Joseph Smith put all of this into perspective when he taught:

> Here, then, is eternal life—to know the only wise and true God; and you have got to learn how to be Gods yourselves, and to be kings and priests to God, the same as all Gods have done before you, namely, by going from one small degree to another, and from a small capacity to a great one; from grace to grace, from exaltation to exaltation, until you attain to the resurrection of the dead, and are able to dwell in everlasting burnings, and to sit in glory, as do those who sit enthroned in everlasting power.[5]

If you are to succeed, all of this doctrine together with all other doctrine that it encompasses becomes part of that which you must consider as you design your practice.

You will want to keep in mind that you have already entered into contracts that will affect other contracts you make and that you may contract away. You are familiar with each of these contracts although you are more accustomed to referring to them by names such as "oath and covenant," "commandments," "obedience," or similar names. But, in reality, they are all based on the very simple principles of contract law that we call "offer and acceptance."

You will remember when you entered into that holy house and in a solemn moment raised your arm to the square and agreed to live the law of consecration. You consecrated for a sacred purpose your time, your talent, and all with which you had been blessed or with which you will be blessed. In that moment, you promised your God all that He might require. Included in that promise was the covenant that you would live in such a way as to magnify your priesthood or your womanhood so as to be worthy and able to render such an offering to the Lord as He might require if and until that time when He requires all. Since that moment, you have received the benefits of your contract. You have received blessings, and because of it you will continue to receive such blessings.

As you now prepare to offer your time, talent, and energy to the practice of law you are designing, if you are to succeed you must recognize the full consequence of that to which you have already committed.

As with all other things with the Lord, certain aspects of the contract are unique to you. As a result, the full extent of its terms can only be known through the power of the Spirit received through the process of prayer.

Sometime later, most of you entered into another contract. Those of you who have not yet will, in the Lord's own time, have that opportunity. In a special place in His holy house, you knelt at an altar and under the guidance of one holding the holy sealing power, which he received under the authority of a prophet of God, you participated in the sacred sealing ordinance.

If you are a man, you took your sweetheart, kneeling across the altar, as your wife. You promised to love her, cherish her, protect her, and care for her. You also promised to provide righteous priesthood leadership and to accept her as a full and equal voting partner in your marriage partnership.

If you are a woman, you gave yourself to your husband and you promised to love him and to sustain and support him. You also promised to be a full partner in the marriage with all of its rights and responsibilities.

Together you promised the Lord that you would multiply and replenish the earth, that you would, in so far as your physical or mental abilities were not impaired, love and raise children unto the Lord. Incorporated by reference into your contract were all of the provisions relating to parents and children including, but not limited to, those set forth in the 68th section of the Doctrine and Covenants, which among other things requires:

> And again, inasmuch as parents have children in Zion, or in any of her stakes which are organized, that teach them not to understand the doctrine of repentance, faith in Christ the Son of the living God, and of baptism and the gift of the Holy Ghost by the laying on of the hands, when eight years old, the sin be upon the heads of the parents.[6]

As you determine the nature of the practice you will conduct, you will, of course, want to consider the time, energy, and attention requirements that you have already contracted to give.

Jointly, the two of you also agreed and promised that you would work together with mutual effort to gain eternal life. Unfortunately, the depth of this doctrine is not well understood by many members of the Church. Expressed in its simplest terms in section 131 of the Doctrine and Covenants we learn:

> In the celestial glory there are three heavens or degrees;
> And in order to obtain the highest, a man must enter into this order of the priesthood [meaning the new and everlasting covenant of marriage].[7]

That doctrinal pronouncement was followed a short time later by D&C section 132, which is the crowning revelation of a long list of revealed truths received by the Prophet Joseph Smith. Inherent in the doctrine is the simple fact that gaining eternal life requires a faithful and spiritually mature husband and wife. Thus, as mutual partners, a husband and wife each has the responsibility of doing everything within their power to ensure that the other partner qualifies for this great reward.

The impact of this doctrine on lawyers is enormous, for as a husband and wife design his or her law practice, they will want to do so with the responsibilities each has to help the other develop so as to enable both to enter into the celestial kingdom. The impact on an unmarried man or woman is no less profound and in one sense has at least one added dimension. Thus, the unmarried lawyer must design his or her practice to allow for the finding of an eternal companion, and then nurturing and working with that companion to ensure that as a couple they qualify for eternal life.

Now, add the one additional thought that you are, by contract, in a full 50-50 partnership where the approval of both partners is required for any decision that might in any way impact the partnership. Among other things, that means that a husband or wife in the process of defining what his or her practice will be must work to see that the companion is made aware of the plan and considers what will be required in time, energy, and emotion. This contractual provision is all too often overlooked in those marriages where the husband "takes care of earning the living" and the wife "takes care of raising the children." While there is some doctrinal validity to this arrangement, carried to its ultimate conclusion, it throws the partnership out of balance and runs the risk of depriving both of achieving the benefits of Christ's work and glory. As a parting thought on this subject, let me remind you of the legal doctrine of informed consent. How can either the husband or the wife give approval to the designed practice if they do not know about it and understand it?

One additional time I remind you that all of these issues present decisions unique to you that must be determined by the partnership in mutual prayer and mutual listening for the answer. I believe this second element to be a much more difficult one than the first. Asking is fairly easy. Listening is hard. As President Boyd K. Packer said over 20 years ago, "The Spirit does not get our attention by shouting or shaking us with a heavy hand. Rather it whispers. It caresses so gently that if we are preoccupied we may not feel it at all."[8]

Let me now raise a question that I believe is running through the minds of many of you. After contemplating all of this, how am I possibly going to be able to compete against others equally bright and capable but who are not subject to the same contract provisions to which I am a party? I believe you are correct in raising the question. All of your professional life you will be facing other attorneys who are just as bright as or brighter than you are. Given all that I have asked you to do, there is not any way, logically, you can serve your God, His church, your wife (or husband),

and your family and still compete unless you have help. That help in the form of the Holy Spirit is exactly what you can have if you live and practice worthily.

We could spend hours on this subject, but the truth is, it is all summarized in one, magnificent scripture. That scripture holds the key of professional success, among other things. It is found in section 88 of the Doctrine and Covenants. As you read it, I urge you to pay particular attention to the qualifier that is so clearly set forth:

> And if your eye be single to my glory, your whole bodies shall be filled with light, [in spiritual matters the word "light" is frequently used in connection with intelligence] and there shall be no darkness in you; and that body which is filled with light *comprehendeth* all things.[9]

Because I have already traveled the road most of you are just beginning, let me assure you that you can have the blessings of comprehending all things in your practice. I witness to you that time and time again I have experienced success where my own efforts alone would have brought failure. That success came because in an instant of revelation I was able to "comprehendeth all things." May that be your blessing as you continue the long line of those who bring credit to an incomparable profession.

This address was given at the J. Reuben Clark Law Society Conference at Georgetown University in Washington, D.C., on February 17, 2006.

Cree-L Kofford received his JD from the University of Southern California in 1961. He served as a member of the Second Quorum of Seventy 1991–94 and First Quorum of the Seventy 1994–2003. He is currently an emeritus General Authority.

Notes

1. From the movie script for *Sabrina*, 1995, http://www.imdb.com/title/tt0114319/quotes.

2. Moses 1:39.

3. *See* John 17:3.

4. *See* 1 John 2:4.

5. Joseph Fielding Smith, comp., *Teachings of the Prophet Joseph Smith*, Salt Lake City: Deseret Book Co., 1976, pp. 346–47.

6. D&C 68:25.

7. D&C 131:1–2.

8. Boyd K. Packer, "The Candle of the Lord," *Ensign*, January 1983, 51.

9. D&C 88:67 (emphasis added).

It Is Given unto You to Judge

Sheila McCleve

For the past eight years, I have been a state trial judge in a court of limited jurisdiction. My court's civil jurisdiction excludes real property, domestic, and probate subjects, with a $20,000 limitation on damages sought. Criminal jurisdiction excludes felony trials. However, I do conduct everything from high-profile preliminary hearings on capital homicides and other felonies to jury or bench misdemeanor trials.

If one were to draw an analogy between serving as a judge in my court and serving as a doctor or a restaurateur, my work would be comparable to that done in a M.A.S.H. unit or a fast-food chain. In my urban court setting, volume is extremely high, caseload pressing. I see thousands of people a year.

Mine is a people career. What I enjoy most about it is the great diversity and the universal threads I see in people's lives. For instance, there isn't a man or a woman who has come before me who hasn't evidenced some relation to loved ones. The people who face me also recognize that they are agents who have made choices that place themselves before me. And everyone I've seen has expressed to some extent his or her views on the purpose and meaning of this existence through the actions that bring them to court.

Individual examples quickly come to mind. A man in his early 20s negligently shoots to death a young girl by sighting her and then pulling the trigger on what he thought was an unloaded rifle. A streetwalker, having been incarcerated repeatedly, dies from the effects of AIDS. An alcoholic, who had been convicted of driving under the influence of alcohol several times, serves the maximum period of incarceration, becomes physically healthy, reunites with his wife and children, is rehired by his employer, and voluntarily promises me he will not return to court on criminal or alcohol-related charges again. In eight years, he hasn't.

People often ask me how it's possible to judge another human being. In the sense of making an ultimate moral pronouncement, I simply respond that that's not my business—not that doing a little moralizing isn't a temptation with all that one sees from the bench. I see everything from police officers who sincerely regard criminals as less than human to lawyers who anonymously pay restitution for food stolen by transients. There are businessmen who forgive debts to resolve disputes and court employees who help the homeless find shelter.

While it is a temptation on the bench to do a little moralizing about people, one can resist by remembering that "all have sinned and come short of the glory of God" (Romans 3:23). Humans—unlike God, who sees our hearts perfectly—discern the intent of the heart from circumstances and acts of the individual, imperfectly listening to the Spirit. Judges, being human—albeit rumors to the contrary—are therefore in no position to issue moral pronouncements.

On the other hand, part of judging is evaluating people. A judge must appraise a lawyer's reliability, preparedness, and truthfulness. And certainly when judges sit as triers of fact, they weigh the credibility of the witnesses, examine their demeanor, and analyze their truthfulness. Similarly, in sentencing, judges assess not only the defendant but his or her family and associates, the victims, and the effects of the crime on society. Consequently, in the evaluation process, it is critical that judges look at people from the same human level we are all on. Otherwise, "'tis high to be a judge" ("Truth Reflects Upon Our Senses," *Hymns* [1985] 273).

When lawyers consider judging, their viewpoints often focus on burdens of proof, rules of evidence, and procedure and substantive law. They know that once a case is taken, winning it depends upon meeting the burden or not, following the rules, and arguing the law.

In judging, regard for the rule of law is critical. Natural laws and God's laws are constant and consequential. To the extent human law can be the same, human beings enjoy order, equal treatment, and fair process. Out of that, freedom is born and survives. It is that rule of law lawyers recognize, consciously or not, in preparing their cases for trial or appeal. It is that same rule of law that judges must follow in order to avoid arbitrary, despotic tyranny by the bench.

Perhaps because its purpose is to resolve conflict, judging offers an opportunity to experience how people act in intense life settings. The forum is public. Society's ability to affect lives is nowhere more powerful. Contest, persuasion, and argument are courtroom tools. Property, freedom, and life itself can be taken away from individuals. And the consequences of choices people make are never more focused in society than they can become in trial.

There are those who believe they would enjoy judging because of the power, prestige, and independence it offers. And there are those who recognize that from a judge's observation point on humankind, the constant inhumanity, conflict, and greed attendant to the office render the position unenticing.

But judging, like anything involving people, is an opportunity to serve. Judging is service when it restores some measure of hope, enforces consequences of actions taken, or resolves disputes. If it's no more than locking people up and awarding people money, it is of little value to humanity and worthy of little regard.

When one renders judgment in any given case, one renders service in at least two ways. One decides the particular issues in the lives of the people present in court—a very specific and immediate act of service. And simultaneously, one defines rules, which can be known and used by all people affected by that court. Service is less direct when it defines rules, but it is still service because it makes a difference in people's lives.

Both appellate and trial courts perform these simultaneous functions. At the appellate level, a judge works with words. At the trial level, a judge sees the faces. At whatever level a judge works, however, experiencing the problems in people's lives will unveil the Christian imperative to serve. Further, the only way to be a judge and not be destroyed by the power, prestige, inhumanity, and conflict attendant to the office is in remembering that judging is serving.

Our Lord, the Creator of the universe, who dwells among us, who redeemed and sustains us, says that His work and His glory is to serve us by bringing to pass our immortality and eternal life. Who are we not to be serving?

Whatever one does professionally makes little difference. I assume that if the gospel is true, it is true seven days a week. It can meet any challenge, withstand any opposition. Therefore, it is not only applicable to but also infused in all that we who espouse it do and are. And I suggest that we ought to be seeing our experiences and life choices in this context, or we have no business holding ourselves out as disciples of Christ.

Because we all share that universe of discipleship, I hope to make some observations about the nature of judging that might strike a universal resonant chord in all our lives.

There are, at this point in my life's observations, three universal issues upon which we constantly state our positions by our living. Over time we will have made our positions clear. Those issues are faith, love, and agency.

Faith involves what one sees as the purpose of life, whether there is a higher power and any meaning beyond this existence. It involves hope and the ability to trust. It makes love possible. It gives us patience with agency and our own limitations. It is the power of the universe.

I see statements on faith in the anguish of alcoholics whose names I know because of their frequent appearances in my court on public intoxication charges. I see statements on faith in cocaine addicts and dealers, in streetwalkers, forgers, thieves, and murderers. I see statements on faith in lawyers who prepare their cases with dedication and thoroughness and in lawyers who push beyond the edge of representing their cases in a light most favorable to their clients.

And I make statements on faith when I walk into the courtroom and try to disregard community or bar approval, to see all the people I serve as children of God, and to allow or reject the Spirit's ability to make up, after all I can do, the difference in what I cannot discern in people before me. Every day in our lives, in all contexts, we each decide our positions on the issue of faith.

Similarly, each day we state our understandings of love. Love is charity, the greatest of all gifts, the pure love of Christ given without condition to endure forever. Charity is that love which the Lord has for us and that love which we are trying to learn to have for Him and for each other. With it, we are able to give and forgive. Because of it, we obey, repent, have faith, and respect agency. It never fails.

I see statements on love in the family who sits watching at the back of the courtroom and exchanges glances with a handcuffed, shackled, convicted defendant. I see statements on love in the tenant who refuses to pay rent, believing the landlord must allow her to remain on the premises because she has children and no job. I see statements on love when a mother appears to have suggested damning testimony to a child about the child's father.

And I make statements on love when I react to mistaken representations or intentional misrepresentations of my rulings from the bench by colleagues or others. I make statements on love in how I treat people who lie to me, try to curry favor with me, or use my reputation or name. I make statements on love in how I sentence, award, or deny judgment, run my courtroom, and determine my availability to lawyers, police, and others. The statements we make are subtle, sometimes not even known to us as statements on love, but they are our statements.

We choose every day, more times than we know, to make statements on these universal issues. That is why agency, which is the forum or context of the other issues, and which, at first, may seem inappropriately paralleled with faith and love, is a universal issue. Because no matter how dim the faith nor absent the feeling, we all understand consequences. We think in terms of cause and effect. We cherish independence and believe liberty a human right. We say we want freedom. Hence, through our choices, we evidence our true desires.

I see statements on agency in the father—also a lawyer—who wants to negate the consequences of his son's negligent traffic collision by "taking care of it" for him. I see statements on agency by all the coke-sniffers and other addicts who daily drag into court. I see statements on agency in lawyers as they confer with one another and with their clients regarding settlement options and outcomes.

And I make statements on agency when I send someone to jail, order parties to appear before me, and respect or reject appellate decisions and legislative actions. I make statements on agency in my conduct with my colleagues on the bench regarding caseload administration, in my treatment of staff personnel, and in my willingness to accept such extra court assignments as speaking at schools or hearing cases for other judges who become unavailable.

These universal issues are always before us because this life is the day we are performing our labors. This life is the time for us to prepare to meet God, who will exercise both judgment and mercy upon us.

Law requires justice. In the broad scheme of things nothing short of an infinite sacrifice could satisfy the whole law and the demands of justice. Not any one of us, save Christ only, could make such a sacrifice. He made the great, infinite sacrifice in order to extend mercy to us, to overpower (as it says in Alma) justice, and to bring about the means for us to have faith unto repentance. God requires that we lean on His arm only, not because He needs our adoration, but because the act of worship draws us to Him and makes His love available to us. Faith, love, and agency seem to me linked not only as the universal issues of life, but as keys to our relationship with God. Because He *loves* us, He offers us the chance in this mortal probation to choose to become like Him, but He doesn't want to lose us. He lets us *choose,* but He beseeches us to come to Him, to have *faith* in Him, because there is no other way we can avoid perishing. Without Him the perils of mortality are insurmountable.

Nor is it possible fully to love His children—each other or ourselves—without first loving Him. It is not possible because we, alone or all together, are incapable of charity without faith in Him. Not any one or all of us could make that infinite sacrifice that restores the repentant person who has done the harm and repairs the harm done to the innocent sufferer. Only He is capable of that everlasting love. And we, therefore, are capable of it only through Him.

At the same time, if we love Him, we love His children because we know by His sacrifice how infinitely priceless His children are to Him. Hence, He tells us if we don't have charity—that is, if we turn away the needy, don't visit the sick and afflicted, don't impart of our substance— then we are as hypocrites who deny the faith. Seeing how we are loved, seeing how to love, we witness our belief in Him and love for Him by treating what is priceless to Him with the same value He perceives in us.

Christ's whole purpose is to bring to pass our immortality and eternal life. His guiding us is His service to us. He, more than we can comprehend, does not want to lose us. Yet we cannot dwell with Him finally—we cannot know as we are known—unless we are like Him. And, to be like Him is something only we can choose for ourselves. This kind of choosing is part of who He is and who we can become.

Underlying the Savior's Atonement for us, agency, as a context or forum for choice, is our Lord's constant expression of His love for us. Only in having the choice to do that which takes us away from Him or alternatively to do that which brings us to Him can we become like Him, preferring good to evil. Out of His great love, He respects our agency. He pleads with us to accept His grace. He tells us that by our life choices we can be subjected and sealed to the devil or have our garments made white by the blood of the lamb. He lets us choose line upon line, step by ever-so-slow step. He exhorts us to choose to come to Him and to help one another choose to come to Him. And if we ask Him, He helps us in this process. That is essentially how we serve, no matter what our life's work.

For me, my life's work thus far has been judging. What I hope I am trying to do, not explicitly but implicitly in the way I live and treat others every day, is to help people better understand the issues of faith, love, and agency so that we all can choose to be with Him and be like Him and not be forever lost from Him. Salvation is social. And then comes His grace.

I will be ever grateful to have held the office of judge. But in a very critical sense, we are all judges.

> For behold, my brethren, it is given unto you to judge, that ye may know good from evil; and the way to judge is as plain, that ye may know with a perfect knowledge, as the daylight is from the dark night. . . .
>
> And now, my brethren, seeing that ye know the light by which ye may judge, which light is the light of Christ, see that ye do not judge wrongfully. [Moroni 7:15, 18]

This article is reprinted from the Clark Memorandum, *spring 1992, 2–7.*

Sheila K. McCleve received her JD *from* BYU *Law School in 1976, studied at Oxford University 1983, and was named* BYU *Honored Alumnus by J. Reuben Clark Law School 1986. She served as a judge on the Utah Circuit Court Third Judicial District 1984–1996, and judge for the Utah District Court Third Judicial District 1996–2009. She is currently an adjunct law professor at J. Reuben Clark Law School.*

On Being Ethical Lawyers

Sandra Day O'Connor

I'm delighted to have the opportunity to address the members of the J. Reuben Clark Law Society. Your organization's commitment to public service, fairness, and virtue in the law is commendable. I am here to talk to you about what you need to do to become ethical lawyers.

I'm sure everyone in this audience both here and participating through satellite broadcast is already firmly committed to being an ethical, moral lawyer. You do not need any more stories of lawyers who pervert the law for their own ends. And I'm sure I don't need to tell you to avoid unethical, shady situations. Your own commitment to your faith has already counseled you in that regard, and I am sure that no one here would engage in behavior that would bring shame on the legal profession.

Instead, I want to talk to you about the hardest part of being an ethical lawyer. There are at least two important parts to being an ethical lawyer. First, as an ethical lawyer, you must refrain from doing things that are wrong. I trust that all of you who are listening will do that without more encouragement on my part.

I want to focus on the second part of being an ethical lawyer. An ethical lawyer must affirmatively choose to do things that are good. I think you will find out as you enter practice that this second part will pose the greater challenge to you.

As you enter the practice of law, you will find that it is not always easy to figure out what is "right" and what is "wrong." On the one hand, it is your duty to act as a zealous advocate for your clients. You need to look out for their interests and advance them, whenever it is proper to do so. You need to hold their confidences in the utmost secrecy. On the other hand, as a lawyer, you are a professional. You are an officer of the courts before which you practice, and you owe the highest duties of fidelity to justice and the rule of law.

You might think it is easy to navigate your way through that maze. But it won't always feel that way. Let me give you an example of a thorny ethical dilemma that a lawyer recently faced. Some of you may recall the Supreme Court's decision in *Atkins v. Virginia,* where the Court decided that it was unconstitutional to execute mentally retarded defendants. But you might not be familiar with its aftermath.

After the Supreme Court's decision, the Virginia courts decided that Atkins was not mentally retarded and therefore could be executed consistently with the Constitution. A few weeks ago, in late January of this year, he was nonetheless removed from death row. The reason had nothing to do with whether Atkins was or was not mentally challenged, nor did it have anything to do with the litigation that had taken place over the decade since he had been convicted. Instead, it was the result of conduct that took place 11 years ago, before Atkins was convicted.

The crucial point in the prosecutor's case against Atkins was that, out of all the other codefendants who were involved in this case, Atkins was the man who pulled the trigger and killed the victim. If Atkins was the actual gunman, he would have been eligible for the death penalty.

If he was not, he could at most have been sentenced to life in prison. The lawyer, whom we will call Mr. Jones, represented a man who testified against Atkins at trial. Mr. Jones' client was one of Atkins' codefendants. The testimony his client offered went to that crucial point at trial: Did Atkins actually shoot the victim?

Mr. Jones had an interesting story to tell. Now, I should caution you that the prosecutor in this case has denied the truth of Mr. Jones' story. But I want to tell you this story for the ethical ramifications. Before Atkins went to trial, Mr. Jones' client gave his side of the story to the prosecutor. The conversation was tape recorded, and the client began by describing the position of the individuals and the firing of the shots.

What Mr. Jones alleges happened when his client started in on that description was that the prosecutor "reached over and stopped the tape recorder." She turned to another individual and said, "Do you see we have a problem here?" According to Mr. Jones, there was a significant problem: Mr. Jones' client's testimony did not match the physical evidence that the police had gathered from the crime scene. The prosecutor realized that the testimony would be damaging to the prosecution. Then, for 15 minutes— off the record, without any tape recording—the prosecutors coached Mr. Jones' client to produce the "right" testimony, that is, testimony that could be used to prove that Atkins fired the fatal gunshot.

Now, if this story is true, and I do not know if it is, there is a problem. No prosecutor should ever attempt to manufacture evidence to obtain a conviction. That obligation is doubly true when the manufactured evidence could spell the difference between life and death for a defendant.

I am sure that none of you would ever consider behaving in this manner. An ethical lawyer must, at all times, refrain from doing that sort of wrong.

But what would you do if you were Mr. Jones? Mr. Jones was present in the room. He only watched these events transpire. He did not ask his client to change his testimony. He did not take part in the conversation. He was not himself a wrongdoer.

What Mr. Jones did was go to his state bar's ethics counsel and ask for advice. He was told in no uncertain terms that he could not make these events known to Atkins' defense or to the public. After all, he was a lawyer. He had an ethical obligation not to prejudice his own client's case. If he spoke the truth, he could have jeopardized his client's deal with the prosecution.

Mr. Jones did not speak, and Atkins was convicted and sentenced to death.

Year after year, stretching over the last decade, Mr. Jones wrote to the bar's ethics counsel, asking if he could now speak up. Year after year they told him that he could not. Finally, after 10 years of silence, Mr. Jones wrote again, emphasizing that his client's case was over. There was no possibility of retrial and no likelihood of any prejudice to his client if he spoke. Under those circumstances, the state bar's ethics counsel finally relented and allowed him to tell his story.

The prosecutor in this case insists that Mr. Jones' story is false. But if it is not, I want you to imagine the ethical dilemma that Mr. Jones shouldered for the last 10 years. On the one hand, he was bound as a lawyer not to prejudice his client's case. On the other hand, he knew that the evidence he had could literally make a life-or-death difference to another man. There was no easy ethical or moral answer for him.

If you were Mr. Jones, what would you do?

Let me give another example that has been much in the news. Move the clock back several years. Suppose you are one of the bright young transactional lawyers who worked for Enron. You are approached by your supervisors, who tell you that they think they've come up with a way to structure transactions in a manner that hides debt and overreports income. Of course, your client and your supervisors both insist that it's all completely—100 percent—within the bounds of the law. You check; you're not sure if they're right. Maybe their actions could be within the letter of the law, but you're pretty sure that what they're suggesting violates the spirit of the law.

But the client did not ask you about either the letter or the spirit of the law. Your client asked you to draw up documents to allow the misleading transactions to go forward. They're not asking you to provide the faulty legal analysis. They're not asking you to fill out misleading reports to the SEC. They're asking only that you write the contract and structure that deal. All they ask is that you do the job you were hired for.

What do you do?

I hope you understand that my point in giving you these examples is to illustrate that being an ethical lawyer is not simple. I hope that none of you are ever faced with these sorts of ethical dilemmas. Being an ethical, moral lawyer can be a tough responsibility.

When you are admitted to the bar of a state, it is not an empty formula. You have to take and pass the bar exam. You must raise your hand and vow to support the law.

Let us look at Mr. Jones' ethical problem. Once he was caught on the horns of his dilemma—once he was forced to choose between keeping his client's case in confidence and allowing a potentially egregious death sentence for another man to stand—there was no good way out. I don't envy him those 10 agonizing years.

But I do want to point out one thing. The account is quite bare. We do not know exactly what happened in that room with the prosecutor. And because they did not tape record those crucial 15 minutes, we will never know. But there is one thing missing from Mr. Jones' version of the tale. When the prosecutor stopped the tape and started prompting Mr. Jones' client to change his testimony, what did Mr. Jones say?

This, you see, was the absolutely crucial moment. I know that this audience intends to be ethical and moral. In order to uphold those standards, you cannot let yourself forget that you are an officer of the court and that you are dedicated first to truth and justice. That moment Mr. Jones experienced in the prosecutor's office is the kind of moment that you need to learn to recognize. If you let it slip by in silence, you will find that events pass you by all too quickly. It is probably one of the hardest moments a lawyer can face. It is a moment when you need to do a lot more than refrain from doing things that are wrong; you need to actively choose to do that which is right.

It would be hard for Jones to interrupt a prosecutor who has promised to deal less harshly with your client in order to say these words: "I am sorry, but I cannot allow you to advise my client to give testimony that may not be true." But that is what Jones should have done.

Think about all the things you may lose for your client by speaking up. If your client does not have useful testimony to give at trial, he may not be able to bargain for a lower sentence. His own version of events could be called into question; perhaps the prosecution might try to pin that fateful shot on him instead. By speaking up, you may well hurt your client's future.

The hardest thing you must accept as an ethical, moral lawyer is that it is not your job to win for your client at all costs. You are an officer of the court; that means that one of the costs you must never pay is to put the law to one side. No matter how much it may prejudice your client, you must never advise him—either through action or inaction—to break the law or tell an untruth.

Now, I don't want to judge Mr. Jones too harshly. His repeated efforts to bring this matter to light show that he is a strongly ethical man who was deeply troubled by the events he witnessed. What this story shows is that if you are not vigilant about those crucial moments, if you let silence reign when you must speak up, even the best-intentioned of us might find ourselves in an unspeakable dilemma.

It is a heavy responsibility that is placed on your shoulders when you become an officer of the court. We ask for your vigilance, not only in the courtroom but out of it. We ask for your constant fidelity to the law. We ask you to do and say things that could make you very unpopular, perhaps with the people who are paying your salary. We demand that each and every one of you stand for truth and the rule of law, no matter the personal consequences.

Now let us look at the matter of the young Enron attorney. You can see that it is similar to the example of Mr. Jones. Even if there is nothing wrong in the duties you perform, you have a duty to your client and to the law to speak up against shady practices. These days, that duty is codified in statute. But even before it was written as law, an ethical lawyer had an obligation to affirmatively do what was right and tell her superiors that she believed that their plan was inconsistent with the obligations imposed on them by law. I think you can all also see in the case of Enron that what might have appeared as "zealous advocacy" for the client in the short term did not serve the company well in the long term.

I bring up the matter of Enron to emphasize to you that when you become an officer of the court, you cannot pooh-pooh the meaning of that term because you plan to become a transactional attorney. Some of you will never stand before a court or address a jury. You may never enter a courtroom. But that does not mean that the obligations imposed on you are in any way lessened.

As a lawyer you are not just an advocate for your client. You are a representative of the law. It is your duty not only to act according to the highest ethical standards but to make sure that you speak up when others intend to do otherwise. Your highest fidelity is to the law; you serve your clients best by making sure that they understand the duties imposed on them both under the letter and under the spirit of the law.

Now, I've spent a lot of time telling you about how hard it may sometimes be to be an ethical lawyer. Hopefully, none of you will face the kind of situation that I've detailed today. But if you do, you must make up your mind well in advance that you will speak up instead of being silent. I know you are all capable not only of refraining from wrongdoing but also of doing and saying what is right.

What I have just asked you to do is very difficult. But I'm going to ask you to do something in addition. There is another extremely important aspect to being an ethical, moral lawyer. Not only must you be sure that your actions with your client meet the highest ethical standards, but you must also strive to be an outstanding citizen lawyer.

Today we do not often use the term *citizen lawyer*. Most Americans today rarely have a favorable opinion of lawyers in general. They are most often thought of as hired guns.

But our country has been shaped by the work of thousands upon thousands of citizen lawyers who have tirelessly labored to make this world a better place. These lawyers have been citizens first. Their role has not been that of just the navigator. Instead, their contributions have been closer to the visionary and the architect. Instead of maneuvering about the law, they have chosen to use the law to build vibrant communities.

As lawyers you also will have the power to shape communities. However, more and more in recent years I have heard that young lawyers often have very little time to act as citizens. You've all heard the statistics, I'm sure. Law firms are increasingly worried about "billable hours." Even jobs spent working for the government, in an era where cash-strapped local, state, and federal officials pull out all the stops to make every dollar go as far as possible, are beginning to turn into heavy workloads. Lawyers today work more hours than lawyers in years past.

But it is also true that our civic need for lawyers has increased at an unprecedented rate. By some estimates, almost 80 percent of the need for pro bono services in our communities goes unmet. Boards of civic organizations claim they see fewer young lawyers volunteering. As a result, our communities are suffering.

I hope to inspire you not only to do right but also to do good. In addition to being an ethical advocate for your clients, I urge you to become advocates for your communities.

I hope to impress upon you the vast difference that individual citizen lawyers have made in this country. Today we live in a country that just celebrated the 400th birthday of Jamestown. That settlement brought us the English common law and the rule of law. It was critically important.

Our country was shaped by some fine lawyers, starting with Thomas Jefferson. Jefferson, as we all know, lived in a period of political upheaval. Instead of seeing himself as a mere navigator of law, Jefferson was brave enough to envision a country in which law, rather than reinforcing a centuries-old social order, could be used to bring about change. Using his skills as a lawyer, he drafted the Declaration of Independence. That document was not composed of dry legalese, detailing the rights and obligations of citizens. It did not hide the details of American independence in fine print. Instead, it contained a startling vision of the future of this great nation. That document stated not only that all men were created equal but that "[g]overnments . . . deriv[e] their just powers from the consent of the governed."

In Jefferson's time, those truths were far from self-evident—they were revolutionary. The Declaration of Independence that Jefferson drafted was not merely a legal document informing Britain it had lost 13 of its finest colonies. Instead, Jefferson's work set forth a vision for our fledgling nation: Our challenge was not just to win independence from taxation but also to forge our country into a refuge from monarchy and tyranny, a place where all citizens could strive to attain life, liberty, and happiness.

That vision, articulated by Jefferson, epitomizes what it means to be a citizen lawyer. There is no question that the Declaration of Independence is a lawyer's document: it sets forth grievances, details the appropriate remedy, and prays for relief. But it did so in a way that created community. At the time it was written, it unified thousands of Americans around the common themes of freedom and equality. Even today the promise of that document inspires citizens to make a positive difference in our world.

After the Americans had won their freedom from British tyranny, they faced a bigger challenge: How were they to enshrine the ideals represented in the Declaration of Independence in their government? The founders of our country knew better than to believe that their government would automatically respect the rights of the people just because they had fought and won a war. They were wary of governmental power, and so when it was time to build our new nation, they knew that the structure of the government had to resist tyranny. They needed to build a structure that was flexible enough to survive the ravages of time but strong enough not to fold under the first great blow.

It is obvious to us now that the solution to this problem is to write a constitution that divides power among those various branches of government. In a nation that is committed to the rule of law, our Constitution establishes what law rules. But when our nation was first conceived, the notion of a federal constitution was not the first thought that occurred to the newly independent states. In fact, the first form of government after the Revolutionary War was the ineffectual Continental Congress, which governed under the Articles of Confederation that left the national government far too weak.

When it became clear that a new form of government was necessary, it was again to lawyers that our nation looked. At the time, it was by no means clear what sort of government we should establish. Most of the states were deeply wary of national government and were loathe to give up the tiniest bit of their power to a potentially tyrannical federal power. It was James Madison who helped to build a legal document that bridged those concerns. Madison proposed establishing three independent branches of government, each of which would act as a check on the others; he restricted the potential reach of the federal government.

After the Constitution was drafted, Madison, along with Alexander Hamilton and John Jay, campaigned tirelessly for its adoption by the states. Instead of hiding the powers of government behind legal maneuvers, he explained the simple provisions of the Constitution and set forth the operation of government. In so doing, Madison built upon the vision of Jefferson: He explained and educated the community about how the Constitution created a government that would be ideally situated to serve the people and bring about the ideals of our young nation.

Madison, like Jefferson, was a citizen lawyer. He envisioned a future and acted to bring that future to fruition. He educated and inspired others to believe in that future.

All good lawyers act as zealous advocates for their clients. Early citizen lawyers acted as zealous advocates for the future, and, in so doing, they shaped our fledgling nation. They defined what it meant for "law" to rule, and they established the necessary conditions for law: democratic consent of the governed and independent executive, legislative, and judicial branches. Without the contributions of those early citizen lawyers to this country's future, the ideals of the American Revolution may well have perished despite our success in gaining independence.

Of course, since those early days, our country has been pushed forward by a great many citizen lawyers who have made important contributions to our society.

One of our great citizen lawyers was Justice Louis Brandeis. Before his appointment to the Supreme Court, Brandeis was famous for submitting a brief to the court that detailed the damaging effects of a lengthy workday on women. Oregon had mandated a maximum workday of 10 hours for women who worked in manufacturing positions. Up until that point, the Supreme Court had regularly struck down similar legislation. But Brandeis submitted a brief that detailed the ill effects of striking down the legislation and convinced the Court to let the Oregon law stand.

As a Supreme Court justice, Brandeis often spoke out for those who were unpopular. He and Justice Oliver Wendell Holmes Jr. regularly spoke out in favor of the free speech rights of political dissidents in the First World War. He favored an expansive view of the Fourth Amendment, one that protected privacy and property rights of u.s. citizens. His service on the Supreme Court drastically altered the character of that institution. Although his views on the First Amendment were first expressed in dissent, today they are recognized as the law of the land.

No discussion of citizen lawyers would be complete without reference to Thurgood Marshall. From the very beginning of his career, Marshall was dedicated to a higher ideal. While he served his clients zealously, he did so with an overarching goal in mind: ending racial segregation. Soon after graduating from law school, Marshall found himself in the thick of the fight for racial equality. In one of his very first court cases, Marshall challenged the University of Maryland's refusal to enroll an African-American student in its law school. He argued that the "separate but equal" mandate of *Plessy v. Ferguson* was inapplicable because there was no law school available to African-Americans. Marshall won his case before the Maryland Supreme Court.

He continued to win victories for black Americans through the years. Of course, his civil rights work culminated in his most famous case. Marshall argued the case for the African-American Kansas schoolchildren before the Supreme Court in *Brown v. Board of Education.* A unanimous Supreme Court agreed with Marshall, and, with that decision, a momentous change was wrought in our country. School districts across our nation desegregated, and the words of Brown soon worked their way into the vision of our nation. We had been told for two centuries that all men were created equal. Now Thurgood Marshall unified that vision of equality with a picture of integration: one in which the racist mantra of "separate but equal" became a contradiction in terms. Thurgood Marshall's exemplary service to the community did not, of course, stop with this monumental change. He was eventually appointed to the Supreme Court, where he continued to work as a tireless champion for individual rights and equality.

Nor was Justice Marshall alone among Supreme Court justices in his service to our legal community. Before his appointment to the Supreme Court, Justice Lewis Powell oversaw school integration efforts in Richmond, Virginia, and served as president of the American Bar Association. Justice Ruth Bader Ginsburg was a staunch advocate for women's rights who cowrote the first law school textbook on sex discrimination.

If we look across our nation today, we will find innumerable lawyers who are dedicated to a vision of the future in which the rule of law brings freedom and equality to all. These people work on issues that range from international affairs down to local interests. They are involved in civic organizations. They sit on corporate boards. They serve in state government and in the judiciary. I am sure that they all serve their clients zealously. But good citizen lawyers undoubtedly know that, in the long run, their clients will be best served by zealous advocacy for the future as well.

I encourage you all to remember that the challenge of being an ethical, moral lawyer is much greater than merely refraining from doing what is wrong. Instead, I expect each and every one of you to do both what is right and what is good in this world. You can act as a powerful force for change, and I expect to hear in the coming years that every one of you has done so.

In that vein, I would like to leave you with the wise words of John Wesley:

Do all the good you can,
By all the means you can,
In all the ways you can,
In all the places you can,
At all the times you can,
To all the people you can
As long as ever you can.

This satellite fireside address was given to the J. Reuben Clark Law Society at Sandra Day O'Connor College of Law at Arizona State University, in Tempe, Arizona, on February 15, 2008. Reprinted from the Clark Memorandum, *spring 2008, 2–7.*

Sandra Day O'Connor received her LLB from Stanford University in 1952, served as Arizona assistant state attorney general 1965–69, Arizona state senator 1969–75, judge for Maricopa County Superior Court 1975–79, and judge for the Arizona State Court of Appeals 1979–81. She served as associate justice on the U.S. Supreme Court 1981–2006. The recipient of numerous honors, she was given a Presidential Medal of Freedom, the United States' highest civil award, in 2009. Currently, she serves as chancellor of the College of William and Mary in Williamsburg, Virginia, promotes the civic learning website http://ourcourts.org and teaches part-time at Sandra Day O'Connor College of Law in Tempe, Arizona.

Learning from Our Conflicts

Gerald R. Williams

Some months ago, when I was invited to speak today, I asked what I should talk about. After a long pause the voice said, "Well, people usually talk about things they're good at." So my topic today is conflict.

I used to think other people had conflicts but that I was immune. Then I came upon two incidents in the life of the Prophet Joseph Smith that completely changed my understanding of conflicts and forced me to admit I probably have as many as anybody else.

What is a conflict? For our purposes today, a conflict is any situation in which both sides feel the other is in the wrong.

I'll begin with seven propositions about conflicts.

1. It is strange, but unless we had a conflict in the last few hours, most of us don't remember our conflicts. This may be good, because it saves us pain, but it creates a problem. If we don't remember our conflicts, we can't learn anything from them.

2. We probably experience conflicts differently—depending on our personalities, our prior experiences (such as the way conflicts were handled in the home where we grew up), and perhaps other factors such as gender and culture.

3. In Mormon culture most people are conflict avoiders. However, some of us are neutral about conflict, and some of us actually enjoy a good conflict.

4. If we are in relationships with others, there will be conflicts. They may be small or they may be large, but there will surely be conflicts. Can you think of any conflicts in your life right now? Perhaps a few hints will help. If you do think of a conflict or two, I hope you will jot them down.

   a. Conflicts with family, such as father, mother, siblings, spouse, children, or in-laws.

b. Conflicts with people you see often who are *not* family: neighbors, landlords, merchants, even people at church. President Brigham Young summed it up in rhyme:

> To live with Saints in Heaven is bliss and glory
> To live with Saints on Earth is another story.[1]

5. It takes two sides to create a conflict. More important, there is almost always fault on *both* sides. As someone said, "It's a mighty thin pancake that only has one side."

6. During a conflict we are usually blind to our own fault and we blame the other side.

7. A final proposition introduces my theme. When we remember our conflicts and reflect on them, they are like mirrors that can teach us things about ourselves that are otherwise difficult to discover. If we permit them, our conflicts will show us where we are weak, defensive, prideful, or otherwise in need of repair.

First Example

I'll illustrate the value of conflicts with three examples. Two are from the life of the Prophet Joseph Smith. These both involve Oliver Cowdery, who, at the time, was Joseph's most trusted associate. These conflicts occurred very close to each other in the summer of 1830, just after the Church was organized. Joseph was 24 years old, and Oliver was 23.

Joseph was busy copying and arranging revelations for publication. Oliver was staying with the Whitmer family in Fayette, 80 miles to the north. Out of the blue, Joseph received a letter from Oliver.

Joseph recorded:

> [Oliver] wrote to inform me that he had discovered an error in one of the commandments—Book of Doctrine and Covenants: "And truly manifest by their works that they have received of the Spirit of Christ unto a remission of their sins" [D&C 20:37].
>
> The above quotation, [Oliver] said, was erroneous, and added: "I command you in the name of God to erase those words, that no priestcraft be amongst us!"

The Prophet continued:

> I immediately wrote to him in reply, in which I asked him by what authority he took upon him to command me to alter or erase, to add to or diminish from, a revelation or commandment from Almighty God.[2]

Doctrinally, Oliver was wrong and Joseph was right. But knowing that doesn't solve the problem. These two trusted friends were now in a conflict—both felt the other was in the wrong. The doctrinal issue could be solved, but what about the bad feelings that had arisen between them?

Realizing his letter had not really answered the doctrinal question and had made the interpersonal problem worse, Joseph traveled 80 miles to the Whitmer home to meet with Oliver and the Whitmers.

Joseph reported:

> I found the [Whitmer] family in general of [Oliver's] opinion concerning the words above quoted, and it was not without both labor and perseverance that I could prevail with any of them to reason calmly on the subject. . . . Finally, with [Christian Whitmer's] assistance, I succeeded in bringing, not only the Whitmer family, but also Oliver Cowdery to acknowledge that they had been in error, and that the sentence in dispute was in accordance with the rest of the commandment.

Joseph then reflected on what he learned from this experience. His conclusions are the centerpiece of my message today:

> And thus was this error rooted out, which having its rise in presumption and rash judgment, was . . . particularly calculated (when once fairly understood) to teach each and all of us the necessity of humility and meekness before the Lord, that He might teach us of His ways.[3]

Judging from his emphasis on humility and meekness, Joseph was commenting not only on Oliver's doctrinal error but also on the interpersonal conflict between them and, I think, on the nature of conflicts in general. With prophetic insight he taught two important lessons. His first point was that conflicts arise "in presumption and rash judgment." *Presumptuous* means overconfident or even offensive. *Rash* means hasty or impetuous. With these definitions in mind, let us look again at Oliver's message to Joseph. He said: "I command you in the name of God to erase those words, that no priestcraft be amongst us!"[4]

Do you see any ways in which Oliver's statement might be considered rash or presumptuous? Certainly commanding another person risks being offensive, especially if it is your ecclesiastical leader. Commanding "in the name of God" would raise offensiveness a degree or two. Accusing your leader of priestcraft would undoubtedly qualify.

I move to the next statement with trepidation, but Joseph invited us to consider the effect of his reply as well. Joseph "immediately wrote to [Oliver]," asking: "By what authority he took upon him to command me to alter or erase, to add to or diminish from, a revelation or commandment from Almighty God."

Are there ways in which Joseph's words might have lacked "humility and meekness"? At a minimum he might have responded with a comment and a question such as, "Oliver, I love you and I value your opinion. Would you help me understand your objection to this passage?"

Joseph's second point added power to the first. He concluded that "[conflicts are] particularly calculated (when once fairly understood) to teach each and all of us."

Three ideas stand out in this statement. First, conflicts are particularly calculated to teach us something. Second, we can't learn from them until they are fairly understood, until we can see both sides—meaning we need to cool off before we can learn from them. Third, in a marvelous illustration of his own humility, Joseph included himself as one who learned something important from this conflict.

If our conflicts are particularly calculated to teach us something, what are we supposed to learn? Joseph's answer goes deep: Conflicts are particularly calculated to teach us "the necessity of humility and meekness before the Lord, that He might teach us of His ways."

Why did Joseph say humility "before the Lord"? Why didn't he say "before the person on the other side"? To learn from our conflicts we must be willing to see our own faults, and we need the Lord's help to do that. Only then can He begin to "teach us of *His* ways" (emphasis added).

We come to the ultimate question: What *are* the Lord's ways for dealing with conflict? They are illustrated in a second conflict between Joseph and Oliver.

Second Example

Just a month after the first conflict, to escape persecution, Joseph and Emma moved 80 miles north to the Whitmer home in Fayette—the home Joseph had so recently visited to resolve the first conflict. Arriving at the Whitmer home, Joseph was grieved to learn that Hiram Page, one of the eight witnesses to the Book of Mormon, had been receiving revelations through a "seer stone" that purported to give instructions on how the Church should operate. Newel Knight was with Joseph, and he described the seriousness of the problem:

> [Hiram Page] had managed to get up some dissension of feeling among the brethren by giving revelations concerning the government of the Church . . . , which he claimed to have received through the medium of a stone he possessed. . . . Even Oliver Cowdery and the Whitmer family had given heed to them.[5]

What could have been more painful and frustrating to Joseph than this? If Joseph had followed his earlier pattern, he would have demanded of Hiram Page by what authority he presumed to receive revelations for the Church, and he would have demanded of Oliver what on earth he was thinking to believe in such things. But Joseph was more aware that a hasty and intemperate response would not solve the problem. Joseph knew what *not* to do, but he wasn't sure what he *ought* to do.

Newel Knight wrote:

Joseph was perplexed and scarcely knew how to meet this new exigency. That night I occupied the same room that he did and the greater part of the night was spent in prayer and supplication.[6]

Rather than react defensively, Joseph patiently sought counsel from the Lord. He was soon granted an answer in the form of a revelation, which is now section 28 of the Doctrine and Covenants.

Doctrine and Covenants, Section 28

Section 28 is well known for answering the question of who *can*—and who *cannot*—receive revelation for the Church. It is also a model of the Lord's willingness to see wrongdoers in the larger context of their lives and to show divine confidence in them while reproving or correcting them.

The Lord spoke in the first person directly to Oliver: "Behold, I say unto thee, Oliver, that it shall be given unto thee that thou shalt be heard by the church in all things whatsoever thou shalt teach them . . ." The Lord's first words were an affirmation of Oliver's good standing in the Lord's eyes. Then He added this stipulation: ". . . by the Comforter, concerning the revelations and commandments which I have given."[7]

After clarifying that only the prophet can receive revelation for the Church, the Lord reaffirmed His divine confidence in Oliver: "And if thou art led at any time by the Comforter to *speak* . . . by the way of command-ment unto the church, thou mayest do it."[8] And then, again, He outlined the limits on Oliver's authority: "But thou shalt not *write* by way of com-mandment, but by wisdom; And thou shalt not command him who is at thy head, and at the head of the church."[9]

The Lord then turned to the source of the problem: Hiram Page. I am struck that He spoke with the same concern for Hiram's feelings as He had shown for Oliver's. This exemplifies the Lord's way, and it makes it much easier for Hiram to accept correction: "Take thy brother, Hiram Page, between him and thee alone, and tell him that those things which he hath written from that stone are not of me."[10]

Instructed and corrected in this loving and reaffirming way, both Oliver Cowdery and Hiram Page recognized their error and continued in full fellowship in the Church for a long while.

Third Example

These two events in the life of the Prophet Joseph prepare us for one other scriptural example—the painful misunderstanding between Moroni and Pahoran in Alma 59 through 62. I wonder if this is where the Prophet Joseph gained his own understanding that conflicts are meaningful and we must learn from them.

Moroni is one of the great military leaders in all of scripture. At the early age of 25 he was made captain over all the Nephite armies. As you will recall, when the prophet Mormon abridged the records of Moroni's military leadership, he called him "a man of a perfect understanding"[11] and honored him with this remarkable endorsement:

> If all men had been, and were, and ever would be, like unto Moroni, behold, the very powers of hell would have been shaken forever; yea, the devil would never have power over the hearts of the children of men.
>
> Behold, he was a man like unto Ammon . . . , and even the other sons of Mosiah, yea, and also Alma and his sons, for they were all men of God.[12]

It has always astonished me that this same Mormon included, as part of his abridged record, a vivid account of Moroni's conflict with Pahoran, the chief judge and governor of the Nephites.

As we learn in Alma 59, Moroni's army was caught in a dangerous situation. Lamanite armies were rapidly gaining ground against them. As chief military leader, Moroni wrote Pahoran for reinforcements. Receiving none, the scripture reports, "Moroni was angry with the government, because of their indifference concerning the freedom of their country."[13]

When no help came from the government, Moroni wrote Pahoran again. He began with the facts: the suffering of his men, the slaughter of thousands of the Nephite people, and other atrocities of war. But Moroni didn't realize that Pahoran had been driven from his throne by the king-men and forced to take refuge in Gideon, and Moroni wrongly accused Pahoran of being a traitor to his own country. Moroni concluded with these challenging words: "Behold, the Lord saith unto me: If those whom ye have appointed your governors do not repent of their sins and iniquities, ye shall go up to battle against them."[14]

We are treading sacred ground here. Is there any question whether the Lord had inspired Moroni to know there were problems at the government level that called for military help? Not at all. However, in his abridgment, Mormon made it clear that Moroni mistakenly assumed Pahoran was part of the problem and threatened to remove him as head of the government.

I have puzzled many years why Mormon would include a detailed account of this uncharacteristic error by the great Captain Moroni. I expect it was for at least two reasons.

One would be to show us that none of us, not even the great Captain Moroni, is immune from presumption and rash judgment. What a comfort it is to me, and I hope to you, that we are in the best of company when we make errors of this kind. This is not to excuse them but to give us permission to admit our mistakes and to learn from them.

The second reason is to show us one of the best examples in all of scripture of how to respond to an unjust accusation. We know very little about Pahoran except that he was an upright ruler committed to standing "fast in that liberty in . . . which God . . . made us free."[15] In chapter 61, Mormon, as editor, gave us Pahoran's entire response to Captain Moroni. I will quote only two of the 20 verses included in his answer:

> I, Pahoran, who am the chief governor of this land, do send these words. . . . Behold, I say unto you, Moroni, that I do not joy in your great afflictions, yea, it grieves my soul. . . .
>
> And now, in your epistle you have censured me, but it mattereth not; I am not angry, but *do rejoice in the greatness of your heart.*[16]

How did Pahoran do it? How could he respond in such humility and meekness before the Lord? He probably sat right down and wrote an angry reply, venting his injured feelings against Moroni. If so, when he was finished, he did what we all must do—he tore it up and threw it away. Then he must have spent long hours in supplication to the Lord to find the strength to overlook the unjust accusations and to reply with such compassion and love.

In Proverbs we read that "grievous words stir up anger" and "a soft answer turneth away wrath."[17] Pahoran's soft answer is a beautiful example of what the Prophet Joseph said about "the necessity of humility and meekness before the Lord, that He might teach us of *His* ways."[18]

Even in this misjudgment Moroni is also our model. When he learned of his error, he was not prideful. He immediately marched to the aid of Pahoran, and with their combined forces they overthrew the king-men and the Lamanites, and peace was restored in the land.

As you reflect on these examples, do they call to mind any other gospel principles? I'm thinking in particular of that favorite scripture, Ether 12:27:

> And if men come unto me I will show unto them their weakness. I give unto men weakness that they may be humble; and my grace is sufficient for all men that humble themselves before me; for if they humble themselves before me, and have faith in me, then will I make weak things become strong unto them.

President Kimball taught this gospel principle in terms of mirrors. He said, "Our vision is completely obscured when we have no mirror to [show us] our own faults and [we] look only for the foibles of others."[19]

Edward Edinger, a wise psychologist, wrote this about mirrors:

> [A mirror] shows us what we otherwise cannot see for ourselves because we are too close to it. Without a mirror, for instance, we would never even know what our face looks like; since we are inside looking out, there can be no self-knowledge, even the elementary self-knowledge of what we look like, unless there is some device that can turn the light back on us.[20]

Final Observations

I conclude with a few final observations about conflicts. Again, more could be said, but you will understand.

1. Conflicts are easy to get into but difficult to get out of. If we have the courage to face them early, they are easier to resolve and to learn from.

2. Conflicts can be dangerous, because they easily fly out of control. They need good containers—such as good friendships and solid marriages—to hold them in. Early detection helps.

3. There are plenty of conflicts. They are also cyclical. If we don't learn from one, that's okay; wait a while, and, sure enough, the conflict will come around again and again until it either destroys a relationship or we learn from it. (If we learn from it, we move on to the next level of conflict, higher up on the plane of progression.)

4. Things often get worse before they get better. But it is generally better to face the problem now than to wait for the next time around.

5. It's cruel that it should be this way, but the thing we're supposed to learn about ourselves is usually obvious to the person we're in conflict with.

6. Even when we are right, we may be wrong. Even when we are right—or *especially* when we are right—if we are presumptuous and rash, we will give offense and become a stumbling block to others.

7. We learn by experience; but experience is not a very good teacher *unless* we remember our conflicts. It is a mark of greatness to remember and to learn from our conflicts.

Conclusion

We should think of our conflicts as mirrors that reflect back upon us things about ourselves we would rather not know. As we learn in Ether 12:27, it is a gift from heaven to be shown our weakness. If we will reflect upon *our* weakness, as the Prophet Joseph did upon his, the Lord will make us strong where we are weak.

I pray we may learn from our conflicts, that the Lord may teach us of *His* ways. In the name of Jesus Christ, amen.

This devotional address was given to the BYU student body on June 27, 2006. Reprinted from Brigham Young University Speeches 2006–2007, 39–50 *and the* Clark Memorandum, *spring 2007, 2–7.*

Gerald R. Williams received his JD from the University of Utah in 1969. He served as a law professor 1973–2008 and Marion G. Romney Professor of Law 2006–2008 at J. Reuben Clark Law School. His textbooks, Legal Negotiation and Settlement *(1983) and co-authored* Legal Negotiating *(2007), are the pioneering works in the field and widely adopted by American law schools. He is currently the director of Scientific Negotiation Research and Training in Provo, Utah, and a faculty member for the Professional Education Group in Minnetonka, Minnesota.*

Notes

1. Barbara Neff Autograph Book, LDS Church Historical Department, Salt Lake City; quoted in Richard Neitzel Holzapfel and Jeni Broberg Holzapfel, *Women of Nauvoo* (Salt Lake City: Bookcraft, 1992), 68.

2. *HC* 1:105.

3. *HC* 1:105.

4. *HC* 1:105.

5. Newel Knight's Journal, in *Scraps of Biography* (Salt Lake City: Juvenile Instructor Office, 1883), 64; also in *They Knew the Prophet*, comp. Hyrum L. Andrus and Helen Mae Andrus (Salt Lake City: Bookcraft, 1974), 13.

6. In *Scraps of Biography*, 65; also *They Knew*, 13.

7. D&C 28:1.

8. D&C 28:4; emphasis added.

9. D&C 28:5–6; emphasis added.

10. D&C 28:11.

11. Alma 48:11.

12. Alma 48:17–18.

13. Alma 59:13.

14. Alma 60:33.

15. Alma 61:9.

16. Alma 61:2, 9; emphasis added.

17. Proverbs 15:1.

18. *HC* 1:105; emphasis added.

19. Spencer W. Kimball, *The Miracle of Forgiveness* (Salt Lake City: Bookcraft, 1969), 269.

20. Edward F. Edinger, *The Eternal Drama: The Inner Meaning of Greek Mythology* (Boston: Shambhala, 1994), 85.

Religiously Affiliated Law Schools: An Added Dimension

Kevin J Worthen

My topic this morning is religiously affiliated law schools. It seems a fitting topic since we are convened on the campus of a very good religiously affiliated law school as members of a society that has its origin and continues to have its base in another. I think it safe to say this is a sympathetic audience—or at least I hope so. Indeed, one may wonder why I need 40 minutes to address something with which we are all so familiar and all in agreement. A story told about the notoriously taciturn Calvin Coolidge illustrates the point. When Coolidge returned home from Sunday services on one occasion, his wife, who was not able to attend, asked him whether he enjoyed the minister's sermon. ""Yes," came the one-word replied. "And what was it about?" "Sin." "Well, what did he say?" she persisted. "He was against it."[1]

Similarly, one might prefer that I simply say: "Religiously affiliated law schools? I am in favor of them." While there is likely not much new in what I will present today, I believe it is worth some elaboration, even if only in the form of a reminder, because the topic is of such importance not only to religious believers but also to those who believe in our legal system.

I want to address three separate, but related, questions about religiously affiliated law schools: First, why should the legal academy and the bar accept religiously affiliated law schools? Second, why would a church start a law school? Third, why should religious believers who attend or graduate from law schools that are not religiously affiliated care about them?

In posing each of these three questions the way I do, I understand that many would suggest that the questions ought to be framed in an even more contingent manner. Instead of asking why the academy and bar should accept religiously affiliated law schools, they would ask whether they should accept them. Similarly, rather than wondering why a church would establish a law school, they would wonder whether a church should do so.

Thus, I recognize that there are many skeptics out there, and their skepticism is not without some foundation. One way to illustrate the basis for this skepticism is to note at the outset that I cannot tell you exactly how many religiously affiliated law schools there are in the country. Contrary to what you might think, my inability to do so is not just the result of my inadequate research or math skills. Even though there is now an association of religiously affiliated law schools (which was formed in 1994), there is no consensus among that group, nor among scholars whose math and research skills are unassailable, as to the exact number of religiously affiliated law schools in the United States today.[2] That fact is instructive in two important ways.

First, it highlights the fact that religiously affiliated law schools are not all alike. Some make religion a prominent feature of their law schools, such that visitors cannot miss their religious affiliation. At the outset of its report, the most recent ABA site inspection team to visit the law school at BYU stated: "First, and obviously, the Law School is an LDS law school. The fact that it is an LDS law school is an essential feature of the School's character, and the faculty, staff, and students consistently demonstrated a deep commitment to this character."[3] They went on to say they were not sure they knew what it meant to be an LDS law school (a question that is much more difficult to answer than many might think), but it's clear that we were one. It's hard to be at BYU for any length of time without realizing that it is a religiously affiliated institution—and we hope it is not just because alcohol and caffeine are noticeably absent from campus events.

The religious nature of some religiously affiliated law schools is less obvious. Steve Barkan, former interim dean at the Marquette Law School, a Jesuit institution, once observed that "[w]ith the exception of occasional elective courses and extra-curricular activities, Jesuit law schools show relatively little objective evidence of their religious affiliation. For the most part, Jesuit law schools . . . are virtually indistinguishable from their secular counterparts."[4] Barkan then observed that "[d]epending on one's perspective, these comments might be either compliments or criticisms,"[5] an observation that applies with full force to schools, like BYU, that are more openly religious.

Second, and more important, the difficulty in identifying the exact number of religiously affiliated law schools reflects the historical fact that most of them (in tandem with the larger universities of which they are a part) have tended to become more secularized over time, so that those that at one point might have been classified as religiously affiliated no longer are. One quick illustration: In his 1937 inaugural address, Yale University President Charles Seymour urged "the maintenance and upbuilding of the Christian religion as a vital part of the university life," calling upon "all members of the faculty . . . freely to recognize the tremendous validity and power of the teachings of Christ in our life-and-death struggle against the forces of selfish materialism."[6] While such a statement by its leader would arguably suffice to classify a law school as religiously affiliated, given the wide range of schools that could fit that description, it is beyond dispute that Yale no longer fits into that category.

Like Yale, many, if not most, major private universities that currently have law schools started out with some form of religious affiliation. Many, if not most, however, would not now fit in that category, and some that do seem headed out the door. That makes it difficult to determine at any given point who is in and who is out. More important, it provides some understanding of why some skepticism exists about religiously affiliated law schools.

Indeed, a somewhat conflated review of the history of legal education in western culture may cause one to wonder whether there is room for any optimism about the future of religion in the legal academy. Harold Berman has noted that from the time formal legal training at a university began in Bologna in the 11th century up until the middle of the 19th century, "legal education in the West . . . always had a very important religious dimension."[7] Religion played a central—if not the central—role in the process. By contrast, in 1985 when Rex Lee addressed the question of the role of religious law schools in American legal education, he correctly observed that "[t]here is a substantial segment of legal educators whose view on that subject can be stated in five words: there is no such role."[8]

It is not, in my view, entirely coincidental that this trend toward secularization—which some applaud and others decry—has occurred largely in tandem with the development of the modern law school. Once Christopher Columbus Langdell and his devotees advanced the "notion that the law is a pure and exact science, consisting of principles which are discoverable through analysis of the embedded logic of reported cases,"[9] learning by faith began to fall into disfavor, so much so that a century later, Roger Cramton, then dean at the Cornell Law School, could conclude that what he called the "Ordinary Religion of the Law School Classroom" left little room for what we would call traditional religious beliefs.[10] Cramton noted that in the modern law school classroom, the unspoken assumptions are that lawyers should be skeptical, value neutral instrumentalists who analyze issues with cold logic and little concern for the ends to which their craft will be put—that decision being made by the client.[11] These characteristics are at least in tension with much of the teachings of traditional faith-based religions, which preach faith, not skepticism, and believe in moral truths, not moral relativism.

Regardless of the exact causes of the trend toward secularization, there is little dispute as to its reality, and that reality poses a challenge for those who believe there is a role for religiously affiliated law schools. As Rex Lee noted in 1985, the "historical pattern of religious schools has been to achieve *either* professional excellence as secular institutions, *or* fidelity to their religious values as so-so law schools."[12] Some remain convinced that this pattern is inevitable. Mark Tushnet has argued that a religiously affiliated university "'will find it extremely difficult' to maintain this affiliation if it also seeks to attain or preserve a national reputation."[13] For many, then, the choice is clear: a law school can be secular or second rate.

It is in this skeptical environment that I pose the three questions I wish to address. I do not purport to provide a full answer to any of the questions but rather hope to provoke further thought and discussion about these issues.

First, why, given the current context, should the legal academy and the bar accept religiously affiliated law schools? Over the last two decades, a growing body of literature has supplied various answers to this question. I highlight three of the more common ones.

First, religiously affiliated law schools can provide a large part of the antidote to a number of the ills that have beset lawyers and the legal profession in the last half century. At an individual level, a growing body of literature reveals an increasing dissatisfaction with the practice of law. A 1990 survey by the ABA Young Lawyers Division revealed that 19 percent of attorneys were generally dissatisfied with their jobs, a 27 percent increase from a similar survey performed just six years earlier.[14] A survey of lawyers in Wisconsin nine years later indicated that 91 percent found the practice of law increasingly stressful every year.[15] Yet another study concluded that lawyers experience depression at a rate that is anywhere from two to six times greater than the general population.[16] As one scholar noted, these surveys demonstrate "a clear . . . decline in lawyers' career satisfaction, physical health and mental health,"[17] a trend that an ABA committee noted, "threatens the well-being of lawyers and firms in every part of the country."[18]

At a macrolevel the concerns are magnified. As faith and other values have been excluded from the legal academy, the nature of the legal practice has itself changed in disturbing ways. Lack of civility is increasingly a concern of the bench and bar. Moreover, questions concerning the usefulness or destructiveness of lawyers who are trained to be value-neutral are arising with greater frequency. As Derrick Bell has observed:

> Lawyers need conscience as well as craft. To borrow an old but picturesque phrase, skilled lawyers without conscience are like loose guns on a sinking ship, their very presence is so disconcerting that they wreak damage whether or not they hit anything.[19]

Religiously affiliated law schools are in a unique position to address these ills because the values that so many find missing in the practice of law and legal education are, to quote Rex Lee, "integral parts of the values that for millennia have constituted the foundation stones of Jewish, Christian, and other religious teachings."[20] This is not to imply that those who are not religious cannot hold these values. Anyone with experience in the world recognizes that is not the case. Some of the most caring, compassionate, and competent lawyers I know have no religious beliefs. But there is often an added dimension that accompanies and sometime magnifies the manifestation of these values if they are rooted in deep-seated religious conviction. Let me illustrate with an experience I shared with our first-year students at last year's orientation.

It concerns one of our graduates who told me of his efforts to apply gospel truths, as he understood them, to the practice of law. He is a litigator—a very good one. As you know, litigation is often contentious, sometimes overly so. On one occasion this lawyer found himself in a deposition involving several attorneys, one of whom repeatedly verbally abused one of the other lawyers, engaging in personal attacks and tirades. Our graduate, somewhat stunned, did little to intervene on behalf of the victim, in part because the issues that sparked the outbursts had nothing to do with his client. That evening, however, he felt terrible because he had done nothing to prevent the attack from continuing. He resolved that he would never again allow that to happen to another attorney or witness when he was present, because he understood the deep truth that we are all sons and daughters of God with a divine nature and destiny.

That story, by itself, could illustrate how an understanding of eternal truths can shape the practice of law in a positive way. But the story does not end there. On further reflection our graduate realized that the abusive attorney was also one of God's children with the same divine nature and potential as everyone else. He concluded that the laws of God required him to be concerned about this overly zealous and somewhat flawed lawyer as well. He knew the opposing attorney somewhat and realized that this behavior was not aberrational. After considerable reflection he concluded that the opposing attorney had some unmet needs that he, our graduate, could never fill. When he was about to let the matter pass, he suddenly realized that there was One—a perfect One—who, because of His infinite atoning sacrifice, could fill the unmet needs of this obviously unhappy attorney and make him whole. At that point our graduate resolved that at minimum he would pray for the well-being and happiness of that—and other—opposing counsel whose own unhappiness spilled out into the lives of others. Thus began his practice of praying for those with whom he worked, even those on the other side of an issue, and especially those whose actions were offensive to him and others. While it is not possible to measure the impact these heavenly importunings have had on the lives of his opposing counsel, this attorney reported that it has made his own professional life more fulfilling. I am also certain this lawyer has internalized the values of civility that so many judicial officials and bar leaders seek to instill in all lawyers.

Again, this is not to imply that those who are not religious will not share or exhibit the same values. But for those who are religious believers, those beliefs add another dimension. Moreover, that kind of story could not be told in that way at a state-sponsored law school; yet it, and similar stories, are the kind that can speak to the souls of many law students and lawyers in ways that will allow them to practice law more effectively and with more satisfaction. Thus, religiously affiliated law schools can provide a distinctively powerful form of teaching the values that the bar, the academy, and society encourage all lawyers to possess.

The second reason that the bar and academy should accept religiously affiliated law schools relates to another issue of importance to those two entities: the need for diversity in legal education. As the Supreme Court noted in *Grutter v. Bollinger,* "The skills needed in today's increasingly global marketplace can only be developed through exposure to widely diverse people, cultures, ideas, and viewpoints."[21] Thus, in order to be effective, legal education must expose lawyers to diverse views. Some will undoubtedly find use of this argument in defense of religiously affiliated law schools surprising, if not objectionable, for one of the common criticisms of such law schools is that they are too narrow, insular, and parochial and therefore insufficiently diverse. While that is a real issue to which religiously affiliated law schools need constantly to be attuned, these same schools have contributed—and continue to contribute—to a diverse environment in ways that often go unrecognized.

As to the past, many Catholic law schools started in the late 19th and early 20th century precisely because the then-established law schools were unwilling to accept Catholic students or immigrants who "either could not afford, or were otherwise excluded from law schools" at the time.[22] Thus, religiously affiliated law schools have opened up legal education and the influence that flows from that education to segments of society that otherwise might have been excluded.

One might counter that the need for such schools has now dissipated in the more enlightened era in which we live, one in which Catholics and members of other previously excluded groups are now found at all top law schools. However, one should not underestimate the impact that the establishment of Catholic schools had—and continues to have—on that enlightenment. The success of Catholic law schools provided an irrefutable rebuttal to the arguments of those who contended, either openly or covertly, that Catholics or immigrants could not flourish in legal education or the legal profession. Moreover, one can argue that the success of well-regarded Catholic schools like Notre Dame and Boston College continues to open doors to Catholics at other law schools because those schools provide a continuing reminder to the world that Catholicism and top-quality legal education are not incompatible, a theme to which I will return at the end of my remarks.

Even if this first contribution of religiously affiliated law schools to the diversity of legal education has run its course, there is another often-overlooked contribution that is perhaps more valuable today than ever. As scholars such as Michael McConnell and Jim Gordon have articulated so well, religiously affiliated universities and law schools contribute to diversity in legal education at a macrolevel in ways that other institutions simply cannot.[23] As Judge McConnell put it, religiously affiliated universities

> enrich our intellectual life by contributing to the diversity of thought and preserving important alternatives to post-Enlightenment secular orthodoxy. Their very distinctiveness makes them better able to resist the popular currents of majoritarian culture and thus to preserve the seeds of dissent and alternative understandings that may later be welcomed by the wider society.[24]

While diversity of thought and viewpoint is an important aspect of legal education, there is a certain irony in the tendency of the legal academy to insist that true diversity can be established only if every institution is diverse in exactly the same way. Religiously affiliated law schools contribute enormously to diversity when one considers diversity at an institutional and not just individual level. As the former dean of the Dayton Law School observed, "The world is a more interesting place . . . when people have beliefs, convictions, and a song to sing."[25]

Religiously affiliated law schools provide the environment in which those beliefs and convictions can be nourished in a legal context. Unless the legal academy and bar have reached the point at which they have concluded with certainty that they have all the answers and that religion has absolutely nothing to offer, they should gratefully accept the diverse voice that religiously affiliated law schools provide, as those voices may otherwise not be heard at all.

That leads to a third reason why the academy and bar should accept religiously affiliated law schools: such schools are essential to religious liberty overall. As Mike McConnell has observed, religiously affiliated universities

> are an important means by which religious faiths can preserve and transmit their teachings from one generation to the next, particularly for nonmainstream religions whose differences from the predominant academic culture are so substantial that they risk annihilation if they cannot retain a degree of separation. The right to develop and pass on religious teachings is at the very heart of the first amendment.[26]

While some might limit that argument to undergraduate education that involves students who are younger and therefore generally more impressionable, similar value transmission is essential in law schools. As the Supreme Court noted in *Grutter*, law schools have historically proven to be institutions that develop leaders,[27] and as Judge McConnell has observed, "Religious colleges and universities do more than transmit creeds; they also raise up leaders and members in the tradition and communion of the faith."[28]

There are other things that could and have been said in support of the proposition that the bar and academy should accept religiously affiliated law schools. I will save those for another day and instead turn to the somewhat-related, but very distinct, and much-less-often-asked question: Why would a church have a law school?

This question is less often considered for a variety of reasons. First, it is of relevance to fewer people. While all the academy and bar have some interest in whether religiously affiliated law schools are allowed to exist, only those who are members of a church that has or will establish a law school are directly concerned with this question. And that universe is even smaller than the universe of religiously affiliated law schools. Many religiously affiliated law schools were started and are controlled not by churches themselves but by members of the faith who seek to promote its values. Thus, some religiously affiliated law schools have limited or no formal ecclesiastical ties with the church with which they are affiliated.[29]

Most of the more limited scholarly writing on this subject has come as a result of the Catholic Church's efforts in the 17 years since the issuance of *Ex Corde Ecclesiae* to more closely regulate Catholic universities, even those not formally initiated by the church itself (such as the Jesuit institutions). Leading among these scholars has been Thomas Shaffer, one of the most thoughtful and influential scholars of our time on the relationship between law and religion.

Professor Shaffer has identified a number of possible reasons why churches—and particularly the Catholic Church, of which he is a member—would have a law school. Dismissing the notion that they do so to make money, he concludes that "a church has a law school because the church wants to do something for God that it can only do by having a law school."[30] He then identifies some of the things that might qualify in that regard. A church law school could, for example, "provide vertical mobility to members of the church."[31] It might "provide a spiritually cordial atmosphere for believers who study law," so they remain close to the faith as they study.[32] Or, Shaffer opines, a church law school may reflect a "theology that says the church should serve the community," and law is one way for that to happen.[33] Finally, Shaffer says—and this is clearly the idea he likes best—the church may have a law school because the church serves a priestly and prophetic function and the law school may help it carry out that mission.[34] This is the most challenging role a law school may play because, just as prophets and priests must on occasion call believers not to follow the ways of the world, churches that have a law school to help them carry out priestly or prophetic functions must at times remain apart from the mainstream. Because it is required to live in the world, the church understands the usefulness of the law.[35] But because it cannot be fully part of the world, the church cannot take its moral guidance from the law.[36] Thus, the church is desirous to use the law to advance its interest but also is wary of the law, and it wants lawyers who understand that tension.[37] It may conclude, Shaffer says, that the best way to do that is to have its own law school.[38] This will allow the church to "focus more carefully and more forcefully on how it understands the practice of law, so that the practice of law will not only be moral but will also be priestly and prophetic."[39]

Not everyone involved in Catholic legal education agrees with Shaffer,[40] but the possible reasons he suggests provide considerable food for thought for anyone interested in any church law school, including the one in Provo, Utah—to which I now turn my remarks.

Many have speculated as to the reasons why The Church of Jesus Christ of Latter-day Saints established a law school. The answers suggested by Shaffer are all plausible: the Church may have wanted to provide vertical mobility for its members, or it may have wanted to provide a spiritually cordial atmosphere in which believers could study the law. President Marion G. Romney's observation that the Law School was established so that there would be "an institution in which [students] may 'obtain a knowledge of . . . [the] laws of . . . man' in the light of the 'laws of God,'" strongly suggests something along the lines of the latter.[41] The Church might also have intended that the Law School aid in the Church's service to the community in ways that the J. Reuben Clark Law Society's pro bono project seems to be doing.

In a 1975 address at the dedication of the Law School building, President Romney provided some other reasons why he used his considerable influence to help establish the Law School, including the Law School's potential impact on the rest of university, the positive impact that the atmosphere of the university would have on the Law School, and—most relevant to this group—his desire to perpetuate "the memory and influence of President J. Reuben Clark Jr." something to which all of you continue to contribute.[42]

For me, however, the most interesting reason posed by President Romney in that address is the one he listed first, one suggesting a role for the Law School in filling the priestly mission of the Church, not in the way that Shaffer had in mind but in a manner that provides a more direct connection with the purposes and doctrines of the Church than the other possible reasons.

In explaining why he advocated for the Church to establish a law school, President Romney stated, "To begin with, I have long felt that no branch of learning is more important to an individual or to society than law."[43] President Romney was not one given to hyperbole, and I don't believe he intended to engage in it on this occasion. With that in mind, reflect for a minute on what he said: "No branch of learning is more important to an individual or to society than law." No other branch of learning? Not philosophy, not medicine, not engineering, not theology? Could he have really meant that?

I believe the answer is yes, and my belief is based on remarks President Romney made two years earlier when speaking to the charter class on its first day of law school in a portion of his address that tends not to get much emphasis in our sound-bite world. At the outset of those remarks, President Romney stated in plain, declarative terms: "To appreciate the reason the Church is establishing a school of law here at Brigham Young University, one must have some understanding of The Church of Jesus Christ of Latter-day Saints, and know and realize something about its nature and its purpose."[44] He then described events that occurred well before any board of trustees meetings in the early 1970s and truths that stretch well beyond the principles found in any casebook.

> First—That we humans "are begotten sons and daughters unto God" (D&C 76:24).
>
> Second—That mortality is but one phase, albeit an indispensable phase, of our total existence.
>
> Third—That God created us that we "might have joy" (2 Nephi 2:25) and that it is His purpose and His work and His glory "to bring to pass the immortality and eternal life of man" (Moses 1:39), which is the highest form and type of joy and happiness.
>
> Next—That God has provided in the Gospel of Jesus Christ the true and only way by which men can achieve that objective.[45]

President Romney then listed other eternal truths and doctrines. In essence, he outlined the plan of salvation. After laying that groundwork, he then discussed some of what the Lord has said in modern revelation about law, quoting specifically from the 42nd and 34th verses of the 88th section of the Doctrine and Covenants: "[God] hath given a law unto all things, by which they move in their times and their seasons; [and] that which is governed by law is also preserved by law and perfected and sanctified by the same." President Romney could have gone on to quote other portions of that section, including the fact that "[a]ll kingdoms have a law given . . . [a]nd unto every kingdom is given a law; and unto every law there are certain bounds also and conditions."[46]

The point seems clear: law extends well beyond this mortal sphere. It is an essential part of our Father in Heaven's eternal plan of happiness for

His children. Thus, when we study law we are truly acquiring an "education for eternity," to borrow President Kimball's phrase.[47] I believe it was with that in mind that President Romney asserted his belief that "no other branch of learning is more important to an individual or to society than law," for as he noted in a different context, "[T]here is no permanent progress made in any field or in any place except it be through obedience to the governing law."[48]

I believe that one cannot fully understand why this Church would establish a law school if one does not first understand how important, how essential, how central, law is to God's eternal plan for us, His children.

When I was midway through law school, I attended a general conference session with my father. Shortly after the session, my father ran into an acquaintance of his and introduced me. My father informed his friend that I was in law school. With all earnestness the man responded, "I once thought about going to law school, but then I realized that there would be no need of lawyers in the celestial kingdom." He did not smile; he was not joking. Somewhat taken aback, I asked him what he did for a living. He said he was a dentist. I am glad that I refrained from asking him whether he seriously thought that teeth would need repair after the resurrection, but I have regretted that I did not have a better answer than that, one that President Romney provided. Yes, there will be need for those who understand law in the celestial kingdom. Indeed, I believe that those who do not understand law will not be there.[49] As Joseph Smith observed:

> If man has grown to wisdom and is capable of discerning the propriety of laws to govern nations, what less can be expected from the Ruler and Upholder of the universe? Can we suppose that He has a kingdom without laws? Or do we believe that it is composed of an innumerable company of beings who are entirely beyond all law? . . . Would not such ideas be a reproach to our Great Parent, and at variance with His glorious intelligence? Would it not be asserting that man had found out a secret beyond Deity? That he had learned that it was good to have laws, while God after existing from eternity and having power to create man, had not found out that it was proper to have laws for His government?[50]

In making these observations I do not suggest that the Church created the Law School so that students could spend three years trying to extract eternal legal principles from the scriptures. The principal focus of the Law School has been and will continue to be to provide a first-rate legal education focused on secular laws. Students have been and will be required to learn the skills and concepts associated with those laws in the same way that they are learned in other top-tier law schools. As President James E. Faust informed our students several years ago:

> Do not expect your professors . . . to concentrate [their] lessons out of the scriptures, although occasionally [they] may wish to do so. [Their] obligation

> is to teach you the secular rules of civil and criminal law and matters that
> relate to them. Your obligation is to learn the rules of law and related matters
> The whisperings of the Holy Spirit will no doubt help you, but you must learn
> the rules of law, using Churchill's phrase, by "blood, sweat, and tears."[51]

I believe, however, we will not understand or achieve the full purposes of
the Law School unless we recognize that the study of law is much more
important and deep than most in the world realize. It is only when we
study the laws of men in the light of the laws of God that we can begin
that process. A school like BYU must be the kind of place where that can
happen if it is to be the law school the Church wants it to be.

Now to the third and final question: Why should religious believers
who do not attend religiously affiliated law schools care about the answers
to the two prior questions?[52] At a general level, one would expect that they
might care to a greater extent than nonbelievers merely because they are
concerned about the well-being of their fellow believers. But I believe the
interest goes much deeper than this and that it turns on things that are
of more direct and practical effect than the more abstract concern for the
well-being of fellow brothers and sisters. I mention three in particular.

First, to the extent that religiously affiliated law schools are essential to
the full enjoyment of religious liberty in the United States, believers, even
those who are not lawyers or law students, have an interest in the success
of those law schools. Indeed, for an organization like the J. Reuben Clark
Society—which maintains that strength is brought to the law by a lawyer's
personal religious convictions—not just the existence but the success of
religiously affiliated law schools is of great importance.

Second, as noted above, I believe the existence of well-respected religiously affiliated law schools improves the environment and the demand
for believing lawyers and law students at nonreligiously affiliated law firms
and law schools. In that regard, I believe that the successes attained by
J. Reuben Clark Law School have helped open doors for all LDS law students and lawyers, even those who never attend a class at BYU. I was at
a meeting of law deans last spring, when the dean of another law school
approached me, introduced himself with a broad smile and announced,
"We have six of your students at our law school and we love them." He
obviously expected me to join in his joy, which I did, even though none
of those students had ever attended BYU Law School. As I have watched
with pleasure the growing number of student chapters of the J. Reuben
Clark Law Society, I believe we at BYU Law School have an obligation to
help those LDS law students who do not attend BYU by being as good a law
school as we can be because I know that at least some of their deans, classmates, and potential employers see them as "our" students.

Similarly, we at BYU Law School benefit from the good works of LDS
students at other law schools. Your successes, especially to the extent you

are affiliated with chapters of the J. Reuben Clark Law Society, clearly redound to our benefit. That is also true of LDS lawyers who are not our graduates. Indeed, the J. Reuben Clark Law Society was founded in large part because Bruce Hafen, then the dean of J. Reuben Clark Law School, and Ralph Hardy, a prominent LDS attorney who was not a BYU Law School graduate, both realized the extent to which their successes and destinies were tied together.

Thus, we are somewhat fellow travelers in this endeavor of bringing together two things that command our time and passion: law and religion. That leads to the third reason why believers who do not attend religiously affiliated law schools should care about the questions such schools face, especially the second one: Why would a church start a law school? I believe that great benefit can come to any LDS lawyer, even those who are not BYU law students or graduates, in considering deeply why the Church would start a law school. I have suggested several reasons. Some are more narrowly focused on the campus at BYU. But I believe the most important reasons extend well beyond that setting both geographically and temporally. As I indicated, it is clear to me from both President Romney's observations and the scriptures that law is of much broader importance than many members of the Church, including many lawyers, may initially suppose. And, while I have given the matter some thought, it is clear to me that I have not—and likely will not—fully comprehend its importance on my own.

I, therefore, invite you to join with me in that exciting ongoing endeavor. For the law is indeed a noble profession, and there truly is "strength brought to the law by a lawyer's personal religious convictions."

This address was given at the J. Reuben Clark Law Society Conference at Pepperdine University in Malibu, California, on February 16, 2007. Reprinted from the Clark Memorandum, *fall 2007, 10–21.*

Kevin J Worthen received his JD from BYU Law School in 1982, clerked for Judge Malcolm R. Wilkey of the U.S. Court of Appeals for the D.C. Circuit 1982–83 and for Justice Byron R. White of the U.S. Supreme Court 1983–84. He has served as a law professor since 1987 and was associate dean 1999–2004 and dean 2004–2008 of J. Reuben Clark Law School. He is currently Hugh W. Colton Professor of Law and advancement vice president at Brigham Young University in Provo, Utah.

Notes

1. PAUL F. BOLLER JR., PRESIDENTIAL ANECDOTES 241–42 (rev. ed. 1996).
2. Within a two-year period, three articles came up with three different numbers. Steven M. Barkan, *The First Conference of Religiously Affiliated Law*

Schools: An Overview, 78 MARQ. L. REV. 247, 247 (1995) (35 religiously affiliated law schools); David L. Gregory, *Where to Pray? A Survey Regarding Prayer Rooms in A.B.A. Accredited, Religiously Affiliated Law Schools*, 1993 BYU L. REV. 1287, 1307 (52); Thomas L. Shaffer, *Erastian and Sectarian Arguments in Religiously Affiliated American Law Schools*, 45 STAN. L. REV. 1859, 1864 n.18 (1993) (48). For a more recent effort at enumeration (including several schools not in existence when the earlier numbers were calculated), see Monte N. Stewart & H. Dennis Tolley, *Investigating Possible Bias: The American Legal Academy's View of Religiously Affiliated Law Schools*, 54 J. LEGAL EDUC. 136, 142 (2004) (44).

3. American Bar Association, Inspection Report on the J. Reuben Clark Law School, 5 (2005).

4. Steven M. Barkan, *Jesuit Legal Education: Focusing the Vision*, 74 MARQ. L. REV. 99, 102–03 (1990).

5. *Id.* at 103.

6. GEORGE M. MARSDEN, THE SOUL OF THE AMERICAN UNIVERSITY: FROM PROTESTANT ESTABLISHMENT TO ESTABLISHED NONBELIEF 11 (1994).

7. Harold J. Berman, *The Secularization of American Legal Education in the Nineteenth and Twentieth Centuries*, 27 J. LEGAL EDUC. 382, 382 (1975).

8. Rex E. Lee, *The Role of the Religious Law School*, 30 VILL. L. REV. 1175, 1175 (1985).

9. Graham B. Strong, *The Lawyer's Left Hand: Nonanalytical Thought in the Practice of Law*, 69 U. COLO. L. REV. 759, 759–60 (1998).

10. Roger C. Cramton, *The Ordinary Religion of the Law School Classroom*, 29 J. LEGAL EDUC. 247 (1978). Cramton notes, for example, that law students tend to be (and are trained to be) "tough minded" rather than "tender minded" and that the former group tends to be "irreligious." *Id.* at 261.

11. More specifically, Cramton notes that an outside observer of a modern law school classroom would conclude that underlying the legal education system are: (1) "a skeptical attitude towards generalizations, principles, and received wisdom," (2) "an instrumental approach to law and lawyering," (3) "a 'tough-minded' and analytical attitude towards lawyer tasks and professional roles," and (4) "a faith that man, by the application of his reason and the use of democratic processes, can make the world better." *Id.* at 248–52.

12. Lee, *supra* note 8, at 1175–76 (1985).

13. Robert John Araujo, *"The Harvest Is Plentiful, but the Laborers Are Few": Hiring Practices and Religiously Affiliated Universities*, 30 U. RICH. L. REV. 713 , 718 (1996) (quoting Mark Tushnet, *Catholic Legal Education at a National Law School: Reflections on the Georgetown Experience*, in GEORGETOWN AT TWO HUNDRED: FACULTY REFLECTIONS ON THE UNIVERSITY'S FUTURE 322 (William C. McFadden ed., 1990).

14. AMIRAM ELWORK, STRESS MANAGEMENT FOR LAWYERS 14 (3d ed. 2007).

15. *Id.* at 15.

16. Susan Daicoff, *Lawyer, Know Thyself: A Review of Empirical Research on Attorney Attributes Bearing on Professionalism*, 46 AM. U. L. REV. 1337, 1347 (1997).

17. ELWORK, *supra* note 15, at 13.

18. *Id.*

19. Derrick A. Bell Jr., *Humanity in Legal Education*, 59 OR. L. REV. 243, 244 (1980).

20. Rex E. Lee, *Today's Religious Law School: Challenges and Opportunities*, 78 MARQ. L. REV. 255, 259 (1995).

21. 539 U.S. 306, 330 (2003).

22. Barkan, *supra* note 4, at 104.

23. *See, e.g.,* James D. Gordon III, Individual and Institutional Academic Freedom at Religious Colleges and Universities, 30 J.C. & U.L. 1 (2003).

24. Michael W. McConnell, *Academic Freedom in Religious Colleges and Universities*, 53 LAW & CONTEMP. PROBS. 303, 312 (1990).

25. Lee, *supra* note 8, at 1180 (quoting Dean Frederick Davis of the University of Dayton School of Law).

26. McConnell, *supra* note 24, at 316.

27. *Grutter*, 539 U.S. at 332.

28. McConnell, *supra* note 24, at 316 n.38.

29. Steven M. Barkan, *supra* note 1, at 247. "The strength of the religious identity of each of [the religiously affiliated] law schools, and the extent to which the religious identity affects the life of each law school, vary greatly." *Id.*

30. Thomas L. Shaffer, *Why Does the Church Have Law Schools?*, 78 MARQ. L. REV. 401, 402 (1995).

31. *Id.*

32. *Id.*

33. *Id.*

34. *Id.* at 402–03.

35. *Id.* at 404.

36. *Id.* at 405.

37. *Id.* at 404–06.

38. *Id.* at 406.

39. *Id.*

40. *See, e.g.,* Mark A. Sargent, *An Alternative to the Sectarian Vision: The Role of the Dean in an Inclusive Catholic Law School*, 33 U. TOL. L. REV. 171 (2001).

41. Marion G. Romney, *Becoming J. Reuben Clark's Law School*, in ADDRESSES AT THE CEREMONY OPENING THE J. REUBEN CLARK LAW SCHOOL, AUGUST 27, 1973 17, 20 (1973).

42. Marion G. Romney, *Why the J. Reuben Clark Law School?*, in DEDICATION: TO JUSTICE, TO EXCELLENCE, TO RESPONSIBILITY: PROCEEDINGS AT THE CONVOCATION AND DEDICATION OF THE J. REUBEN CLARK COLLEGE OF LAW, Brigham Young University, Provo, Utah, September 5, 1975 43, 43–44 (1975).

43. *Id.* at 43.

44. Romney, *supra* note 37, at 17.

45. *Id.*

46. *Doctrine and Covenants* 88:34, 36.

47. Spencer W. Kimball, *Climbing the Hills Just Ahead: Three Addresses*, in EDUCATING ZION 43 (John H. Welch & Don E. Norton eds., 1996).

48. Marion G. Romney, *The Rule of Law*, ENSIGN, Feb. 1973, at 2, 2.

49. *See, Doctrine and Covenants* 88:22.

50. TEACHINGS OF THE PROPHET JOSEPH SMITH 55 (Joseph Fielding Smith comp., 1976).

51. James E. Faust, *The Study and Practice of the Laws of Men in the Light of the Laws of God, in* LIFE IN THE LAW: ANSWERING GOD'S INTERROGATORIES 37 (Galen L. Fletcher & Jane H. Wise eds., 2002).

52. With respect to the first question, the real inquiry here is why this group should care more than a nonbelieving lawyer or law student since all lawyers and law students presumably have some interest in the first question.

BE HEALERS

The Doctrine of Religious Freedom

W. Cole Durham Jr.

I would be remiss on this occasion if I did not express gratitude for the opportunities I have had during one of the great transformative epochs in human history—the decade after the collapse of communism—to visit almost every post-communist country and to work with leaders in their homelands on implementing the ideals of religious freedom. I am grateful beyond measure for blessings that have been given and keys that have been exercised to allow me to participate in the high adventure of opening the doors of nations.

Several years ago a close friend and Church leader gave me a blessing promising that I would be able to invoke the witness of the Holy Ghost when I spoke with others about religious freedom. In fulfillment of that blessing, I have seen the influence of the Spirit change the hearts and minds and, indeed, the entire outlook of many of the governmental leaders with whom I have met, the "gatekeepers" who stand at the doors of nations. I pray that the Spirit will be with me again today as I have the chance to bear witness of this great principle among my own people.

The Doctrine of Religious Freedom

The title of my address—"The Doctrine of Religious Freedom"—is intended to remind us that religious freedom is not merely an important constitutional and human right.[1] There can be no doubt that it is a "first" freedom.[2] But for us it is even more: it is a matter of doctrine. Our 11th article of faith reads:

> We claim the privilege of worshiping Almighty God according to the dictates of our own conscience, and allow all men the same privilege, let them worship how, where, or what they may.

Moreover, this is not merely doctrinal for us—it is a core doctrine. Yet, as I will explain, it is a paradoxical doctrine. And it is a doctrine of prophecy.

Religious Freedom Is a Core Doctrine

That religious freedom is a core doctrine has been reemphasized to my mind by the following remarkable statement from Elder Bruce R. McConkie:

> Freedom of worship is one of the basic doctrines of the gospel. Indeed, in one manner of speaking *it is the most basic of all doctrines,* even taking precedence over the nature and kind of being that God is, or the atoning sacrifice of the Son of God, or the vesting of priesthood and keys and saving power in the one true church. By this we mean that if there were no freedom of worship, there would be no God, no redemption, and no salvation in the kingdom of God.[3]

Note two things about this statement. First, Elder McConkie does not say this is the most *important* doctrine. He said that "it is the most basic of all doctrines." It is the most basic because none of the other doctrines could become operative or have any meaning or authenticity if we did not have the option to choose them freely. The exercise of this right is in fact an attribute of divinity.[4] The atoning sacrifice of Christ would be meaningless if we could not avail ourselves of its power to save and exalt through freely chosen acts of faith, repentance, and covenanting. Part of the reason the Messiah is "the Lamb slain from the foundation of the world"[5] is that at the key moment in the premortal existence, He recommended the Father's plan of freedom, knowing its cost. He knew the price that He personally would pay to atone for all our abuses of freedom. He also knew that despite His payment of that price, countless numbers of His beloved brothers and sisters—individuals He loves with a depth and intensity that passes our understanding—would be lost forever because of their own decision "to choose captivity and death."[6]

This brings me to the second point about Elder McConkie's statement. Note that he did not say that it made no difference *how* we exercise this freedom; to the contrary, everything depends on learning to follow the divine pattern set by the Master of worship in every thought and deed and with all our "heart, . . . might, mind, and strength."[7]

The Paradox of Religious Freedom

Paradoxically, following the pattern set by the Master includes learning to respect the beliefs and choices made by others, even while standing firm in witnessing and teaching doctrinal truths. Indeed, following the pattern means standing for the rights and freedoms of others, even at the cost of our own lives—and surely also even at the lesser cost of inconvenience or discomfort.

This paradoxical nature of the doctrine of religious freedom needs to be emphasized and understood more deeply. Most of our doctrines are teachings that we affirm and agree to follow. In contrast, although religious freedom is basic and foundational for the system of gospel truth, it demands that we respect the views of those who adhere to other systems of belief. What is paradoxical is that our belief in religious freedom obligates us to tolerate and respect beliefs with which we disagree—though it does not require us to accept, endorse, or support them.

Part of the paradox is explained by the fact, attested by all the modern prophets, that the gospel embraces all truth.[8] But more is involved in the doctrine of religious freedom than an admonition to accept truth wherever we find it.[9] It is a recognition of the realities of human dignity and conscience and of the obligation to respect agency at the precious core of the human spirit. This doctrine has had great practical meaning for our leaders.[10] Just a year before his martyrdom, Joseph Smith declared:

> The Saints can testify whether I am willing to lay down my life for my brethren. If it has been demonstrated that I have been willing to die for a "Mormon[,]" I am bold to declare before Heaven that I am just as ready to die in defending the rights of a Presbyterian, a Baptist, or a good man of any other denomination; for the same principle which would trample upon the rights of the Latter-day Saints would trample upon the rights of the Roman Catholics, or of any other denomination who may be unpopular and too weak to defend themselves.
>
> It is a love of liberty which inspires my soul—civil and religious liberty to the whole of the human race.[11]

Forgetting the paradox of religious freedom has been a cause of incalculable suffering during human history. Too often, groups who have pleaded for tolerance while they were a persecuted minority have turned into persecutors as soon as they acquired political power. Joseph Smith was very conscious of this tragic tendency toward unrighteous dominion and repudiated it.[12] We as members of The Church of Jesus Christ of Latter-day Saints should not be guilty of insensitivity in this area. Having so often suffered from religious intolerance in the past, we should go the extra mile in assuring that others are not exposed to similar pain.[13] What those who forget this paradox do not understand is that the mere possession of truth does not carry with it a right to impose that truth on others. God possesses all truth, yet He has left us our freedom.

In the end, the paradox of religious freedom is linked to many of the deepest truths of the gospel, which share a similar paradoxical structure. "Whosoever will lose his life for my sake shall find it."[14] "I, the Lord, will forgive whom I will forgive, but of you it is required to forgive all men."[15] What ultimately lies behind this paradox is the second great commandment: "Thou shalt love thy neighbour as thyself."[16] Love lies at the heart of the paradox and at the core of religious freedom.

> Love your enemies, bless them that curse you, do good to them that hate you, and pray for them which despitefully use you, and persecute you;
>
> That ye may be the children of your Father which is in heaven: for he maketh his sun to rise on the evil and on the good, and sendeth rain on the just and on the unjust.[17]

Stated differently, what makes the doctrine of religious freedom paradoxical is that the right to enjoy religious freedom for ourselves carries with it a reciprocal obligation to respect the religious freedom of others. In the words of the Golden Rule, Do unto others as you would have them do unto you.[18] Or as the Lord said at the Last Supper, "As I have loved you, . . . love one another."[19]

Religious Freedom and Prophecy

Religious freedom is not only a matter of doctrine; it is a focus of prophecy. You are all familiar with the great description of the last days found in Isaiah 2:

> And it shall come to pass in the last days, that the mountain of the Lord's house shall be established in the top of the mountains, and shall be exalted above the hills; and all nations shall flow unto it.
>
> And many people shall go and say, Come ye, and let us go up to the mountain of the Lord, to the house of the God of Jacob; and he will teach us of his ways, and we will walk in his paths: *for out of Zion shall go forth the law,* and the word of the Lord from Jerusalem. . . .
>
> O house of Jacob, come ye, and let us walk in the light of the Lord.[20]

For me, Isaiah's great vision of the last days has taken on greater meaning ever since I read a commentary on this passage by President Harold B. Lee,[21] in which he pointed to an interpretation of the phrase "out of Zion shall go forth the law" that is found in the dedicatory prayer of the Idaho Falls Temple. The relevant portion of that prayer reads as follows:

> We pray that kings and rulers and the peoples of all nations under heaven may be persuaded of the blessings enjoyed by the people of this land [the United States] by reason of their freedom under thy guidance and be constrained to adopt *similar* governmental systems, *thus to fulfil the ancient prophecy of Isaiah that "out of Zion shall go forth the law and the word of the Lord from Jerusalem."*[22]

The Idaho Falls Temple was dedicated on September 23, 1945, immediately following the end of World War II. With that in mind, it is worth reflecting on developments that have occurred since 1945 that bear on the fulfillment of this prophecy.

First, virtually all currently enforceable international human rights treaties have been adopted since 1945. Moreover, the entire approach to international human rights law has changed. It is now taken for granted that it is legitimate for one sovereign nation to be concerned about the human rights practices of other nations.[23]

At the national level, with only a handful of exceptions, all the countries on earth have adopted their current constitutions since 1945.[24] In short, we are witnessing a remarkable historical process in the field of international law and comparative constitutional law that is the subject of prophecy. This to my mind is one of the many ways that we see the tracings of the Spirit of Christ in history.

The Significance of Religious Freedom for Church Growth

Let me now give you a graphic sense for the implications that global religious freedom has for the growth of The Church of Jesus Christ of Latter-day Saints. Look first at a map of the globe that attempts to plot the status of religious freedom around the world [Map 1]. The information in this map is based primarily on the latest annual report on religious freedom provided by the u.s. State Department.[25] The countries shown in gray are countries that have either no constitutional protection of religious freedom or that do not respect this ideal in practice. Some states protect religious freedom to some extent but have significant qualifications that make it difficult to found a new religious community in the country. Restrictions on proselyting are particularly problematic. As the map shows, most of the world now has normal-to-strong protection of religious freedom. No country has a perfect record, but the situation is markedly better than it was even 10 years ago.

Now look at the map showing the presence of the Church of Jesus Christ worldwide [Map 2]. Darker gray shows the countries where the Church has not yet achieved formal recognition. As you can see, this band of the world includes China and most Islamic nations. Not surprisingly, since the Church always follows the policy of going "in the front door" and entering a country only when it is legal for it to do so,[26] there is a high correlation between low religious freedom and lack of formal presence of the Church of Jesus Christ.

The third map shows that religious freedom also has considerable significance for general patterns of Church growth [Map 3]. One of the things that is striking from the map is that concentrations are higher in what the scriptures refer to as the "promised land" of the Americas and certain "islands of the sea." Second, one is beginning to see the impact of growth in parts of Africa and the former socialist bloc, where we lacked significant presence until recently. Finally, what the map shows is that Church population remains very thin virtually everywhere. Aside from the United Kingdom, Portugal, and South Korea, there are no countries in these three vast continents of Europe, Africa, or Asia that have as much as one Latter-day Saint per 1,000 in its population. Even in the Americas population exceeds 3 percent only in Chile. Utah remains the only place where the Church is in the majority. The point is that we remain a tiny minority virtually everywhere—so religious freedom protections continue to be of tremendous significance to the Church and its members.

Global Challenges to Implementing Religious Freedom

With this background, let me turn now to some of the global challenges to implementing religious freedom. We live in a world that is peopled with an odd mixture of Sherems[27] and Korihors.[28] Sherem, as you remember, is the Book of Mormon figure who criticized prophets and revelations concerning Christ on the basis of fundamentalist or supposedly "orthodox" interpretations of religious texts. At the other pole stands Korihor, the secular anti-Christ who prefigured in his thought the great masters of suspicion of the 19th and 20th centuries—Darwin, Marx, Nietzsche, and Freud.

Both secularism and fundamentalism or orthodoxy in other traditions can pose profound problems for religious freedom. Further problems emanate from nationalism, ethnicity, and efforts to exploit these for the retention of political power. The recent arrest of Slobodan Milosevic reminds us of the terrible ways a power-hungry leader can use these forces, often manipulating religion in the process to cause terrible devastation.[29] Finally, fears associated with stereotypical images of "dangerous sects"—often fanned by virulent anticult forces[30]—are leading to infringements of religious freedom both in areas of Western Europe and in many other parts of the world.

The Church has outgrown the "dangerous sect" label, but just barely, and we are constantly at risk that overbroad reactions to supposedly "dangerous" religions will create problems for us as well. Even if this were not the case, however, our own experience with religious persecution should encourage us to stand firm for the rights of the currently less fortunate groups.

Time is limited, but let me give a few concrete examples of how religious freedom is protected in practice.

Technical Legal Assistance

A year ago in January I stopped for three days in Romania because I had a few extra days between two other conferences in Europe. I was aware that very problematic legislation was pending that, among other things, would have made it virtually impossible for the Church of Jesus Christ and many other religious groups to find places of worship in that country. On the first day of my visit I stopped in to see the head of religious affairs, who I had met at a conference a few months earlier. By coincidence, or something more, I was in his office when he received a call indicating that the ruling coalition in Romania would consider whether to withdraw the proposed law from Parliament three days later. Armed with that alert, it was possible to help mobilize response from many groups and government leaders both within and outside of Romania, with the result that the legislation was withdrawn. With a kind of clarity that is seldom so clear-cut, I knew that my three days in Romania had been blessed, and blessed with success.

More typical of efforts working on legislation has been the experience of the past few weeks working in Kazakhstan and Kyrgyzstan through the Organization for Security and Cooperation in Europe (OSCE). Through this international organization I have been privileged to help provide technical advice to these central Asian republics as they grapple with the difficult problem of dealing with Muslim extremists coming into their countries from other parts of the Islamic world. Their initial reaction has been to clamp down on any transborder activity, restrict missionary work, and make it more difficult for religious groups to be registered so that they can operate legally in the country. OSCE efforts will help contribute to better laws for these countries and may help set patterns that can be utilized elsewhere in the Muslim world.

The Influence of Academic Conferences and Consultations

Academic conferences provide an important setting for contributing to religious freedom. Let me describe a few incidents that have grown out of this type of activity. Each fall for the past several years we have held an international conference at BYU dealing with religious freedom. The minister of justice from Peru attended one of these two or three years ago. At the time the Church had just learned that it had exhausted missionary quotas for the year in Peru. A Church official working with visas mentioned this to the minister of justice during a break at the conference. He was quite surprised that such a quota existed at all and indicated he would check into the matter when he returned home. Within a few weeks there were no more missionary quotas in Peru.

The people who come to BYU for our annual conference are often deeply moved by what they experience here. One of my favorite statements comes from another friend who is currently the head of religious affairs in Albania. He had the opportunity last fall, the day before our academic conference started, to attend the Sunday morning session of general conference in the new Conference Center. Some of you who stood in lines to get into conference this past weekend can appreciate what he saw. This is what he said about the experience:

> I have been in [my position as head of religious affairs] for a year, and I have seen a lot. But now I am totally convinced that religion should be an essential part of people's lives. In my country, people line up for bread; today I saw thousands of your people standing in line . . . to worship.

This kind of impression changes perspectives on the importance of religious freedom. I returned a month ago from a conference that same man had organized in Albania, aimed at pointing the way toward a good law on religious associations that can bless the lives of people in that poor and struggling country for years to come. These stories indicate only a few of the many approaches that can help promote religious freedom.

Implications

In the end, what ultimately carries the day is that religious freedom is a true principle. It is a principle of justice. The just and honorable people of this earth recognize its validity. A nation that fails to respect it cannot claim to be just. We must do all in our power to make it a common heritage of all mankind. As the maps suggest, the gospel flourishes best under conditions of liberty. God Himself respects this principle. Were it otherwise, He would not be just. His kingdom must be freely chosen. It will not be imposed on anyone anymore than worship in the temple is imposed on nonbelievers. The celestial kingdom is, among other things, a type of worship that will be imposed only on those who have chosen it. But choosing the Lord's kingdom has implications; you cannot arrive in Zion without having chosen to get there. You cannot ascend the mountain of the Lord's house without leaving other things behind. Part of the paradox of freedom is that the Lord allows people not to return to Him. Allowing freedom reflects the nature of a just God, but it cannot compromise divine truth. Just as mercy cannot rob justice, so justice cannot rob truth.

With this in mind, let me conclude by saying a few things about what the doctrine of religious freedom should mean for each of us. I am convinced that many in your generation will have opportunities to make important contributions to the cause of religious freedom. Hannah Smith, a law student, and Elizabeth Clark, the associate director of the BYU International Center for Law and Religion Studies, each played crucial roles in a recent visit to France to help oppose problematic anticult legislation there. Hannah's husband, John, also a law student, is helping to organize a conference on religious freedom in Ukraine. Others could be mentioned. In time there will be more and more such individuals with knowledge, experience, expertise, and contacts who will be able to help monitor religious freedom developments worldwide and provide assistance and positive contributions when called upon to do so.

Another young Latter-day Saint lawyer played a crucial role last year in helping to set up a conference on religious freedom with the constitutional court of Azerbaijan. His work had taken him to Azerbaijan at the time. He recognized the opportunity and checked with appropriate authorities. A way was found to organize the conference. I want to underscore the fact that this brother checked with appropriate authorities. Matters of religious freedom often raise a variety of sensitive issues, and it is important before working on these matters to follow the guidance of those holding the keys for the work. There are a number of unfortunate incidents in Church history where well-intended Church members exerted "zeal without knowledge," and set Church progress back by years.

The story of the founding of the Church in Kazakhstan suggests another role that some adventurous Church families will play. About three years ago a major law firm approached the Law School looking for a business lawyer willing to go to its office in Almaty, Kazakhstan. One of our graduates who had been in practice for several years responded. He and his family have now been in Kazakhstan about three years. Two other expatriate families have moved in. As recently reported in the *Church News*,[31] the Church is now organized in Kazakhstan. These founding families are praying for someone to come with greater fluency in Russian, or with other gifts, so that they can teach and train new Church members more effectively.

During conference over the past weekend, you heard several talks about the need for couples. Let me tell you a secret. You don't have to wait until you are 65. I have been convinced as long as I have been teaching at the Law School that one of the great waves of missionary work we will see in our lifetime is that performed by families who, like Ammon, decide to go out to the frontiers of the kingdom, dedicated to serving those they find there and hoping to build the kingdom in these locations. This activity will not be for everyone, and there is much to be done on the home front.[32] But some of you will feel this call and will see unparalleled growth in the Church as a result of your faithfulness and witness.

Consider one other example that suggests another kind of role we all can play. I have a nonmember friend who has played a very important role in a country sensitive enough that I will not name it. He tells me that over the past few years, through a chain of coincidences, he has found himself being befriended by Church members at almost every turn. When he first came to the U.S., the librarian at his university was a Latter-day Saint who helped him immeasurably. Later he studied at another university, where he met additional Latter-day Saints. I heard of him through yet another organization and invited him to our BYU conference. He has subsequently met some Church members in his own country. He was ultimately retained to help secure legal recognition for the Church. In connection with rendering this service, he was asked what he would charge. The lawyer who asked him told me that at the time he was silent for several minutes. Then he said, "I really don't know what to do. I have been benefited so much by friends in your Church that I don't know whether I should charge at all." In the end he was persuaded to take some compensation, but I'm sure it was much less than his help was worth.

This leads me to a final set of comments about how we should implement the doctrine of religious freedom in our lives. Most of you will not in fact be engaged in legal defense of religious freedom in various parts of the world. For you, what will be most important is the paradoxical part of this doctrine—not the part that underlies all our doctrine and protects our rights to worship but the reciprocal part in which you show tolerance and respect and love for others.

A few years ago, precisely as much of my work in Eastern Europe was heating up, I became involved in an effort to revise provisions of the Utah Constitution dealing with religious freedom.[33] During the political process I had numerous opportunities to speak around the state. Two things concerned me. First was the number of Church members who felt it was part of their duty as Church members to impose their views on other members of our community. Too many of them, it seemed to me, had forgotten the vital lesson at the core of the paradox of the doctrine of religious freedom: the mere possession of truth does not carry with it a right to impose that truth on others. Second, I heard countless nonmember parents talking about pain their children had suffered because of either intentional or more often unintentional exclusion of their children in our communities.

I believe that President Hinckley has also sensed their concerns. I don't know if you have paid attention to this, but in virtually every conference for the past few years he has emphasized the importance of being tolerant, of being civil, and of being good neighbors. I cannot repeat his numerous statements on this theme.[34] I can only say that he has been an exemplary advocate of religious freedom. I was immeasurably proud when he greeted the arrival of the Southern Baptist Convention and its plans to "evangelize the Mormons" with counsel that we should be as courteous to them as we would hope others would be to our missionaries.[35] Again and again he has reminded us of our obligation to be true to the hard side of religious freedom: respecting the beliefs of others.

Let me conclude with a statement that some of you here may have heard President Hinckley give at his devotional on November 4, 1997. In that address he stated:

> I hope that [Brigham Young University] will give to you a great sense of tolerance and respect for others not of your faith. The true gospel of Jesus Christ never led to bigotry. It never led to self-righteousness. It never led to arrogance. The true gospel of Jesus Christ leads to brotherhood, to friendship, to appreciation of others, to respect and kindness and love.[36]

After teaching this principle he told a remarkable story. He had been visited the week before by Shimon Peres, a former prime minister of Israel and one of the elder statesmen of the world. Mr. Peres told him the following story about a Jewish rabbi, which appropriately enough had been told to the prime minister by a Muslim. President Hinckley recounted the story as follows:

> A Jewish rabbi . . . was conversing with two of his friends. The rabbi asked one of the men, "How do you know when the night is over and the day has begun?"
>
> His friend replied, "When you look into the distance and can distinguish a sheep from a goat, then you know the night is over and the day has begun."
>
> The second was asked the same question. He replied, "When you look into the distance and can distinguish an olive tree from a fig tree, that is how you know."
>
> They then asked the rabbi how he could tell when the night is over and the day has begun. He thought for a time and then said, "When you look into the distance and see the face of a woman and you can say, 'She is my sister.' And when you look into the distance and see the face of a man and can say, 'He is my brother.' Then you will know the light has come."[37]

I am reminded of the first line of a hymn by my great-grandfather, Thomas Durham: "Stars of morning, shout for joy; Sing redemption's mystery."[38]

The morning is coming. You are the stars of morning. We are the stars of morning. We are witnessing the Church coming "forth out of obscurity and out of darkness."[39] Part of "redemption's mystery" is our paradoxical—and yet ultimately not paradoxical—obligation to respect and love and protect the rights of others not of our faith.

May we sing this mystery well. May we be true children of our Father in Heaven, never forgetting—and never forgetting to live—the song learned in Primary: "As I have loved you, Love one another."[40] In the name of Jesus Christ, amen.

Notes

1. Religious liberty is protected by a vast array of constitutions, treaties, and other international human rights instruments. See, e.g., U.S. Constitution,

amendment 1; *Universal Declaration of Human Rights,* adopted and proclaimed by
u.n. General Assembly Resolution 217A (III) (1948), art. 18; *International Covenant
on Civil and Political Rights,* adopted and opened for signature by u.n. General
Assembly Resolution 2200A (XXI) (1966), art. 18.

2. See Franklin Delano Roosevelt, "The Four Freedoms," address to 77th
Congress, 6 January 1941; available online at <http://www.libertynet.org/edcivic/
fdr.html>.

3. Bruce R. McConkie, *A New Witness for the Articles of Faith* (Salt Lake City:
Deseret Book, 1985), 655; emphasis added.

4. The members of the Godhead Themselves worship each other freely as a
natural, yet free response to the glory of Their beings. For example, the Father can
be seen as worshiping the Son—not a worship of subordination, but surely worship
in the sense of love and respect—when He declared, "This is my beloved Son." See
2 Peter 1:17: "For he received from God the Father honour and glory, when there
came such a voice to him from the excellent glory, This is my beloved Son, in whom
I am well pleased." The members of the Godhead bear witness of each other. See 3
Nephi 11:32: "I bear record of the Father, and the Father beareth record of me, and
the Holy Ghost beareth record of the Father and me."

If C. S. Lewis is correct in pointing out that praise is a natural and willing
response to "the worthiest object of all," then it is reasonable to assume that an
attitude of worship and praise characterizes the reciprocal relations of members
of the Godhead (*Reflections on the Psalms* [New York: Harcourt, Brace and World,
1958], 96). As Lewis says, "All enjoyment spontaneously overflows into praise. . . .
I think we delight to praise what we enjoy because the praise not merely expresses
but completes the enjoyment; it is its appointed consummation" (*Reflections,* 94, 95;
see also entire chapter, "A Word About Praising," 90–98).

5. Revelation 13:8.

6. 2 Nephi 2:27.

7. D&C 59:5.

8. There are countless statements supporting this proposition. Only a few of
the more notable ones are listed here. Joseph Smith wrote:

> The first and fundamental principle of our holy religion is, that we believe that we
> have a right to embrace all, and every item of truth, without limitation or with-
> out being circumscribed or prohibited by the creeds or superstitious notions of
> men. [Letter to Isaac Galland, written from Liberty Jail, 22 March 1839, in Dean
> C. Jessee, comp. and ed., *The Personal Writings of Joseph Smith* (Salt Lake City:
> Deseret Book, 1984), 420]

Brigham Young taught:

> "Mormonism," so-called, embraces every principle pertaining to life and salvation,
> for time and eternity. No matter who has it. If the infidel has got truth it belongs
> to "Mormonism." The truth and sound doctrine possessed by the sectarian world,
> and they have a great deal, all belong to this church. . . . There is no truth but what
> belongs to the gospel. [JD 11:375]
>
> I want to say to my friends that we believe in all good. If you can find a truth
> in heaven, earth or hell, it belongs to our doctrine. We believe it; it is ours; we claim
> it. [JD 13:335]

Further, he stated:

For me, the plan of salvation must . . . circumscribe the knowledge that is upon the face of the earth, or it is not from God. Such a plan incorporates every system of true doctrine on the earth, whether it be ecclesiastical, moral, philosophical, or civil: it incorporates all good laws that have been made from the days of Adam until now; it swallows up the laws of nations, for it exceeds them all in knowledge and purity; it circumscribes the doctrines of the day, and takes from the right and the left, and brings all truth together in one system, and leaves the chaff to be scattered hither and thither. [*JD* 7:148]

A wonderful passage from John Taylor is worth quoting at length:

We wish to comprehend and embrace all truth and seek for and obtain everything that is calculated to exalt, ennoble and dignify the human family; and wherever we find truth, no matter where, or from what source it may come, it becomes part and parcel of our religious creed, if you please, or our political creed, or our moral creed, or our philosophy, as the case may be, or whatever you may please to term it. *We are open for the reception of all truth, of whatever nature it may be, and are desirous to obtain and possess it, to search after it as we would for hidden treasures; and to use all the knowledge God gives to us to possess ourselves of all the intelligence that he has given to others; and to ask at his hands to reveal unto us his will, in regard to things that are the best calculated to promote the happiness and well-being of human society.* If there are any good principles, any moral philosophy that we have not yet attained to we are desirous to learn them. If there is anything in the scientific world that we do not yet comprehend we desire to become acquainted with it. If there is any branch of philosophy calculated to promote the well-being of humanity, that we have not yet grasped, we wish to possess ourselves of it. If there is anything pertaining to the rule and government of nations, or politics . . . that we are not acquainted with, we desire to possess it. If there are any religious ideas, any theological truths, any principles pertaining to God, that we have not learned, we ask mankind, and we pray God, our heavenly Father, to enlighten our minds that we may comprehend, realize, embrace and live up to them as part of our religious faith. *Thus our ideas and thoughts would extend as far as the wide world spreads, embracing everything pertaining to light, life, or existence pertaining to this world or the world that is to come.* [John Taylor, *JD* 14:337; emphasis added]

Wilford Woodruff stated, "If any man has got a truth that we have not got, let us have it. Truth is what we are after. . . . If we have not the truth, that is what we are after, we want it" (*JD* 17:194).

Joseph F. Smith proclaimed:

We believe in all truth, no matter to what subject it may refer. No sect or religious denomination in the world possesses a single principle of truth that we do not accept or that we will reject. We are willing to receive all truth, from whatever source it may come; for truth will stand, truth will endure. [*GD*, 1]

Coming down to the present, President Howard W. Hunter stated:

As members of the Church of Jesus Christ, we seek to bring all truth together. We seek to enlarge the circle of love and understanding among all the people of the earth. Thus we strive to establish peace and happiness, not only within Christianity but among all mankind. ["The Gospel—A Global Faith," *Ensign*, November 1991, 18]

Note the interesting linkage here between the notion of embracing all truth and enlarging the circle of love and understanding.

Finally, President Gordon B. Hinckley has restated the theme as follows:

> I love to learn. I relish any opportunity to acquire knowledge. Indeed,
> I believe in and have vigorously supported, throughout my life, the pursuit of
> education—for myself and for others. . . .
>
> The learning process is endless. We must read, we must observe, we must
> assimilate, and we must ponder that to which we expose our minds. I believe in the
> evolution of the mind, the heart, and the soul of humanity. I believe in improve-
> ment. I believe in growth. . . .
>
> . . . It therefore behooves us, and is our charge, to grow constantly toward
> eternity in what must be a ceaseless quest for truth. And as we search for truth, let
> us look for the good, the beautiful, and the positive. [*Standing for Something* (New
> York: Times Books, 2000), 59, 62, 64]

9. Clearly that is part of our obligation, but it is not all. The light of Christ
"lighteth every man that cometh into the world" (John 1:9; D&C 93:2), and we
should be responsive to that light wherever it shines. In seeking wisdom "out of
the best books" (D&C 88:118), my experience has been that although others may
not have the fullness of the gospel with the authority and keys that have come with
the Restoration, they often understand those portions that they have been given
in greater depth. We can benefit immensely from their knowledge. For example, a
modern physicist may not understand the fullness of the gospel, but as to the truths
of the fundamental structure of matter, he no doubt knows more than most of us,
and to the extent his knowledge corresponds to reality, he has knowledge of truths
that are embraced by our religion. The same is true in other domains of knowledge.
In this regard it is worth remembering Brigham Young's statement:

> Our religion measures, weighs, and circumscribes all the wisdom in the world—
> all that God has ever revealed to man. God has revealed all the truth that is now in
> the possession of the world, whether it be scientific or religious. [JD 8:162]

10. When Nauvoo was founded, the Prophet Joseph Smith stated that he
designed its charter "for the salvation of the Church, and on principles so broad,
that every honest man might dwell secure under its protective influence *without
distinction of sect or party*" (HC 4:249; emphasis added). In this same spirit, the
city council of Nauvoo passed one of the early "anti–hate crime" ordinances in
American history. Section 1 of the ordinance reads as follows:

> Be it ordained by the City Council of the City of Nauvoo, that the Catholics,
> Presbyterians, Methodists, Baptists, Latter-day Saints, Quakers, Episcopals,
> Universalists, Unitarians, Mohammedans, and all other religious sects and denom-
> inations whatever, shall have free toleration, and equal privileges, in this city; and
> should any person be guilty of ridiculing, and abusing or otherwise depreciating
> another in consequence of his religion, or of disturbing or interrupting any reli-
> gious meeting within the limits of this city, he shall, on conviction thereof before
> the Mayor or Municipal Court, be considered a disturber of the public peace, and
> fined in any sum not exceeding five hundred dollars, or imprisoned not exceeding
> six months, or both, at the discretion of said Mayor or Court. [HC 4:306]

Significantly, Brigham Young clearly taught that even during the Millennium
there will be just and honorable people of other faiths who will be protected in their
rights to freedom of religion (see JD 2:309).

11. HC 5:498.

12. See D&C 121:37. For an example of Joseph Smith's critical view of the tendency of the persecuted to assume the role of oppressors, see his comments on intolerance in Massachusetts (HC 2:464–65).

13. For an excellent discussion of this principle, see John K. Carmack, *Tolerance: Principles, Practices, Obstacles, Limits* (Salt Lake City: Bookcraft, 1993).

14. Matthew 16:25; see also 10:39; Mark 8:35; Luke 9:24; 17:33.

15. D&C 64:10.

16. Matthew 22:39.

17. Matthew 5:44–45.

18. See Matthew 7:12: "Therefore all things whatsoever ye would that men should do to you, do ye even so to them: for this is the law and the prophets." A version of this great teaching of the Master is found in virtually every major religious tradition. See, e.g., *The Analects of Confucius* 15:23 ("What you do not want done to yourself, do not do to others"—Confucianism); *Mahabharata* 5:1517 ("This is the sum of duty: do naught unto others which would cause you pain if done to you"—Hinduism); Talmud, Shabbat 31a ("What is hateful to you, do not do to your fellow man"—Judaism); *Udanavarga* 5:18 ("Hurt not others in ways that you yourself would find hurtful"—Buddhism); *Dadistan-i Dinik* 94:5 ("That nature only is good when it shall not do unto another what-ever is not good for its own self"—Zoroastrianism); *Forty Hadith of an-Nawawi* 13 ("Not one of you is a believer until he loves for his brother what he loves for himself"—Islamism); *Tablets of Bahá'u'lláh* 71:26 ("Blessed is he who preferreth his brother before himself"—Bahaism); *Sutrakritanga* 1.11.33 ("A man should wander about treating all creatures as he himself would be treated"—Jainism); Guru Arjan Dev 259, *Guru Granth Sahib* ("Don't create enmity with anyone as God is within everyone"—Sikhism).

19. John 13:34.

20. Isaiah 2:2–5; emphasis added.

21. Harold B. Lee, "The Way to Eternal Life," *Ensign*, November 1971, 15; quoted in Jay M. Todd, "A Standard of Freedom for This Dispensation," *Ensign*, September 1987, 16.

22. George Albert Smith, "Dedicatory Prayer for the Idaho Falls Temple," *Improvement Era*, October 1945, 564; quoted by Harold B. Lee in Todd, "A Standard," 16; emphasis added.

23. See Henry J. Steiner and Philip Alston, *International Human Rights in Context: Law, Politics, Morals* (Oxford: Clarendon Press, 1996), 148–65. Moreover, a number of regional international treaties have been adopted. Most notable of these is the European Convention for the Protection of Human Rights and Fundamental Freedoms. The European Court of Human Rights, which monitors compliance with this convention, is now the most significant constitutional court in the world. It has approximately 800,000,000 people within its jurisdiction, including all the former socialist bloc countries with the exception of those in Central Asia, and its pronouncements on human rights issues are now given effect throughout this vast region. See P. van Dijk and G. J. H. van Hoof, *Theory and Practice of the European Convention on Human Rights*, 3rd ed. (The Hague: Kluwer Law, 1998), 1–2, 31–36. For a brief overview of the current status of the court, see European Court of Human Rights, FAQ, <http://www.echr.coe.int/50/en/#faq>.

24. To the best of my knowledge, the only exceptions are the following 10 countries, which adopted their constitutions prior to World War II: the United

States in 1788, Norway in 1814, Liberia in 1847, Luxembourg in 1868, Switzerland in 1874, Tonga in 1875, Australia in 1901, Liechtenstein in 1921, Lebanon in 1926, and Ireland in 1937. The only other exceptions are the United Kingdom, Bhutan, Israel, and Libya, which do not have written constitutions.

25. U.S. State Department, *2000 Annual Report on International Religious Freedom* (5 September 2000) (available online at <http://www.state.gov/www/global/human_rights/irf/irf_rpt/irf_index.html>). The differentiation between "normal" and "strong" protection is subjective, based on personal perceptions and interactions with comparative constitutional law experts.

26. "Wherever we go, we go in the front door. Our representatives honor the laws of the nations to which they go and teach the people to be good citizens" ("President Hinckley Addresses World Affairs Council," *Ensign*, August 1999, 75). Similar statements have been regularly made by other Church leaders as well. See, e.g., Spencer W. Kimball, quoted in Martin B. Hickman, *David Matthew Kennedy: Banker, Statesman, Churchman* (Salt Lake City: Deseret Book, 1987), 342; also see Dallin H. Oaks and Lance B. Wickman, "The Missionary Work of The Church of Jesus Christ of Latter-day Saints," in John Witte Jr., and Richard C. Martin, eds., *Sharing the Book: Religious Perspectives on the Rights and Wrongs of Proselytism* (Maryknoll, New York: Orbis Books, 1999), 270.

27. Jacob 7.

28. Alma 30.

29. See "Siege Ends as Milosevic Surrenders," *Deseret News*, 1 April 2001, A1.

30. W. Cole Durham Jr., "The United States' Experience with New Religious Movements," *European Journal for Church and State Research* (1998), 5:215.

31. "Kazakhstan Recognizes Church," *Church News*, 17 February 2001, 5.

32. See Bruce D. Porter, "Building the Kingdom" *Ensign*, May 2001, 80–81. Elder Porter provided a vital reminder that

sometimes, perhaps, we may be inclined to see the building of the kingdom as something that takes place beyond the horizon, far away from our own branch or ward. In truth, the Church advances both by outward expansion and by inward refinement. . . .

We do not have to be called to serve far from home, nor do we have to hold a prominent place in the Church or in the world to build up the Lord's kingdom. [Porter, "Building the Kingdom," 80]

33. Because of what I regard as one of the great decisions in the history of our state supreme court, *Society of Separationists v. Whitehead*, it ultimately became unnecessary to pursue the constitutional amendment in question (870 P.2d 916 [Utah 1993]).

34. See, e.g., Gordon B. Hinckley, "A Time of New Beginnings," *Ensign*, May 2000, 87–88; "The Work Moves Forward," *Ensign*, May 1999, 4–5; and "We Bear Witness of Him," *Ensign*, May 1998, 4–6. One statement that seemed particularly impressive to me is the following:

> In many communities where our people are in the majority, accusations are heard that we are intolerant, that we display an attitude of self-righteousness, and that we are uncooperative in advancing causes which are for the common good. . . . It has been reported that some parents, out of a desire to protect their children, have told them that they should not associate in school with those not of their faith.

It seems anomalous that some would keep their sons and daughters from so doing while they are in the elementary schools, and yet make great sacrifice when they grow older to send them into the mission field.

Let us not forget that we believe in being benevolent and in doing good to all men. I am convinced that we can teach our children effectively enough that we need not fear that they will lose their faith while being friendly and considerate with those who do not subscribe to the doctrine of this Church. Let us reach out to those in our community who are not of our faith. Let us be good neighbors, kind and generous and gracious. Let us be involved in good community causes. There may be situations, there will be situations, where, with serious moral issues involved, we cannot bend on matters of principle. But in such instances we can politely disagree without being disagreeable. We can acknowledge the sincerity of those whose positions we cannot accept. We can speak of principles rather than personalities. In those causes which enhance the environment of the community, and which are designed for the blessing of all of its citizens, let us step forward and be helpful. An attitude of self-righteousness is unbecoming a Latter-day Saint. [*TGBH*, 661–62]

35. See, e.g., "'We Are a Biblical Church, Atlanta Members Told,'" *Church News*, 23 May 1998, 5, quoting President Gordon B. Hinckley as saying:

I don't know how many will be there [at the Southern Baptist Convention]. I have heard everything from 12,000 to 18,000. I hope there are 20,000 of them. I hope they have a wonderful time. I hope that our people are hospitable toward them and will reach out the hand of fellowship and show love for them.

36. Gordon B. Hinckley, "The BYU Experience," *BYU 1997–98 Speeches* (Provo: BYU, 1998), 63.

37. Hinckley, "BYU Experience," 64.

38. "Stars of Morning, Shout for Joy," *Hymns*, 1948, no. 164.

39. D&C 1:30.

40. "Love One Another," *Hymns*, 1985, no. 308. I am indebted to Elder Bruce D. Porter for highlighting this image to beautifully teach this concept in his recent general conference address. See Porter, "Building the Kingdom," 80.

This devotional address was given to the BYU student body on April 3, 2001. Reprinted from Brigham Young University Speeches 2000–2001, 213–226 *and the* Clark Memorandum, *fall 2001, 2–13.*

W. Cole Durham Jr. received his JD from Harvard University in 1975 and clerked for Judge Robert A. Ainsworth of the U.S. Court of Appeals for the Fifth Circuit 1975–76. He received the International First Freedom Award from the First Freedom Center in Richmond, Virginia, in 2009. He currently is the Susa Young Gates University Professor of Law and director of the International Center for Law and Religion Studies at J. Reuben Clark Law School in Provo, Utah.

Be Healers

James E. Faust

I am humbled to have been invited by Dean H. Reese Hansen, dean of J. Reuben Clark Law School, and William Atkin, chair of the J. Reuben Clark Law Society, to participate in this historic fireside. I am advised that the J. Reuben Clark Law Society, founded in 1988, has a membership of 6,000 Latter-day Saint attorneys and law students in approximately 40 chapters throughout the world. I am grateful for the generous use of the Church satellite broadcasting system, which makes it possible for all of you to participate without traveling to a central location. Both J. Reuben Clark Law School and this society were established for a noble purpose. President Marion G. Romney, who supported the establishment of J. Reuben Clark Law School, stated that a principal purpose was to permit the study of the "laws of man in light of the laws of God."

I would like to expand on President Romney's statement beyond the study of the laws of men in light of the laws of God to *involvement with* the laws of men in light of the laws of God. In our own standards of personal conduct we must remember that the laws of men are the lesser law. I cite to you that the laws of many jurisdictions do not require or encourage being a Good Samaritan. As I have said before, there is a great risk in justifying what we do individually and professionally on the basis of what is "legal" rather than what is "right." In so doing, we put our very souls at risk. The philosophy that what is legal is also right will rob us of what is highest and best in our nature. What conduct is actually legal is, in many instances, way below the standards of a civilized society and light years below the teachings of the Christ. If you accept what is legal as your standard of personal or professional conduct, you will deny yourself of that which is truly noble in your personal dignity and worth.

A lawyer's own careful conscience and his own standard of high integrity ultimately must govern his conduct. The Doctrine and Covenants reminds us that "he that keepeth the laws of God hath no need to break the laws of the land" (D&C 58:21).

Surely the higher law requires us to not only just seek justice but to eliminate injustice. The Savior taught if any person has done an injustice to another so that the injured party needs to seek redress, the offender should do more than merely pay that which is due, he should in spirit give his cloak also (see Matthew 5:40). Efforts of conciliation and reconciliation and compromise are elements of the higher law.

The mission statement of the J. Reuben Clark Law Society is: "We affirm the strength brought to the law by a lawyer's personal religious conviction. We strive through public service and professional excellence to promote fairness and virtue founded on the rule of law." These two statements suggest that there is a higher standard of conduct expected of the graduates of the Law School and members of this Law Society. Wherever we live we may need to break with certain trends of the legal establishment as it is today. When the profession has in some ways strayed from high professional principles, perhaps we have some duty to point the way.

I presume that most if not all of you have had the gift of the Holy Ghost bestowed upon you. By this transcending gift we are told that we can learn all things and "know the truth of all things" (Moroni 10:5). Thus we can enjoy discernment of things that cannot come in any other way. This is true not only in our professional lives but also in our family, Church, and public lives. Advocates even as angels need to speak "by the power of the Holy Ghost" (Moroni 10:5). The great truths taught by King Benjamin were given to him by an angel who said unto him, "[H]ear the words which I shall tell thee" (Mosiah 3:3). This is a pretty reliable source of information. The founders and supporters of J. Reuben Clark Law School have hoped that you could be men and women of profound legal competence without being tainted by any of the pernicious selfish influences that tend to corrupt and abuse the legal system. One can't help wondering if in some instances the tort judicial system in the United States is being abused because of the exorbitant punitive damages that are sometimes being awarded. A few of them bear no relationship to reasonable compensation. The lawyers must bear some of the responsibility for this, because some of the cases are taken on a contingent fee basis. It is hard to change human nature, because greed is a basic human weakness. The compensation a lawyer receives ought not to be his primary interest. The interest of the client always has to be the first consideration. If you will follow that rule, you and your family will be taken care of.

The day when a young lawyer passes the bar and hangs out his shingle (as I did) and hopes some clients will come to him is probably over. My first month after paying my expenses I made three dollars, and it didn't improve very rapidly. But my wife and I took comfort from my patriarchal blessing, which said that I would have sufficient means to take care of my

wife, my family, and myself. She stayed home with the children, and looking back on it, I don't know how we did it, but my patriarchal blessing in
that regard was completely fulfilled. I could have made more money by
simply charging more for my services, but that was a conscious decision on
my part. The Lord's hand is in the affairs of those who seek to do His will.
Things work out in unexpected ways. When I was a 28-year-old bishop,
only a few months in the practice of the law, we had a Relief Society bazaar
in our ward. I was flat broke, and my wife and I wondered how we were
going to support the Relief Society bazaar. The very day of the bazaar some
money came in that was totally unexpected, which strengthened my faith
and made it possible for the bishop to do his duty. I believe that if you con-
scientiously render the service to your clients, and strive to be worthy, the
Lord will take care of you.

To you law students who are in attendance tonight, I pass on a warning
written in July 1850 by Abraham Lincoln:

> There is a vague popular belief that lawyers are necessarily dishonest.
> I say vague, because when we consider to what extent confidence and honors
> are reposed in and conferred upon lawyers by the people, it appears improb-
> able that their impression of dishonesty is very distinct and vivid. Yet the
> impression is common, almost universal. Let no young man choosing the law
> for a calling for a moment yield to the popular belief—resolve to be honest
> at all events; and if in your own judgment you cannot be an honest lawyer,
> resolve to be honest without being a lawyer. [*The Collected Works of Abraham
> Lincoln,* vol. 2 (Rutgers University Press, 1953, 1990), p. 81]

When I was a young practicing lawyer, there was an older member of
the bar who was considered a very skilled advocate, but as a person he was
nothing more. He was a fierce opponent and knew all of the tricks of the
trial advocacy. His personal life was reprehensible. He was never involved
in humanitarian efforts. To my knowledge, he never served on a community committee, never ran for nor held public office. He did not evidence one scintilla of spirituality. Others with less natural talent but more
character were far more successful and much happier.

To be fully successful in the law, one does not have to be brilliant or
exceptionally gifted. The most effective work of the world is done by ordinary people who put forth extraordinary effort. This is true of lawyers. Our
strengths are magnified with experience and inspiration. I also believe that
while practicing law we can still maintain our humanity, that we ought to
be patient and forgiving—although, as some witty person quipped, "To err
is human; to forgive would put a lot of attorneys out of work."

Our lawyers need to be more than successful advocates. We need to
bring our sacred religious convictions and standards to the practice of
law. To do otherwise would bring an inconsistency to our character. There
always needs to be a connection between having an involvement in the

law and living the gospel. In a sense we are all "able ministers of the new testament; not of the letter, but of the spirit: for the letter killeth, but the spirit giveth life" (2 Corinthians 3:6).

The kind of a lawyer you are depends in large measure upon your character. If you are going to point the way, you need to be more than skilled advocates. You need to be decent human beings trying to solve problems. You need to be teachers as well as advocates and draftsmen. You can do this best by personifying the lessons learned from being a good example. To be a good example it will be necessary for you to carefully guard your good name. As William Shakespeare said,

> Good name in man and woman, . . .
> Is the immediate jewel of their souls:
> Who steals my purse steals trash; 'tis something, nothing;
> 'Twas mine, 'tis his, and has been slave to thousands;
> But he that filches from me my good name
> Robs me of that which not enriches him,
> And makes me poor indeed.
> [William Shakespeare, *Othello*, Act iii, Scene 3]

Despite all of the lawyer jokes, such as Shakespeare's quip through Dick in his play King Henry vi Part ii, "Let's kill all the lawyers," as an individual you may be accorded respect and positions of honor and trust. This may be in public life as well as Church callings that may come to you. While as a group, lawyers are often criticized, as individuals most are appreciated. As Lincoln said, "They are accorded honor and confidence." Your clients often become lifetime friends. They continue to seek counsel on nonlegal matters.

I now wish to comment briefly on some special privileges practicing lawyers enjoy. You should be different from the typical citizen. You can ask questions of people which, when asked by others, would be considered unthinkable. Some of the answers you receive are privileged and, as you know, protected by law. They contain some of your clients' deepest feelings and confidences. Some things disclosed may be embarrassing and others sacred. These answers are to be held inviolate. I do not wish to be unfair, but I have observed that some law students and lawyers are inclined to have inflated egos. They think they have the answer to everything. Speaking for myself, however, I know I don't. When some questions come up I find myself saying, along with Yogi Berra, "I wish I had an answer to that because I'm tired of answering that question. If you ask me anything I don't know, I'm not going to answer." I commend to you the words of Shakespeare, "There's nothing so becomes a man / As modest stillness and humility" (*King Henry v*, Act iii. Sc. 1). Even after we have gained some experience, it doesn't do to get complacent or smug about our ability. It's good to remember what Will Rogers once said, "Even if you're on the right track, you'll get run over if you just sit there!"

To those of you who are practitioners, a few simple suggestions learned the hard way over half a century at the bar might include:

Don't get so overly involved in your client's cause that you lose your balance, good judgment, and sense of humor.

Sublimate your own ego to the greater need of helping your client.

At all costs, keep your own integrity.

Don't let your client establish the rules of your conduct.

Communicate: keep your client informed, and without compromising your client's cause, keep communication open with your opponent.

Never commingle other people's money with your own.

Protect yourself by making an adequate record.

This can all be summed up in the principle that we should never do anything to offend the spirit.

Thirty years ago when I was first called as a General Authority of the Church, I had an office full of matters, some of which had been pending for some time. It took a few months to get them resolved. The remarkable thing that happened was that I never had to go back into court again on a contested matter. It was like the waters of the Red Sea had parted. One longstanding, complex case got quickly resolved when my opposing attorney and I sat down and began to communicate. One by one the complexities got adjusted, and when it came to the settlement of the money claim, my opponent was so pleased to have the other issues settled that he offered to pay more money than we had asked. I informed him that we would stand by our previous figure, which was less than he eventually paid, because he insisted on paying more to get the whole matter settled.

The adversary system has been proven over the centuries to be the best way to get to the ultimate truth of the facts. However, my sons who are lawyers tell me the system has become far too contentious and disagreeable. In my lifetime I have seen the majesty of the law cheapened under the theory that the end of winning justifies the means. To many the trial of the O. J. Simpson case was a soap opera. We have seen the legal system abused by having the issues tried in the newspapers before and during the trials rather than on the law and the facts. Historically the legal system developed as a means of resolving differences and preserving peace. I find much wisdom in the statement in Proverbs, "When a man's ways please the Lord, he maketh even his enemies to be at peace with him" (Proverbs 16:7). The spiritual gifts we can enjoy by obedience to our religious convictions can work in remarkable ways in our attempts to help resolve differences. The pursuit of justice is a very noble path, but obtaining justice is often very elusive, because what is justice to one is considered injustice to another. In some ways a more noble effort is to resolve differences by being a peacemaker. I quote again from Abraham Lincoln, who advised:

"Discourage litigation. Persuade your neighbors to compromise whenever you can. Point out to them how the nominal winner is often a real
loser—in fees, expenses, and waste of time. As a peacemaker the lawyer
has a superior opportunity of being a good man. There will still be enough
business" ("Notes for a Law Lecture" (July 1, 1850?)," *The Collected Works of
Abraham Lincoln*, vol. 2 (Rutgers University Press, 1953, 1990) p. 81).

John W. Davis, senior member of the New York City law firm of Davis,
Polk, spoke about promoting peace:

> True, we build no bridges. We raise no towers. We construct no engines. We
> paint no pictures—unless as amateurs for our own amusement. There is little
> of all that we do which the eye of man can see. But we smooth out difficulties;
> we relieve stress; we correct mistakes; we take up other men's burdens and by
> our efforts we make possible the peaceful life of men in a peaceful state. [John
> W. Davis, Address at 75th Anniversary Proceedings of the Association of the
> Bar of the City of New York, March 16, 1946]

Before the wounds of injustice can heal, there must first come a feeling
of peace. So, in a sense, a lawyer who helps make peace becomes something of a healer. A good beginning for settling controversy is to try to
lower the tension between the real parties in interest. This may require
some persuasion of your own client. A lawyer acquaintance of mine invariably became so intense in his client's cause that as a tactic before trial he
would threaten, browbeat, and insult opposing counsel. In one instance,
he gratuitously but personally insulted opposing counsel in a parking lot
while they were going to their cars. His opponent was older and bigger
and responded by putting a headlock on him. The gossip from that event
traveled fast through the bar circles. My acquaintance became the butt
of unkind jokes and was unfairly branded. Unfortunately, he didn't learn
from that experience. He never apologized to his adversary or tried to
make it right in any way. As a result of his personal belligerency he was
rarely able to settle matters and thus did a disservice to his clients. He was
always trying to make big waves instead of calming the waters.

All professionals, including lawyers, need to find a balance between
the demands as servants of God, as parents, and as advocates and lawyers.
As a wise person once said, "The things that matter most cannot be left to
the mercy of the things that matter the least." I think the Savior Himself
established the priorities well in the book of Matthew (Joseph Smith
Translation) 6:38, when he said, "Wherefore, seek not the things of this
world but seek ye first to build up the kingdom of God, and to establish his
righteousness; and all these things shall be added unto you."

I bear witness of the truthfulness of the restored gospel and pray that
the mercy of that gospel will bless us all, in the name of Jesus Christ, amen.

This satellite fireside address was given to the J. Reuben Clark Law Society at the Conference Center in Salt Lake City on February 28, 2003. Reprinted from the Clark Memorandum, *spring 2003, 2–7.*

James E. Faust (1920–2007) received his JD from the University of Utah in 1948 and was president of the Utah Bar Association 1962–63. He received the Distinguished Lawyer Emeritus Award from the Utah Bar Association in 1996, an honorary Doctor of Laws degree from the University of Utah in 2002, and the Marion G. Romney Law and Public Service Award from BYU Law School in 2003. President Faust served as a General Authority 1972–2007, member of the Quorum of Twelve Apostles 1978–1995, and second counselor in the First Presidency of The Church of Jesus Christ of Latter-day Saints 1995–2007.

Words of Hate, Words of Love

Constance K. Lundberg

Good morning. I am happy to be here today, though I feel like the speaker in church who said she felt inadequate standing before the congregation. One sister said to another, "Isn't she humble?" And the other responded, "That's no real accomplishment, she has a lot to be humble about."

Some of my students are sitting here thinking, "No joke!"

I do feel overwhelmed at the prospect of attempting to share something new and of value as I stand in the footsteps of the great men and women who have been here before me. I pray I can share some of my life and thoughts in a way that may help some of you have a new and useful perspective about words and their place in a Christ-centered life.

Words are my tools. As a librarian I collect, catalog, and preserve them. As a lawyer, which is my principal profession, I search them out, savoring the power, sound, feel, and nuance of them. As a mother, words are something I teach, and teach with—a method of motivation, reward, and reprimand. As a person of faith, they are second only to spiritual promptings as a form of guidance, comfort, and inspiration.

Lately, however, I have observed a distressing escalation of the use of words to hurt, anger, divide, and make war. Perhaps as a law professor I should approve of the trend. It does, after all, make well-paying work for many of our graduates. However, I have viewed myself as a solver of problems and a peacemaker, not as a warrior. I have not found entertainment in *L.A. Law* or its more recent progeny. Neither am I comfortable with the wars of words that rage around us.

Today I would like to talk about the power of words. I would like to remind you of some of their magic. There is nothing arcane about words. They are not supernatural. They are like light and gravity—they are central to our existence, and, because they are pervasive, we often fail to see them or recognize their power and worth.

John sets us on the right path:

> In the beginning was the Word, and the Word was with God, and the Word was God.
> The same was in the beginning with God.
> All things were made by him; and without him was not any thing made that was made. [John 1:1–3]

The Savior is the Word. Let us consider whether our words are worthy of Him.

Words are among the most marvelous gifts we have as human beings. Words are tools used by God to build the necessary framework to lift us from our mortal existence and carry us back to His presence. He uses words for making and keeping binding commitments. The difference between an eternal marriage and anything else is a few words.

This is made clear in one of the most loved films of the BYU community, past and present:

BUTTERCUP:
Oh, Westley, will you ever forgive me?

WESTLEY:
What hideous sin have you committed lately?

BUTTERCUP:
I got married. I didn't want to. It all happened so fast.

WESTLEY:
Never happened.

BUTTERCUP:
What?

WESTLEY:
Never happened.

BUTTERCUP:
But it did. I was there. This old man said "man and wife."

WESTLEY:
Did you say "I do"?

BUTTERCUP:
Uh, no. We sort of skipped that part.

WESTLEY:
Then you're not married. If you didn't say it, you didn't do it.
[From the movie script for *The Princess Bride*, http://www.awesomefilm.com/script/princess.html]

Our words in the marriage vows, and those of the priesthood-holding sealer who binds us together for eternity, are not symbols of the marriage. Words are the mechanism for making the vows and for our Father's accepting our commitment and granting us the opportunity to extend those vows into eternity. The vows are the wedding—the binding.

As we bind ourselves to our eternal companions through vows, we also bind ourselves to God. We are members of a covenant church. We enter into covenants with our Father in Heaven, as did Abraham, his son, and his grandson. Our Father makes great promises to us through those covenants: eternal life, eternal marriage, blessings poured from the windows of heaven. "I, the Lord, am bound when ye do what I say; but when ye do not what I say, ye have no promise" (D&C 82:10).

The individual covenants we make are set out in specific sacred words. The baptism prayer, the sacrament prayer, and portions of the prayer of confirmation use precise words. Why must a baptism or sacrament prayer, a sealing prayer, or any other prayer or blessing in the temple be witnessed and spoken exactly as it is set out in scripture or otherwise revealed? Because the exact pattern of those words is a sacred act—an ordinance— an exercise of the priesthood of God. If you didn't say it, you didn't do it.

Used in the context of our relationship with God, words are real, and their power is real. Repentance can be real and sincere, but our acceptance of the Atonement is not sufficient if we only have a change of heart. We must also be baptized. The act, and the words of the prayer, are more than symbols. They effect real change. The acceptance and understanding of that change is part of the act of repentance and of our preparation for baptism. Contemplating those vows enables us to test the reality of our commitment to repentance, to a forsaking of past sins and a covenant to take upon ourselves the name of Jesus Christ—more words. More words that are the acts we cherish and revere (see D&C 76:50–54).

As a lawyer, I understand that. Mutually enforceable promises to act or pay constitute a contract. One relying upon the representations or promises of another can legally bind the promisor. The promisor cannot change his mind or say, "King's X, I didn't really mean it." The time of agreement may alter tax liabilities or the validity of the agreement itself. The parties cannot lawfully misrecord the time or date when it is an element of the agreement. The law views those words as binding, just as our Father does in the spiritual context.

For this reason I am always shocked when I learn of a law student or lawyer who blithely alters the facts recited in an agreement. He has not made a legally valid change but has committed fraud—deception with intent to achieve a benefit to which the client is not legally entitled. If caught, he will suffer the appropriate penalties—think Enron. If not, he remains at risk of discovery. The false words may fool some people, but they do not make an invalid document valid. If we lie in a document, can we expect the courts to honor the document?

However, we are mortal and can be deceived. It is possible that the liar can cover up a lie, and it will live so long that it is accepted as truth and the law does not allow the question to be reopened. That does not make it true, but it takes the lie beyond the power of the court to undo its consequences. The term for this is *statute of limitations*. It means a limitation of action: the services of the courts are no longer available to a petitioner who seeks to overturn a result based on the lie. The law provides for a limitation of actions because otherwise there would be no certainty in our temporal lives. Contracts, deeds, and other transactions would never be final. It would be impossible for us to have certainty in our temporal affairs.

Temporal affairs are reciprocal of eternal ones. In an eternal world, with an immortal Father and omniscient judge, we cannot lie. We can say we have repented and been baptized, but if we do not in our hearts make the covenants that go with the words, can we expect our Father to honor them? We can fool ourselves, our bishops, our mission presidents, and our spouses, but we cannot lie to our judge, our Father. It is not an accident that Satan is known as the father of lies:

> And because he had fallen from heaven, and had become miserable forever, he sought also the misery of all mankind. Wherefore, he said unto Eve, yea, even that old serpent, who is the devil, who is the father of all lies, wherefore he said: Partake of the forbidden fruit, and ye shall not die, but ye shall be as God, knowing good and evil. [2 Nephi 2:18]

On the other hand, our Father is the Father of Truth.

I have a personal vision, not a comfortable one, of the Judgment. I think the book that is the record of each life is the heart and mind of the person. Judgment is ultimately a stripping away of all lies. We are faced with our own selves, the absence of all deceit, excuse, rationalization, or obfuscation. Further, we know that our Father and our Savior have a perfect knowledge of us, as we now are. They love us anyway. However, they also know the exact degree of our sin, our repentance, and our acceptance of the proffered Atonement. Stripped bare of all pretense, we are not so much judged as we come to fully understand the justice, the mercy, and the inevitability of our ultimate fate.

Until that day we must live with an imperfect knowledge of the truth of words. So I will turn from the perfection of words and understanding to which we come in the next life to the more difficult, even trying confusion we bring to each other as we use and misuse words each day.

I want to talk about the mundane uses of words for the rest of our time together because their consequences are not mundane. I think these uses are the ones that get us into the most difficulty. In our daily speech we use words casually. We toss them out, sometimes careless of their effect. We drum up a phrase for its immediate impact without thinking of its long-term consequences.

My father would not tolerate a vulgarity, much less an obscenity or profanity, to be used in the home or by his children. Once, when I was about 11, I used a word often used by my friends and classmates and also used, though not in my father's presence, by my siblings. It was a mild expletive, one that had once had a specific biological connotation, lost through millions of thoughtless repetitions. He asked, in the disappointed tone that always stirred the guilt I was carefully trying to ignore, if I was so bereft of imagination that I couldn't think of a creative way to express myself. He was disappointed if my education from my parents had left me so stunted in vocabulary that I could find nothing to say of greater grace or meaning.

My parents and their siblings were pioneers. As an adult I had the occasion to read the journals and autobiographies of other late 19th- and early 20th-century settlers as well as historical novels, including my favorite, *The Virginian,* which tells the story, thinly disguised, of the in-laws and grandparents of some of my dearest friends. Most of these men and women had a few years of education in a local schoolhouse or home. They lacked degrees or academic distinction. However, it was central to their self-definition that they expressed themselves well. Their stories were works of art. Their descriptions were careful and precise. In *The Virginian* the protagonist brings a train car full of cowboys on the verge of rebellion into happy, though abashed obedience by selling them as truth a tall tale of such magnificence that they bow to his obvious superiority. (See Owen Wister, *The Virginian: A Horseman of the Plains* [1902], pp. 157–166.)

My relatives of the same generation viewed speech and especially storytelling as entertainment, art, and a way to build and maintain subtle and nuanced relationships of love and respect within the family and the community. Many of the stories were funny, many tender, but the art of well-chosen language was a hallmark of intelligence and leadership. Or, as Elder Dallin H. Oaks said:

> A speaker who mouths profanity or vulgarity to punctuate or emphasize speech confesses inadequacy in his or her own language skills. Properly used, modern languages require no such artificial boosters. ["Reverent and Clean," *Ensign*, May 1986, 51]

I compare that with the mindless gutter language that washes over us as we watch television, movies, or walk down the street. I loved the movie *Apollo 13* but was interested, and relieved, when I read an interview of one of the astronauts from that amazing flight. Commenting on the film, he said it was pretty accurate except that no one on the crew swore, there was no antagonism between crew members, and they did not drink alcohol while in training. Apparently the makers of the movie felt the need to use profanity to pump some energy into dialogue that lacked, in their minds, vigor or interest—sort of like adding too much salt to watery soup to cover the absence of more nutritious ingredients. Surely this story had enough body that it did not require those extra few handfuls of salt.

The law has a term, *fighting words,* for insults so foul that the victim of such insults is entitled to fight back. In the words of one court, "[Fighting words] by their very utterance provoke a swift physical retaliation and incite an immediate breach of the peace" (*Skelton v. City of Birmingham,* 342 So.2d 933, 936-37 [Ala. Crim. App.], *remanded on other grounds,* 342 So.2d 937 [Ala. 1976]). The words themselves constitute assaults. If you are interested in what words those might be, listen to some of the more popular rap recordings. I have been dismayed to read in legal literature that some scholars think these words have become so common in general public discourse that, except for one or two racial epithets, there may no longer be words that meet the legal standard of fighting words. I disagree and would like to share two experiences I had this year.

My son is a basketball player. In the last seven years I have seen perhaps 120 high school or Junior Jazz basketball games. I have also heard perhaps every fighting word in the book on the lips of players, coaches, or referees. It has become an accepted strategy for some players to subject their opponents to a stream of foul language to upset them, put them off their game, or (best of all, it seems) to goad them into fouling. In one game, one of my son's teammates was subjected to a continuing verbal assault from a referee, who told the boy he intended to make him behave so badly that the ref could throw him out of the game.

An even sadder instance involved a different ballplayer at a different game. A boy about 10 years old was sitting on the floor underneath the home team's basket, yelling every obscenity and profanity the mind could recall at one of our boys who was waiting to rebound. Here was a 16-year-old basketball player trying to stay calm and focused being riveted by a barrage of filth, his teammates yelling his name repeatedly to refocus him on the game. Parents, teachers, principals, coaches, and referees took it for granted. What does it say when we consider foul language to be an acceptable strategy in school sports competitions?

I love the grace, strength, and skill of basketball. But sitting in the stands I sometimes find my heart racing and my blood pressure shooting up as if I were being mugged when I am surrounded by booing, shouting, disrespect, and harassment of players and referees. If we really love the game, as opposed to a gladiatorial contest, we don't want garbage. In too many sports events, and in television shows like *The Weakest Link* and *American Idol,* the real sport is the abuse.

The referee should have known better. The parents, teachers, and players should have known better. They were not witless or helpless. They made choices about the language they used and tolerated. Those choices tell us much about them—and ourselves when in the same position.

Elder Charles Didier taught us to remember:

> Words are a form of personal expression. They differentiate us as well as fingerprints do. They reflect what kind of person we are, and tell of our background, and depict our way of life. They describe our thinking as well as our inner feelings. ["Language: A Divine Way of Communicating," *Ensign*, November 1979, 25]

Elder Didier went on to say:

> Language is of divine origin. Only man speaks (and women do even better), and he does so because of the purpose for which he was created. Let us listen to Paul when he said: "Though I speak with the tongues of men and of angels, and have not charity, I am become as sounding brass, or a tinkling cymbal" (1 Cor. 13:1). Anacharsis, when asked what was the best part of man, answered: "The tongue." When asked what was the worst, the answer was the same: "The tongue."
>
> "Therewith bless we God, even the Father; and therewith curse we men, which are made after the similitude of God.
>
> "Out of the same mouth proceedeth blessing and cursing. My brethren, these things ought not so to be.
>
> "Doth a fountain send forth at the same place sweet water and bitter?
>
> "Can the fig tree, my brethren, bear olive berries? either a vine, figs? so can no fountain both yield salt water and fresh" (James 3:9–12). [Didier, "Language," 25]

Words can be healing balm or gasoline on a fire in disputes with neighbors, friends, or colleagues. Television and movies create a tolerance for overblown emotion. Where once we sought the subtle or understated, now we often feel the need to heat up our vocabulary. Consider these different ways to make the same point:

1. "I don't remember things that way" or "You are lying." Or, my personal favorite, "You are a fraudulent malfeasor!"

2. "Let's think together to try to solve this problem" or "That's dumb. Let me do it. I know the right way."

3. Or, turning back to my basketball stories, consider the parent of one of my son's teammates, who proposed that our parent rooting core quit yelling negative comments to referees who were doing a poor job but praise them when they did well and encourage our boys on in the face of adversity. It seems to be making an impact in the tenor of games and has even perhaps reduced, though it has not stopped, the foul language.

When we attack people with whom we disagree, we injure or even end our ability to resolve disputes. Each time we raise the temperature in the discourse it is harder to reconcile differences. We raise a barrier of hate and anger. Elder Richard L. Evans counseled: "We are in a sense as much responsible for what we do to others with our words as we could be with weapons. In a sense, you can hit a man with words—'words as hard as cannon balls' as [Ralph Waldo] Emerson said it [*Self-Reliance*]" ("The Spoken Word: 'Words as Hard as Cannon Balls,'" *New Era,* December 1971, 34).

Words can be powerful in a positive way. Think of Alma's experience with the Zoramites:

> And now, as the preaching of the word had a great tendency to lead the people to do that which was just—yea, it had had more powerful effect upon the minds of the people than the sword, or anything else, which had happened unto them—therefore Alma thought it was expedient that they should try the virtue of the word of God. [Alma 31:5]

The Apostle Paul admonished us: "But now ye also put off all these; anger, wrath, malice, blasphemy, filthy communication out of your mouth" (Colossians 3:8).

Tenderness and loving speech are more important in families than anywhere else. My mother and I were at a dinner with a large family that was, for the most part, loving. There was one particularly attractive young couple. Their three beautiful children were talented and bright. The parents were successful in the community and apparently had everything. Later we were talking, and Mother grieved over the couple because of the pain in their relationship. I questioned her judgment. They were joking, laughing—the life of the party. She was not fooled by the jokes. Each one had an edge, she said. Every funny comment by one put the other in a bad light. Two years later they were divorced. Mother saw, as I did not, that cutting, hurtful words are not ameliorated by humor—just disguised to the inattentive.

Loyalty in a family means that we are loving in word. Again, Elder Didier gives great guidance:

> Language is divine. Some may know this but do not realize its implications in their daily family life. Love at home starts with loving language. This need is so important that, without loving words, some become mentally unbalanced, others emotionally disturbed, and some may even die. No society can survive after its family life has deteriorated, and this deterioration has always started with one word. [Didier, "Language," 26]

And it is always a hurtful word.

Studies of couples who stay married for 30 or more years show that they are kind to each other. Their criticisms, when they come, are couched as exceptions in a nest of praise and love. I did a Google search on the term *lasting marriage*. The results? There were over a quarter of a million entries. I did not tally all the suggestions. I did page through the first 50 or so. The overriding theme was to be loving, resolve conflict, and be respectful of each other.

Elder Lynn G. Robbins wrote of Satan's efforts to destroy families:

> He damages and often destroys families within the walls of their own
> homes. His strategy is to stir up *anger* between family members. Satan is the
> "father of contention, and he stirreth up the hearts of men to contend with
> *anger,* one with another" (3 Ne. 11:29; emphasis added). The verb *stir* sounds
> like a recipe for disaster: Put tempers on medium heat, stir in a few choice
> words, and bring to a boil; continue stirring until thick; cool off; let feelings
> chill for several days; serve cold; lots of leftovers. ["Agency and Anger," *Ensign,*
> May 1998, 80; emphasis in original]

Finally, as a mother, grandmother, great-grandmother, and Primary
president, I must talk a bit about words that heal children and words that
wound them. Children are tender. They want to please. They want to do
right. Sometimes they do not know how to do so, but they will strive to do
right unless they are beaten down. We have all lost our temper on occasion with a particularly persistent child. But remember the Savior's love for
them. His admonition, repeatedly, is that we should seek to be like them.

> But whoso shall offend one of these little ones which believe in me, it
> were better for him that a millstone were hanged about his neck, and that he
> were drowned in the depth of the sea. [Matthew 18:6]

A child may, and will, make mistakes. She may do bad things, but she
is not bad. Psychological studies suggest that a child's brain is forming and
reforming, building connections and synapses. When we discipline or reprimand a child, we are truly building that child. If we teach a child she is
bad, we teach her to be bad. If we teach a child she is good, she strives to
become good.

My son Philip persisted in asking me, when he was a child, if he was
perfect. I had a rare moment of insight and knew that either a yes or no
answer had pitfalls. If he was perfect, there was no room for growth. But
he was clearly telling me he wanted and needed approval. I hit upon a
compromise: "You are a perfect five-year-old." This was not exactly what
he wanted to hear. What was a perfect five-year-old? It gave us a chance
to talk about all the things he did well, how he was loved by his heavenly
and earthly parents, and how he could grow to be a wonderful adult and
return to his heavenly parents—not just a perfect five-year-old but one day
perfected. Although he wanted another answer, he found mine acceptable.
Through the years he has asked me if he is perfect. At about the age of 12
he came to accept my answer. "You are a perfect 12-year-old." Over time
he has developed an understanding of the doctrine of eternal progression.
He still desires to be better. He knows he has ample room to grow and
improve, though sometimes his lack of perfection frustrates him as it did
when he was five. But he accepts the process.

President David O. McKay counseled:

Three influences in home life awaken reverence in children and contribute to its development in their souls. These are: *first,* firm but *Gentle Guidance; second, Courtesy* shown by parents to each other, and to children; and *third, Prayer* in which children participate. [*Conference Report,* October 1956, 6–7; emphasis in original]

All of these three influences involve words.

Everything given to us by our Father is given for our eternal salvation. However, any gift can be abused or turned to evil purposes. Words, the power of language, are among the greatest gifts. I pray we can use words for our edification and bless the lives of others, and I do so in the sacred name of Jesus Christ, amen.

This devotional address was given to the BYU student body on March 11, 2003. Reprinted from Brigham Young University Speeches 2002–2003, *211–217 and the* Clark Memorandum, *fall 2003, 2–9.*

Constance K. Lundberg received her JD from the University of Utah in 1973. She served as a law professor 1982–2005 and associate dean 1989–2005 of J. Reuben Clark Law School, and director of the Howard W. Hunter Law Library 1990–2005. She is currently an attorney at the law firm Jones, Waldo, Holbrook & McDonough in Salt Lake City, Utah.

Peacemaking: Our Essential Work in the Last Days

Chieko N. Okazaki[1]

A couple of years ago when my grandson, Kenzo, was four or five, I picked him up to take him to the museum or the library and asked, "How's your mom? How's your dad?" Kenzo said, "Oh, they're fine. Daddy was walking back and forth in the living room last night talking to himself."

"What was he doing that for?" I asked.

"Oh," said Kenzo matter-of-factly, "he was doing his litigation."

Well, when I was invited to give this address, I thought it would be a great opportunity to get Ken's thoughts on peacemaking, since he's quite well regarded (and this isn't just his mom speaking) as a negotiator and mediator as well as a litigator. I know that it's important to him to do superb representations of his clients but that he exhausts every possible avenue short of litigation to find a fair solution that both parties can live with.

So I asked him about peacemaking. He just laughed out loud. Then he gave me a lengthy lecture, the bottom line of which was that talking about peacemaking and the law in the same sentence was a fantasy. He pointed out that the courts are set up as adversarial arenas. Lawyers and clients want to win. Judges and juries don't notice or reward efforts at peacemaking. His job as an attorney is to win for his client, which has nothing to do with peacemaking. He tries to work with the other side out of court; but when the other side wants to fight, then he gets busy and constructs the best case he can to win for his client.

After reading me this lecture, he sighed and said, "Maybe you can talk about trust, Mom, or civility, but I don't think you can talk about peacemaking." There was a long pause, and this tough, accomplished, highly regarded litigator son of mine said, "I wish we could make peace."

Well, you and I and Ken all know that peacemaking is pretty much of a fantasy right now in our international and national lives, as well as in our courtrooms. One of the signs of the last days is:

> And there went another horse that was red: and power was given to him that sat thereon to take peace from the earth, and that they should kill one another: and there was given unto him a great sword.[2]

Anyone who doesn't believe that this sword has been unsheathed hasn't seen the news recently.

So, is the idea of peacemaking a fantasy? I say no, and I want to talk about three ideas about peacemaking in these last days. And I want to speak to you specifically because you're involved with law. You have, in my opinion, a crucial and perhaps even essential role as peacemakers. The first point I want to make is that we can and, indeed, must achieve peace of conscience. Second, we can and, indeed, must achieve peace in our own homes. And third, an essential element of peacemaking is the ability to love others.

Achieving Peace of Conscience

Let's begin with peace in the most important place: peace of conscience. Brothers and sisters, the two factors that you have in common here today are that you're all attorneys (or your spouse is) and you're all graduates of Brigham Young University. You may have had moments of being irritated at the Honor Code when you were there, but you had the great blessing of being at a school where the word *honor* was taken seriously. Words like *honesty* and *integrity* count for something. Those qualities are part of who you are, and their ideal is something you reach for and will keep reaching for, in both your personal and your professional lives.

When you pass the bar and are sworn in, you take a serious oath to pursue, defend, and preserve justice. This oath—we might call it a covenant—puts you in a special category in our society. It's one that promises desirable rewards but it also makes heavy demands on you. Part of who you are is your code of professional ethics. You're responsible to your peers and to the standards of your profession for the quality of your behavior. Each of you participates in pro bono work, making your expertise available to those who can't afford to buy it, and works in your community. These are heavy responsibilities that you owe the community and your profession because of the esteem in which law is held.

It should go without saying that maintaining your personal and professional honor requires that you do your absolute best—the best job of research, the most persuasive writing, the more resourceful defenses, and the most carefully conducted prosecutions. The theory underlying the adversarial system of law that prevails in the United States is that the truth—and therefore justice—is most likely to emerge from the open clash of strongly opposed ideas.

I truly believe in this system of justice. Although it does not work perfectly—and sometimes does not work at all—I don't see how the alternatives can produce a better chance of justice, especially since all of them involve either random chance or placing inordinate trust in the ability of either one person or a very small group to intuit the truth. As a minority woman and as a member of a religion against which the United States of America sent an army in the 19th century, I strongly prefer our adversarial system.

So part of having peace of conscience involves doing your absolute level professional best. To me that means doing absolutely honest research, honest writing, and honest arguments. This doesn't always mean that you'll win, but it does mean that you'll have peace of conscience about your efforts.

Having peace of conscience means that you cannot ever justify shady behavior by the results. The worthiness of the end does not justify using unworthy means to achieve it.

Even though the media rejoice to feature bad-tempered and grandstanding attorneys, you cannot become one of their number. I understand that the California State Bar has launched a "civility initiative and may consider adopting a civility code with hopes of convincing judges to sanction rude behavior."[3] Gus Chin, president of the Utah State Bar, in a special issue of the *Utah Bar Journal* devoted to professionalism and civility, points out the fact that the Utah Supreme Court in 2003 adopted standards of professionalism and civility, and states: "Despite being treated unkindly, one can prevail by maintaining a high degree of personal professional dignity and control. Furthermore, the constitutional guarantee of freedom of speech does not amount to an open license to engage in invective, rudeness, and uncooperative conduct."[4]

Justice Christine M. Durham, now serving her second term as chief justice of the Utah Supreme Court, has pointed out: "The consequences of incivility are grave—it increases litigation costs, fails to promote clients' legitimate interests, and diminishes the public's respect for the legal profession and its ability to benefit society."[5]

Justice Richard D. Fybel, associate justice of the California Court of Appeals in Santa Ana, specifically challenged the argument that "clients really like tough-guy and tough-gal lawyers. You know, the junkyard dog that attacks, salivates, and then attacks some more? Why shouldn't I be the toughest, nastiest representative out there? Who cares about expertise and ethics anyway?" Justice Fybel, drawing on his long years of experience as an attorney and as a judge counters: "Quite simply, [mean lawyers] don't usually win." People—sometimes their own clients—don't want to work with them and "simply, don't rely on their judgment and representations." That's the issue of trustworthiness.

He also points out that attorneys have to persuade someone: the other side, a court, an agency, or their own client. "People are not persuaded by obnoxious or unethical tactics. Intimidation is overrated as a litigation tool. It does not work in the widest range of my experience—from business cases to criminal pleas and trials. . . . [Obnoxiousness] may make for good TV from time to time, but in real life, over time, persuasion by use of reason and appeal to self-interest works best."[6]

Since I'm a teacher, I'll say it in second-grade terms. Nobody likes tantrums, and they're especially unappealing when it's adults who are having them.

Brothers and sisters, anger is a useful and helpful emotion. It tells us that something is wrong, and it mobilizes our energy to do something about it. Part of maturity, however, is learning the difference between feeling anger and acting on it. A sign of maturity is being able to recognize the difference between injustice and merely not getting our own way. Most of the behaviors President Chin and Justice Durham are talking about are the manifestations of mean-spiritedness, name-calling, rudeness, the desire to hurt verbally—in short, the inability to control one's temper.

You're all well aware of that famous passage in Ephesians that talks about putting on the "whole armour of God." Particularly relevant to our discussion is the verse in which the Apostle Paul urges his readers to have "your feet shod with the preparation of the gospel of peace."[7] I think it's extremely important that the Lord not only repeated a version of this "whole armour" passage in a revelation to Joseph Smith but then expanded it this way: "And [have] your feet shod with the preparation of the gospel of peace, *which I have sent mine angels to commit unto you.*"[8] It's the last phrase that's new in this modern scripture: "the gospel of peace which I have sent mine angels to commit unto you."

I think that if something is important enough that God sends angels to give it to us, then we need to pay attention. Anger may be a good spark plug, but it's a bad motor. If you find yourself taking parts of your profession too personally and especially if you find yourself relishing and even counting on feelings of anger and using anger as the justification for behaving badly, then I'm calling you to repentance, right here and now. I greatly enjoyed a book that compiled one-sentence lessons from ordinary people about life lessons. This one came from a seventy-one-year-old, who said: "I've learned that no situation is so bad that losing your temper won't make it worse."[9]

Brothers and sisters, you are all people of conscience. You know how quickly dishonesty, pride, and anger can cloud your conscience. As the book of Proverbs reminds us: "He that is slow to anger is better than the mighty; and he that ruleth his spirit than he that taketh a city."[10]

Peace in Our Own Homes

Now let's talk about the second place of achieving peace: peace in our own homes. I remembered reading a book called *The 10 Greatest Gifts I Give My Children*. The author, Stephen Vannoy, asked his son, Jeremy, who was not quite three, if he wanted a piece of cheese with his lunch. "No," said Jeremy, "I want peace and quiet."[11] Well, I think that parents, especially the parents of young children, have moments when that's what they want, too.

So let me ask you: Do you want the person you are in the courtroom or in the office to be the person who is raising your children? In other words, if you aspire to be a killer litigator or the brainiac researcher, is that litigator or researcher also your goal as a parent? Almost certainly not.

I accept and acknowledge that some of the skills you need to do your job with integrity and excellence may be counterproductive in your all-important relationships as a spouse and a parent. But I ask you to think intelligently and insightfully about the list of qualities that makes you a good attorney and see how and to what extent they may also make you a good parent.

Let's get back to my question: What job skills do you have that can also help you be a good parent? Obviously, we can see respect for others, respect for the sometimes abstract principle of fairness, placing a high priority on the value of rules, the ability to listen carefully, and the ability to creatively work at finding acceptable compromises. I also want to make the obvious point that being a good parent develops very valuable skills that can enhance your professional performance.

I'm suggesting this approach because I think we sometimes try to meet this particular challenge by being two people. We have one personality for the office and another one for home. But I've found that people who think it's okay to yell at the secretary at the office also think it's okay to yell at their daughter. Everything we've just said about peace of conscience applies here as well. If you can be a whole person and be your essential self in both the professional and personal settings, that will go far toward giving your children the kind of parent you want them to have and your spouse the kind of partner he or she deserves.

I realize that I'm describing something of an ideal here and that reality has other demands that you have to accommodate as well. So after having given you this excellent advice about integrating the parts of your roles as much as possible, I'm also going to ask you to do the exact opposite and find ways to keep your roles separate.

Let me explain. Does your work involve stress and tension? Absolutely. What do you do about it? Some people thrive on the juggling, the split-second decision making, the adrenalin rush of packing 90 minutes worth of activity into a 60-minute hour, even the contests in the courtroom—the thrust and parry of the mental combat and expert maneuvering. But most of us don't thrive on that kind of around-the-clock stress, and I'm pretty sure that high-speed, high-tension lifestyle is not a healthy mode for children. So I'm suggesting advice you've all heard since your first year at law school about leaving your problems at the office.

Love and Peacemaking

We've talked about peace of conscience and achieving peace in our own homes. My third point is that essential to peacemaking in these last days is the ability to love. I want to be very specific on this point; and even though I've already disclaimed any insider knowledge of your professional responsibilities and duties, I want to talk specifically about love in your professional setting. I'm talking about your relationships with your clients and, to a lesser extent, your staffs, your colleagues, opposing counsel, the judges, and courtroom staffs.

Brothers and sisters, you must respect the office held by expert witnesses, the judges, the bailiffs, other officers of the court, and opposing counsel. You don't have to respect the person who holds that office unless that person earns your respect by his or her behavior. You don't have to trust that person, even though you must trust the system. You don't have to like that person or choose to spend time voluntarily with him or her, but it is absolutely incumbent upon you as a Christian and Latter-day Saint to love that person.

I know exactly how impossible that sounds—even how undesirable it sounds, but I mean exactly what I say. Jesus told His disciples, "A new commandment I give unto you, That ye love one another; as I have loved you."[12] This isn't a suggestion or a handy hint. It's a commandment.

It cuts through all of the relationships that require reciprocation. Respect requires reciprocation. Trust requires reciprocation. Courtesy doesn't require reciprocation but it can only flourish when there is. Liking and friendship definitely require reciprocation.

Jesus isn't talking about any of those things. He's talking about love—the kind of love that He had for us. And what kind of love was that? It was love that went to Gethsemane and to the cross. It was love that suffered from betrayal, abandonment, and torture but without withdrawing itself. It was love that persisted to the very uttermost. When humankind did its worst to Jesus, He did His uttermost for us. That's why we worship and adore Him.

Can we do the same thing? Not on our own. Not from our own resources. Not by our own kindly thought and self-discipline and will-power. Not without Him. When Jesus says, "I am the way," He means that literally. He not only imposes this impossible commandment on us of loving one another as He loves us, He not only insists that we take that commandment seriously, but He also foresees that we will fail and that our own pitifully small wells of charity can last no longer than an ice cube on the sidewalk at the 24th of July parade—that is, unless He helps us.

He is the vine. We are the branches. As long as we are firmly connected to Him, then His own power, energy, passion, and compassion flow through to us from Him. We can't do it without Him and, God be thanked, we don't have to even try without Him. He is the living water, springing up everlastingly, if we will partake in obedience and faith.

Now, think about what faces you when you return to your offices and your courtrooms Tuesday morning. Some of you will be protecting widows and orphans from greedy landlords. You can probably love them without too much trouble.

Some of you will be dealing with much more difficult situations: with clients whom you may have every reason to believe are guilty of murder, the sexual abuse of children, traffic in mind-destroying drugs, and corruption in the institutions that we rely on to protect democracy. These are exactly the people I'm saying you must love. You don't have to like them—in fact, you probably can't. You don't have to respect them—in fact, there would probably be something wrong with your value system if you did. You don't have to trust them—in fact, you'd be a fool to. But you *do* have to love them. Jesus died for that murderer, that child molester, that insurance defrauder, that drug lord.

Your duty as an attorney is to prosecute or to defend, to the very best of your ability, the worst of the worst that human beings can become, those who have made simple errors, and those in between who are adrift in the judicial system without a moral compass of their own. Your duty to society is to see that justice is done, and for litigators that means doing your very best to win for your client. It also means, if that is your duty, to do your best to remove from society those who, by breaking the law, are unworthy of its freedoms. You will not have the first kind of peace—peace of conscience—unless you do your best.

But you also have a Christian duty: the duty to love that individual for whom Christ died, that individual who is your spiritual brother or sister.

This means that, along with doing your research, preparing your briefs, filing your motions, and arguing your case, you must, as Mormon puts it, "pray unto the Father with all the energy of heart, that ye may be filled with this love, which he hath bestowed upon all who are true followers of his Son, Jesus Christ."[13] God's message of love is not reserved for those who are looking for it or even for those who want it.

If God has a message of love for one of your clients, maybe you're the only messenger who can deliver it. I'm not saying you need to pass out copies of the Book of Mormon or make pious speeches or somehow weave your testimony into your closing argument. I *am* saying that if you can provide a clear channel for the Holy Ghost, one that is not cluttered with your own ego or anger or pride, then you can rely on the Holy Ghost to deliver that message. I think it was St. Francis of Assisi who said, "At all times, preach the gospel. If necessary, use words."

Brothers and sisters, you have joined a profession of warriors, and you serve under the banner of hope: hope that the rule of law will be stronger than individual selfishness, hope that justice may roll forth, and hope that truth is mighty and will prevail. You have prepared yourself with your education, with your skills, by observing respected mentors in your field, by gaining knowledge, and by seeking wisdom. You will have to walk through some very dark places and see into still darker places. Please remember that you have the power to bring light into those dark places. You must not let the darkness overwhelm you.

At times the darkness must seem strong. Be strong to combat it. Strengthen yourselves through prayer. Work for peace of conscience through absolute integrity and honesty. Establish peace in your own homes by building trust and respect and by loving self-sacrifice. Remember who you want to raise your children. And love. Seek the abundant, never-failing source of love in our Savior. Make kindness and love your pathway and the light by which you walk. Teilhard de Chardin, a French Catholic theologian, said: "Some day, after we have mastered the winds, the waves, the tides and gravity we shall harness the energies of love. Then, for the second time in the history of the world, [we] will have discovered fire."[14] I feel to bless us all in the words of the Apostle Paul to the Roman Saints:

> Who shall separate us from the love of Christ? shall tribulation, or distress, or persecution, or famine, or nakedness, or peril, or sword? . . .
>
> Nay, in all these things we are more than conquerors through him that loved us.
>
> For I am persuaded, that neither death, nor life, nor angels, nor principalities, nor powers, nor things present, nor things to come,
>
> Nor height, nor depth, nor any other creature, shall be able to separate us from the love of God, which is in Christ Jesus our Lord.[15]

I testify to you of that love; I know that we are surrounded by that love. May we be filled with that love and therefore be about the Master's work of peacemaking in these last days. If we do, we have the sacred promise that "the peace of God, which passeth all understanding, shall keep your hearts and minds through Christ Jesus."[16] I ask His blessing upon us in the holy name of the Lord Jesus Christ, amen.

This address was given at the J. Reuben Clark Law Society Conference at Pepperdine University in Malibu, California, on February 16, 2007. Reprinted from the Clark Memorandum, *fall 2007, 22–29.*

Chieko N. Okazaki received her MA *in curriculum from the University of Northern Colorado in 1977 and her Administration Certificate from Colorado State University in 1978. She served as a member of the Young Women General Board 1960–66 and 1971–72, member of the Primary General Board 1988–90, and first counselor in the Relief Society General Presidency 1990–97. The author of several award-winning books, including* Cat's Cradle *(1993),* Disciples *(1998),* Lighten Up! *(2003), and* Sanctuary *(2007), she currently speaks nationally and internationally to men and women on personal development and education.*

Notes

1. Copyright 2007 by Chieko N. Okazaki. Please do not make copies of all or portions of this address without permission. Address requests for permission to Chieko N. Okazaki.

2. Revelation 6:4.

3. Gus Chin, "Civility, the Hallmark of Our Profession," President's Message, *Utah Bar Journal* 19, no. 7 (November–December 2006): 6.

4. Ibid.

5. Christine M. Durham, "Promoting the Standards of Professionalism and Civility," *Utah Bar Journal* 19, no. 7 (November–December 2006): 8.

6. Justice Richard D. Fybel, "Honest Lawyers Make Good Lawyers: Thoughts on Ethics and Civility in the Legal Profession," *Utah Bar Journal* 19, no. 7 (November–December 2006): 12–13.

7. Ephesians 6:15.

8. D&C 27:16; emphasis added.

9. H. Jackson Brown Jr., comp. *Live and Learn and Pass It On*, vol. 2 (Nashville, TN: Rutledge Hill Press, 1955), 22.

10. Proverbs 16:32.

11. Steven W. Vannoy, *The 10 Greatest Gifts I Give My Children* (New York, NY: Fireside, 1994), 195.

12. John 13:34.

13. Moroni 7:48.

14. As quoted in Editors of Conari Press, *Random Acts of Kindness* (Berkeley, California: Conari Press, 1993), 53.

15. Romans 8:35, 37–39.

16. Philippians 4:7.

Law School: A Sacred Experience

Jane H. Wise

I have heard many law students describe their decision to come to law school as a "calling" and—because when you choose to follow a path, you also choose its destination—a calling to the law as well. Students' stories of this "call" illustrate a spiritual impetus that moved them here with a hunger to acquire legal skills. I think all of us were called to law school. I wonder how many law school graduates remember that initial call and still feel a spiritual impetus in their professional lives?

"Many Are Called"[1]

Heeding this call isn't for the fainthearted. Law school's reputation is one of hard work, endless preparation, the Socratic method, and razor-sharp competition. Why would anyone choose to do this? Because law school prepares lawyers. Everyone who graduates from law school can practice in a profession of power.

I spent the weekend reading essays on the reasons why 27 first-year law students decided to become lawyers. Some of them knew from early on that they wanted law as a profession. The events of September 11, 2001, figured prominently in others' decisions. Some were kindly or unkindly nudged by a parent, teacher, or friend. All stated that once planted, the idea of coming to law school gained a life of its own.

It brought back memories of how I was "called" to the law. My college graduation was looming with undergraduate degrees in English and theatre performance. I had not acquired many practical or employable skills and was wondering what on earth I was going to do: Graduate school? Find a "real" job? In one of my last literature classes I recognized a woman who had been in elementary school with me. I asked her what she was going to do after graduation. "I'm going to law school," she said. She spoke in a nonchalant and even blasé way about this plan, but as I heard what she was saying, I felt the earth move under my feet.

It was 1972. I knew many attorneys—my father was an attorney—but I knew no women who were going to law school. My women friends were either married, planning for marriage, still in school, teaching, nursing, or pounding typewriters.

The idea of going to law school swirled around in my mind making me dizzy. Here was a possibility I had never considered. The more I thought about it, the more possible it seemed for me, too. The seed was planted, and just as Alma described, it was a good seed because it began to swell in my heart.[2] I could do that—go to law school. I loved school. I loved reading. The idea began to "enlarge my soul and be delicious to me."[3]

I met my closest friend for lunch soon after and announced, "I'm going to take the LSAT next week. I think I'll go to law school." She, too, was floored by such an announcement. Let me set the stage for those who don't remember more than 30 years ago. In 1973 when I started law school at the University of Utah, there were less than half a dozen women who would graduate that year in a class of one hundred. There were 15 women graduates in 1976, the year I graduated. I took the bar and became the 100th woman admitted to the Utah State Bar. The first woman had been admitted in 1873 before the Territorial Bar, and 103 intervening years passed before another 99 women joined her in the ranks. In 1972 for a woman to casually announce she was going to law school was out of the ordinary.

"I think I'll go, too," said my friend. It didn't take long for her to plant the seed and for it to grow and become delicious to her. There was also the fact that she would have a friend there—me.

It was not a blinding flash of light or an audible voice that issued my call to the law. It was planting a seed of an idea, feeling it swell and enlarge, believing it was good, and having it become delicious to me. The beginnings of transforming events may happen simply and quietly in the planting of a good idea. That doesn't mean that the repercussions of that good idea won't mean thunder and lightning later on, but the start can begin in a quiet thought, the remark of a trusted friend, a new and sweet inspiration that brings light.

I'd like to share some of the stories from the entering class of 2003 first-year law students and their calls to law school. The stories are embedded in circumstances from the quiet to the dramatic, but all of them involve planting an idea that brought good feelings that law school was the right thing to do.

For some students the idea of law school grew up with them. "I always knew that I wanted to go to law school, but from a young age people told me I should think about something else. I welcome a challenge, however, and realize that without it we cannot grow." Another student wrote, "I can't remember when I first formulated the idea of going to law school. I grew up knowing it and living it as if it was the most natural thing in the world."

Some students thought they'd go to law school because a parent was a lawyer. One student remembers a second-grade back-to-school night when he unveiled an art project to his mother and attorney father: "It was a stiff sheet of white paper that began, 'When I grow up I want to be a lawyer.'" The word *lawyer* was spelled out in pennies.

Other students had experiences that showed them the importance of legal skills, like drafting laws to protect people. They wanted those skills to help right wrongs. One student wrote of surveying migrant workers:

> The surveys were designed to see if the farmers were following safety regulations. We asked about things like notification of pesticide treatments, the availability of proper equipment, sanitary living conditions, and other safety-related issues. While spending time with these workers and hearing some of their stories, I became extremely grateful for the laws that were designed to protect them. I began to see that being a lawyer would fit into the life I wanted to live.

Another student wrote:

> I began to think about my dreams growing up. I remembered an experience I had in high school where I interned at the Utah State Capitol and had the chance to read over bills that were being proposed. I fell in love with the atmosphere of many men and women working together to create laws for the good of the citizens of the country, realizing that the law could be used to bring to pass good purposes and protect good people and programs. I realized that good lawyers were needed to promote these causes.

There were stories of frustration with systems where rules were not obeyed that made the idea of acquiring legal skills attractive. Work in China was the seminal event that led one student to law school, seeing what she saw as a lack of adherence to rules and regulations there:

> Cars did not yield the right-of-way to ambulances. Bicyclists, mopeds, and pedestrians fought to be on the sidewalk. I was pushed, shoved, and stepped on as others moved in front of me to get on a bus, to get into the subway, to pay for groceries, or to conduct banking transactions. My students at the university were casual in sharing work on exams and in papers and disregarded the ground rules I had tried to establish and reiterated throughout the semester.

Another student wrote of his experience as a collection agent for a rent-to-own company and determining there must be a better way to earn a living:

> I was looking at going into management soon, but the merits of the rent-to-own industry were wearing thin. The majority of our customers were people who could not manage money. Many lived in trailers rented by the week

with no required deposit; however, the cumulative monthly payment was more than the rent on a nice apartment or house payment. Many individuals were in a constant cycle of addiction, eviction, and then temporary cleanup. Or, if a customer did stay with us, he or she would end up paying triple the cost for a houseful of basic furniture. I asked myself, "What do I really want to do? What is important to me?" As I pondered on this, the word *justice* came to mind. I made up my mind to go to law school and become a lawyer.

Two years after the events of September 11, the memory of that day figured in some of the essays as a call to self-examination and reevaluation of future plans:

> September 11, 2001, was a bad day for me. I would in no way wish to make light of how devastating that day was for others in saying that for me it was particularly bad. It hit close to home. It jarred the sense of civility that I held for my life, specifically and for my country at large, and it prompted me to scrutinize my purpose on the earth. That disastrous Tuesday was the beginning of a serious self-reflection period.

Another student wrote:

> The morning of September 11, 2001, I was on my way to another sales call in Crystal City, Virginia—just across an interstate highway from the Pentagon. My appointment was for 10:00 a.m., but I never made it close to the area. I was able to get turned around and make it home several hours later, where I watched the rest of the day's events unfold on television. After that, my wife and I sat down and asked ourselves what we really wanted to do with the rest of our lives, like living where we wanted to live and working in something we wanted to work in.

Many students expressed the notion that a law school education would further a life of service. One wrote, "I've always wanted to help others, and through my public education experience, I met many people who felt trapped and taken advantage of. Regardless of the type of law I eventually practice, I want to assist those who feel helpless." Another student expressed her love for children and a desire to help them: "At an early age I decided that I wanted to enter into a field where I could help protect children from the harshness sometimes found in the world." One student came to law school because of "a desire to help people find justice, equality, and a better life" and because "the desire to be of service to others is at the core of my life."

Finally, several students wrote about the connection between spiritual promptings and pursuing an education in law. One student summed it up by saying, "I am in law school because of the teachings of the Church regarding personal revelation and regarding my relationship with a loving Father who gives direction to His children concerning His will for them. Such teachings have given me the knowledge, the opportunity, and the faith to know that law school is the place where I should be."

Some calls to law school seemed the most natural thing in the world, while other calls were born from frustration with systems as they were and wanting justice and protection for others. Others were inspired with knowing law school was the place they should be. For many, the call to law school began with students imagining the end of that education culminating in justice, service, and protection.

Students who come to law school are called to a special preparation, but that is a different thing from being spiritually chosen for the profession of law. To be spiritually chosen for the work means first we choose God and His kingdom; He then chooses us for the work.

"Why Are They Not Chosen?"[4]

Section 121 of the Doctrine and Covenants explains why those who are called, who receive promptings of the spirit to proceed in a certain direction, may not later be chosen and approved by God for that work.

> Behold, there are many called, but few are chosen. And why are they not chosen?
>
> Because their hearts are set so much upon the things of this world, and aspire to the honors of men.[5]

It comes down to this: If we are called to law school and the law, and in that journey we choose God and his kingdom and righteousness over the things of the world, we will be chosen by Him for the work. We choose obedience to His laws and enter willingly into His ordinances. But if instead we set our hearts on achieving honors, power, and money or choose to exercise dominion over others, we are choosing the world.[6] Ultimately, those who don't choose God will be left spiritually alone.[7]

Interestingly, this choosing usually happens through the everyday, routine, small and simple choices in life[8] involving how our time and resources are spent. You have decided to use some of those resources on a legal education because you have felt called to law school. After law school you will be faced with the same kind of choices involving your time, which is your most important resource as an attorney. Most of these defining choices will be cumulative. Don't lose your perspective of the importance of everyday choices. "No man can serve two masters: for either he will hate the one, and love the other; or else he will hold to the one, and despise the other. Ye cannot serve God and mammon.[9]

It isn't just the importance of day-to-day work, school, and service choices that will tip the balance on whether we will be chosen by God. Our most sacred experiences are bound to us in quiet ways. We choose to be baptized and make a covenant of obedience. We choose to enter temples to make covenants of obedience. We receive promises that God will reveal Himself to us in the sanctifying of our *ordinary* lives in our education and in our work. What does that look like? How do we make our schooling and our work sacred?

"In the Name of the Lord"[10]

There was much that had to be set in motion for you to enter the doors of this school. In reading these essays I see that the motivation to attend law school came out of desires to serve, desires to live life more fully, desires for justice, and desires to make a difference in the world. These are all ideas of great things that will swell and grow from learning and working.[11] Merely seeking for these things, however, won't make the study and practice of law sacred—and for disciples of Christ, the work we engage in should be sacred and sanctifying.

Section 88 of the Doctrine and Covenants was designated the "olive leaf" by Joseph Smith, "plucked from the Tree of Paradise, the Lord's message of peace to us."[12] From verses 34 to 50, there is a discussion of law, but in verses 119 and 120, there is the suggestion that in establishing a "house of learning," disciples of Christ will make the experience of learning sacred and holy because it will be done in His holy name. "That your incomings may be in the name of the Lord; that your outgoings may be in the name of the Lord; that all your salutations may be in the name of the Lord, with uplifted hands unto the Most High."[13]

The implications of this shake the heavens and the earth. To make your education and work sacred because it is in the name of the Lord connotes learning to be a *priestly* function. What might at first appear challenging, difficult, and an ordinary, day-to-day grind is in reality sacred work. We make it sacred by doing it in the Lord's name. It is the same later on as we make our professional work sacred by doing it in the Lord's name.

When we do our work in His holy name, His mission becomes ours. Christ announced that mission when He read a passage of Isaiah to His fellow Nazarenes in the synagogue at the beginning of His ministry:

> The Spirit of the Lord is upon me, because he hath anointed me to preach the gospel to the poor; he hath sent me to heal the brokenhearted, to preach deliverance to the captives, and recovering of sight to the blind, to set at liberty them that are bruised,
>
> To preach the acceptable year of the Lord.
>
> And he closed the book, and he gave it again to the minister, and sat down. And the eyes of all them that were in the synagogue were fastened on him.
>
> And he began to say unto them, This day is this scripture fulfilled in your ears.[14]

His mission was and is to serve all mankind: to heal, to deliver, to set free, and to bring comfort. As I look back at these student essays, I see that J. Reuben Clark law students see their mission is the same—promoting justice for healing and deliverance, fairness and protection for freedom and comfort.

I pray that this law school experience will become sacred as you go about it in His holy name, choosing Him and His kingdom, and I ask for His blessings to be upon you in that same sacred name of Jesus Christ, amen.

This Women's Law Forum address was presented at BYU *Law School on September 1, 2002. Reprinted from the* Clark Memorandum, *spring 2003, 14–19.*

Jane H. Wise received her JD *from the University of Utah in 1976, clerked for Justice Henri Henriod of the Utah Supreme Court 1975–76, and co-edited* Life in the Law: Answering God's Interrogatories *(2002). She is currently professor of legal writing at Concord Law School, editor of the* Clark Memorandum, *and adjunct law professor at J. Reuben Clark Law School.*

Notes

1. *See* D&C 121:34.
2. *See* Alma 32:28.
3. *Id.*
4. D&C 121:34.
5. D&C 121 34–35.
6. D&C 121:37.
7. *See* D&C 121:35–40, 45–46.
8. *See* Alma 37:6.
9. Matthew 6:24.
10. D&C 88:120.
11. D&C 64:33.
12. *See* headnote to D&C 88.
13. D&C 88:120.
14. Luke 4:18–21.

The Relevance of Religious Freedom

Michael K. Young

Tonight I will talk about some of the lessons I've learned about religious liberty as I've worked in academics and government—I want to discuss how those lessons can teach us what needs to be done, and how we as committed members of The Church of Jesus Christ of Latter-day Saints can fill those needs.

I've spent 25 years as an academic studying Asian economic trends, political trends, and human rights, and I spent four years in government service in the George H. W. Bush administration. The timing in that administration gave me an opportunity to work closely on the issue of German unification as well as on some significant trade and human rights treaties. After my work in the Bush administration, I returned to Columbia University to direct and organize a program on international human rights and freedom of religion. I also served on the U.S. Commission on International Religious Freedom, a statutorily created watchdog commission designed to give the State Department, the NSC, and the president advice on how to integrate issues of human rights more deeply into our foreign policy, especially issues related to freedom of religion. Through all of this I was an observant, dedicated, committed member of The Church of Jesus Christ of Latter-day Saints. Each of these roles informed my understanding of the world and particularly of people who are religiously observant and hope to remain so.

What did I learn from academics and government? Religion is very important in every geopolitical event I have ever studied or participated in. For instance, in the 1930s and '40s, the Japanese government manipulated an indigenous set of morals and ethics into a religion that became known as State Shinto, a form of the Shinto religion allowing the government to control the priests and the doctrine and eventually to manipulate the religion into a form of nationalism.

We all know the role that the Catholic Church played in the solidarity movement in Poland, but lesser known is the role that the church has played in Germany. There has been a religious influence in a number of different countries such as Hungary and Russia. China had an extraordinarily extreme reaction to Falun Gong, a combination of Daoism and Buddhism, and repressed the religion with enormous ferocity. Why were the Chinese so concerned about this seemingly harmless form of meditation? It has to do with the astute sense of history that Chinese leaders have possessed as they have seen political movements derived out of religiously based organizations. For example, the White Lotus Rebellion, the Taiping Rebellion, and the Boxer Rebellion all came during times when the present government was viewed as morally corrupt and relatively weak, so alternate sources of loyalty began to develop. In each instance the Chinese government reacted and successfully suppressed the rebellions, only to lose power within a few years because the cost of suppression was so high and because the very rise of the movements demonstrated the fundamental weakness and invalidity of that government. Chinese leaders are no fools. They understand the threat that something even as innocuous as Falun Gong presents to them.

So here is point one: Throughout my career in academics and in government, I have seen again and again that religion is important—profoundly important—to virtually every major geopolitical event. It seems like a simple point, but it is the first point, and one not shared very commonly by many policy makers around the world.

The second point I want to make I learned from my experience at Columbia as well as from my work on the U.S. Commission on International Religious Freedom. Again, this commission was created by Congress to provide input into our foreign policy formation process that would ensure that our foreign policy was better designed to advance human rights, particularly human rights related to freedom of religion. This was in part because of congressional mistrust of the State Department and of the administration. We had a chance to study religion and how it was being treated in a variety of countries around the world and to then formulate ideas about how those repressed people might be helped by our persuading their governments to repress them a little less vigorously.

So what did I learn from that? I learned that religion is important not only to geopolitical movements but also to individuals. Geopolitical movements are amalgams of people's preferences, their views, and their beliefs. Religion is important geopolitically precisely because, to the vast majority of the world's population, religion is profoundly important individually: Why are we here? Where did we come from? How do we live a life with meaning and purpose? How do we raise our children? What do we teach our children? What happens when we die? The most basic human elements of human dignity are found in those sets of questions—what it means to be human—and, therefore, to individuals, religion is profoundly important. It is how we define ourselves. We are not defined by the government; we are not defined by our external circumstances. Religion is the opportunity for us to reflect and define ourselves.

This is important to governments precisely because it is important to individuals, who act collectively as a nation. People who are religiously observant necessarily have an allegiance to something higher than the state. And for some governments it is very threatening to know there may be organizations out there more likely than the government to secure the allegiance and the adherence of their members. It also means that those who are religiously oriented believe there are some areas of life into which the government can't intrude. There are things an individual can do that the state cannot suppress and is not entitled to suppress. That's why religion is important to governments, particularly governments that seem to be insecure or authoritarian. Religious liberties are often the first rights to be suppressed—the canary in the coal mine of human rights. (I use that analogy and nobody under the age of 40 ever understands it, so I'm going to ask you who are under 40 to ask your parents what "canary in the coal mine" means.) Suppression of religion is an early warning signal of more repression to come. Religion is fundamental and profound; therefore it is threatening in some ways to governments that are themselves insecure in their power.

While on the commission I learned that governments are capable of extraordinary repression and can be remarkably vicious. I met persecuted people face-to-face: Christians in China, southern Sudan, Vietnam, and North Korea; Jehovah's Witnesses in Belgium; Muslims in India and Gujarat; Buddhists in Vietnam, Laos, Pakistan, and Mahis; Jews in Iran; Scientologists in Germany; and members of the Unification Church in Japan. Many were persecuted, humiliated, and discriminated against, and, believe me, there is significant death and torture out there. The reasons for suppression vary from government to government, but they are in the end very relevant to what we think about as we think about the world going forward.

Authoritarian governments are one example of governments that are often insecure with respect to religion. They impose and maintain social and political control, their leaders aren't chosen by the people, and people have little say over state decisions. Religion can be seen in those cases as an alternate source of loyalty and therefore very threat-ening. Examples of nations with such governments are North Korea, Turkmenistan, Uzbekistan, and China.

Then there are governments that on their own cannot garner adequate support and so rely on some identification with the majority religion to remain in power. These are countries that may establish official religious laws conforming to the main religion but apply them to everybody, whether a person is a member of that religion or not. There is often an overlap between official authority and religious authority.

My third point is that governments are divided between majority and minority religions and don't have the authority, the power, or the capability to mediate between those religious differences. Think of Indonesia and the tremendous outbreak of violence there in '98 or the conflict in Malacca in '99. Think of the slaughter of the Muslims by the Hindus in Gujarat, India.

I was asked a year ago if I would be willing to do a presentation for the Area Committee of the Church, which consists of a number of General Authorities who help watch over Church activities throughout the world. It includes a number of members of the Twelve and the Seventy. I was told to cover a few countries in 10 minutes, leaving some time for questions and answers. I talked about Russia and the former Russian republics as well as countries in Asia, Latin America, and Africa. Interestingly, it was a useful exercise because, as I looked at the patterns of repression, I realized that governments that suppress religious freedom for reasons relating to political control may do it quite differently from governments that do it in an attempt to repress intercommunal violence. The former countries are actually loosening their restrictions around the world. One may look at China, Vietnam, and Cambodia—not free, to be sure, but certainly freer than they were a decade ago. On the other hand, countries that control religious expression because of concerns over intercommunal violence— such as Pakistan, India, and Turkey—are getting substantially worse in terms of freedom. Circumstances have an enormously powerful impact on how governments deal with the issue of religious freedom.

This is a point that I want to turn to now. The other thing I realized in the course of this presentation was that the world is in a very good place in terms not only of religious freedom but of many things. We read the newspapers and we continue to think the world is a violent, disastrous, terrible place going downhill. But let me read you some statistics. As we think about human rights, let me cite some important statistics from a report by the Human Security Centre at the University of British Columbia. It found that by the end of the Cold War in 1990, armed conflicts had declined by 40 percent around the world. The number of deadly conflicts—those that kill more than 1,000 people—have declined by 80 percent. Civil wars have dropped by 80 percent. The number of military coups has dropped dramatically. Genocides have dropped by more than 80 percent. Not only that, the number of people killed in an average conflict has dropped extraordinarily. In 1950 the number of people killed in an average conflict was 38,000. Today it is 600. From 38,000 to 600 is a 50-fold decline. Now, for those who were killed, I don't mean to diminish the horror and the terror of war as it does exist, but what we have to understand is that we are in a very different place than we were even 15 years ago. I can talk about a substantial decline of the number of refugees, and the list goes on.

Now, why is that the case? Well, part of it has to do with the end of the Cold War. Also, countries are no longer fighting surrogate wars through smaller countries, and that has dramatically reduced the need for battles in Nicaragua, Iran, and other places. Additionally, the decline is due to the spread of democracy. I think at the end of World War II there were approximately 20 countries that you could have identified as having most of the characteristics of a democracy. Now the number is close to 90. That's an extraordinary difference.

Professor Amartya Sen, a Nobel lawyer and economist at Harvard, spoke at our university recently and made the point, quite profoundly I thought, that no two democracies have ever fought a war against each other. Tom Friedman, who wrote the famous book *The World Is Flat,* describes it differently. He said, "No two countries with a McDonald's have ever fought a war against each other." But whatever the touchstone is, the point is that the world may be in a place where there's more opportunity to do good than at any time since the end of World War II. That is an exciting development.

Nevertheless, the third point I want to make is that this challenge is complex. This is what I learned at Columbia. The program we designed was to bring the secular human rights community—which is not faith-based, and, indeed, is sometimes a bit dismissive of expressions of faith—together with the religious liberties community—which is generally faith-based and somewhat mistrustful of the Godless humanists who run the secular human rights community. One of the things we learned as we tried to bring these groups together is how complicated these issues are. It's very easy to agree that people should stop killing each other, but after that it becomes more complicated.

For instance: head scarves. On the one hand, we say it should be a matter of freedom whether somebody wears a head scarf or not. On the other hand, some say that to reject the head scarf is a political signal of rejection of certain fundamental values for which the government stands. So maybe they should be able to stop head scarves and not allow driver's license pictures of people showing only their eyes. If you start from the supposition that covering one's head is a sign of respect and a reflection of a view that perhaps people, men in particular, will be less tempted if they don't see anything and therefore more capable of living their religion, then this becomes a different issue, an issue that if put in the context of pornography we perhaps will begin to understand in a different way.

And there are issues relating to proselytization, for example. You may have seen the recent article in the paper about how the World Council of Churches has created protocols on proselytization. There is a concern in many developing countries that rich religions are coming in, buying up converts, and disadvantaging the indigenous religion that may not have the resources to do that. Well, that sounds plausible, but isn't the most profound purpose of religion to perform work for the needy? Isn't that the message of every single major sermon in the Book of Mormon?

It's easy to think that our Church doesn't really confront any of those issues because we are very respectful in proselytizing. But in Europe one finds that there is an increasingly powerful gay and lesbian movement with perfectly appropriate people demanding rights. What are some of the mechanisms they are thinking about for enforcing that? Well, organizations that may not provide equal rights would not be entitled to government benefits like the right to establishment, the right to own property, and the right for tax deductions. Well, this is appalling, we think. Yet here in the United States we have done precisely that with respect to racial discrimination. In a major case, Bob Jones University's tax-exempt status was denied, and deductions given to Bob Jones University were no longer considered tax deductible, because of the school's racial discrimination. These are complex, difficult issues that require serious, sustained thought.

Religion is profoundly important intellectually. We cannot understand geopolitical movement, economics, politics, and history without taking seriously the role and the nature of religion in the process. I think, by and large, the academies in America, and indeed the world, have failed. Religion has been largely written out of the curriculum. That's not as important as the fact that as a powerful component of various intellectual disciplines, rebellion is almost totally absent. That has to change.

We also must take religiously oriented people seriously. We can no longer dismiss their claims and their concerns. Four-fifths of the world's people are profoundly religious, and religion matters enormously in their lives. We cannot structure policies without taking their views seriously. That's very hard. That emphasizes my third point: *These are complex and difficult issues.*

Let me conclude with one last thought. It comes from a longtime membership in our Church and an enormous amount of thought about what that means. What I've concluded, a bit to my surprise, is that freedom of religion is not merely a practical, prudential, and wise policy. It is in fact profoundly theological, and it may be more theological than it is practical and political.

Let me give you a couple examples of this in the Book of Mormon. First, take Alma's interaction with the anti-Christ Korihor in chapter 30 of the book of Alma. Korihor begins to preach against the prophecies that had been spoken by the prophets. The Book of Mormon makes it clear, however, that this was not a concern of the law. Even before we learn how pernicious Korihor's teachings were, we learn that "the law could have no hold upon him" (Alma 30:12). Now, in case we miss the point, the scriptures tell us that "there was no law against a man's belief" (v. 7); this is beginning to get kind of repetitive. But they don't leave it at that; three more verses say it was strictly contrary to the commands of God that there should be a law that should bring men onto unequal grounds. This teaching is not prudential—this is a commandment. But it's a commandment because it is essential to keep people on equal grounds. And the very next verse tells us why: "For thus saith the scripture: Choose ye this day, whom ye will serve" (v.8). In other words, this command from God is essential; it's predicated on the most profound principle of all, and that is agency. Anything else, whether it's designed to give us choice or someone else choice, even if it's a choice we don't like very much, is contrary to the commands of God. In fact, this is said in the context of Korihor, who is saying things about as repugnant as one can imagine.

Pahoran says the same thing in Alma 61 when he gives that tremendously temperate reply to Moroni's rather intemperate letter to him. As you recall, the Lamanites were knocking at the door while some grasping Nephites were attempting to take over the country. Moroni is very unhappy; there are no supplies coming. At this point he writes a rather scathing letter to Pahoran. Pahoran writes a scathing letter back, but he puts it in a drawer and then later writes a more temperate letter. In it he says that he understands the problem and wants to send supplies, but he can't because he's defending his people. Would Moroni come and beat back the Nephites who are trying to destroy the kingdom? But Pahoran doesn't want to leave the other people undefended, so he says to send Lehi and Teancum to contend with the invaders. He urges Moroni to give them "power to conduct the war . . . according to the Spirit of God" (v.15). Not a surprising injunction to be given to such spiritual people! He goes on to say that this spirit "is also the spirit of freedom which is in them" (v.15).

I'm going to stop here and just say that as I look at the world, I stand back and think that not only have I had an intellectual and a professional interest in religious liberty, but for me there is a sense of religious urgency to this mission as well. I feel like when the last day comes, be it my last day or the world's last day, I want to be found with my shirtsleeves rolled up. I want to be found with sweat coming down my brow. I want to be found with my lip a bit bloody from the fight to protect not only my freedom and your freedom but also the freedom of everyone around the world, because even if others make choices with which I profoundly disagree, the imperative to give them the same opportunity that I have is one that finds profound and important support in the scriptures—it is an obligation that goes to the very heart of the gospel. I say this in the name of Jesus Christ, amen.

This Education Week fireside address was given to the J. Reuben Clark Law Society at Brigham Young University on August 21, 2007. Reprinted from the Clark Memorandum, *spring 2008, 14–19.*

Michael K. Young received his JD *from Harvard University in 1976 and clerked for Associate Justice William H. Rehnquist of the* U.S. *Supreme Court 1977–78. He served as the Fuyo Professor of Japanese Law and Legal Institutions and director of the Center for Japanese Legal Studies, the Center for Korean Legal Studies, and the Project on Religion, Human Rights and Religious Freedom at Columbia University 1978–1998. He served as law school dean and Lobingier Professor of Comparative Law and Jurisprudence at George Washington University 1998–2004 and as a member of the* U.S. *Commission on International Religious Freedom 1998–2005. He is currently president of the University of Utah in Salt Lake City.*

BE PROFESSIONAL

A Personal Philosophy of Professionalism

Cecil O. Samuelson

While I appreciate the invitation to be with you, I admit to being somewhat intimidated. The last time I appeared before so many lawyers was many years ago as a then young medical school dean. A previous faculty member had been accused of research fraud, and I was "invited" to a deposition. Each of the several universities involved had its own team of lawyers, and since the issue of federal funding for research was part of the inquiry, the Justice Department also was there in force. Even though I was frankly irritated with the alleged perpetrator, I admit that I felt sorry for him because his side seemed to have only five or six lawyers to face the hordes. I had some good advice from my university's counsel who was trying to prepare me for the deposition and who apparently had had uneven prior experiences with the testimony of physicians. In trying to assist me, he took a rather long time to give basically the same advice that President Franklin Roosevelt gave to his son James when counsel was sought concerning a speaking engagement: "Be sincere, be brief, and be seated." I will try to do all three.

I must also confess that I am not looking for speaking engagements at this time of transition in my life. I'll not speak about the matters most pressing on my mind today, because I am not yet the president of BYU and also do not consider myself yet well enough informed to represent the institution with the distinction it deserves. Hopefully, that will be possible as time passes.

The primary reason I accepted Oscar W. McConkie Jr.'s kind invitation is that I have owed him a great deal for many years. I have never been his personal client, but he has been my mentor and friend since the days over three decades years ago when he was my stake president, and I had the privilege of serving as president of an elders quorum under his direction. His influence was profound and persistent and, in fact, has contributed to much of what I wish to discuss with you today. An interesting dimension is that while serving under his direct leadership, I appreciated only in part the things that have been the most helpful. Much has come in the years that have passed, in spite of sporadic personal contact, because the lessons of life and the passage of time have amplified principles he modeled and taught at a time when they could not be fully valued without the context of later experience.

I fear that the title given for my remarks sounds more pretentious than is intended. The real reason I chose it was that my secretary, and Oscar's, applied some pressure to provide a title when I was not yet at all prepared. I looked for something that would cover anything that I decided to say and viewed the advertised topic as appropriately vague for the circumstances. Please notice that I said *a philosophy*, not *the philosophy*. Mine has developed over time and is still a work in progress, I suppose.

Merriam-Webster's dictionary defines professionalism as "the conduct, aims, or qualities that characterize or mark a profession or a professional person" (Tenth Edition). Conduct, aims, and qualities all seem fairly straightforward, and yet each must be viewed or considered in the context of not only what a particular profession—such as the law—means to the public generally but also what the particular profession means to the individual member or practitioner.

As a young man making the decision to pursue medicine as a career and profession, I knew relatively little about the realities and nuances of the life of a physician, and yet the notions of professionalism seemed straightforward. Over time, as my knowledge and experience increased, the ideals of professionalism continued to seem clear, but the applications invariably became more complicated. It was Grace Williams who said, "We learn from experience. A man never wakes up his second baby just to see it smile."

Perhaps a couple of examples that seem to me to have clear analogies with the practice of law may be helpful.

In my training, particularly as a resident and postdoctoral fellow at Duke University, I met some teachers and mentors who were terribly impressive and wonderful examples of the art and practice of medicine. Some of their influences and philosophical imprinting remain with me even now. All that they did professionally was worthy of emulation, and yet I was able to identify values they held to firmly that created dissonance with some of my own dearest standards. One that was dramatic then and is increasingly so now was the obvious relegation of their families to a distant second place in their hierarchy of important things. Because of what I had learned from my parents, other influentials like President McConkie, and my wife, Sharon—as well as my own experiences—I was able to recognize the differences in our philosophies, and this perception also helped me in making career decisions that some others, including important mentors, have thought to be foolish or unfortunate. (By the way, some of my best friends, especially those not of the LDS faith, believe that my most recent career change is a real whopper!)

Over the years as I have followed the courses of the lives and careers of some who I have admired and appreciated, I have been both glad with the major choices I have made (even in the face of some rather silly mistakes) and sad at the disasters that I have seen in the lives and families of some dear friends who have reaped the consequences of their priorities. Please understand that I do not hold up my family or my behaviors to be commendable or exemplary but only that I am increasingly and profoundly grateful that I have understood that there was and is much more to professionalism than the laboratory, courtroom, or classroom.

A second example has to do with a later professional assignment. I was asked to chair the Council on Continuing Medical Education for the American Medical Association. The activities of this council had to do with accrediting formal learning opportunities for practicing physicians. You may be aware that for a time there was a fair amount of concern raised in the media that continuing education for physicians really meant continuing vacations in exotic places.

As we reviewed standards for these courses, it became apparent that some of our colleagues met the letter of the law while avoiding the spirit. That is, a psychiatrist might attend a plastic surgery course in Hawaii and earn the required educational credits while not learning anything that applied to his actual practice. I know you are shocked, and such a thing would never occur with attorneys, but it was a small and yet significant problem in medicine. Now physicians actually need to demonstrate that the continuing education courses they take have demonstrable applicability to their individual practices to count against the requirements of licensure and certification. You might say that this could be an issue for the ethics committee. It might well be, but certainly it is a dimension of professionalism.

Having said all of the above, within the boundaries of proper professionalism lie many opportunities to personalize our approaches to our life's work. I have come to believe that the apparent separation of our public and private lives is really not possible. I am not suggesting that we mow the lawn in coat and tie. What I am suggesting—and believe with increasing intensity—is that there must be integrity and consistency in what we are and what we do. In other words, while we may perform with excellence in certain aspects of our professional responsibilities and yet have other major parts of our lives in disarray, complete or optimal professionalism requires consistency between our public and private behaviors. I suspect that most of you will agree and consider this assertion to be consistent with the values of J. Reuben Clark Jr.

In a similar vein, I confess that while I may be showing only my age, I worry that some of the basics of professionalism are being eroded by members of the professions themselves. I won't comment on what I see happening with practitioners of the law, but I admit to being very troubled by the rather blatant advertising and competition I see today in medicine and health care that virtually everyone in the profession would have thought to be unseemly just a few short years ago.

Not that everything is bad. There are some things that are much better. In medical education today, for example, the law now mandates that a house officer in training—an intern or resident—should not work over 80 hours a week. That seems like a modest requirement to most people, but the facts are that in my day, sleep deprivation was one of the rites of passage, however dangerous to patient or even physician health. I think Thurman Wesley Arnold, an American lawyer, probably set the balance right when he said, "The principles of Washington's farewell address are still sources of wisdom when cures for social ills are sought. The methods of Washington's physicians, however, are no longer studied."

Another risk of our professions that must be considered is that by virtue of the recognition society grants to various professionals, come freedoms not typically accorded to the average citizen. As attorneys you are allowed and expected to ask questions of clients and others that would be considered offensive, impertinent, or rude when asked by anyone else. I know that being officers of the court does not grant complete immunity in this area, but the general principle applies. You will be the holder of some of your client's deepest secrets or confidences—some of which are sacred, some of which may be embarrassing, and all of which are private.

In brief, you are seen in an entirely different light than most people, the recipient of special prerogatives restricted to only a few but also carrying the tremendous responsibilities that are inextricably connected to them. We always need to remember that Jesus taught, "For . . . unto whom much is given much is required" (D&C 82:3; see also Luke 12:48). One of the heavy burdens you bear is the need to be constantly self-monitoring and totally honest with the face you find in the mirror—your own! As talented as you are, you are not invincible. With privileges come special risks that you all recognize.

In speaking of the risks we face, President James E. Faust—who has been rightly honored by your society—once said, "Living on the edge can also mean being perilously close to the Bottomless Pit. . . . Some of you may think that you will discover your strengths and abilities by living on the edge. . . . There will always be enough risks that will come to you naturally without your having to seek them out" (*Ensign,* Nov. 1995, 46).

I applaud this counsel but also admit to feelings of optimism about life and our professions, even in the face of current troubles and challenges. In his recollections about the difficult times of the Second World War, Winston Churchill is reported to have said, "When I look back on all these worries, I remember the story of the old man who said on his deathbed that he had had a lot of trouble in his life, most of which never happened." I myself remember hearing Paul Harvey on the radio many years ago in the midst of some crisis—the specifics of which I have long forgotten—say something like, "In times like these, it is important to remember that there have always been times like these."

Let me conclude by offering some suggestions that I believe deserve regular review by all professionals as they hone their personal philosophies. You will recognize that these are neither new nor original.

1. Be totally honest—not only with others but with yourself.

2. Get help when you need it. Not only should you regularly seek the consultation and advice of colleagues and those more experienced than you with respect to a particular aspect of your work, but also you should be anxious to receive counsel in your family and personal lives.

3. Learn to become an even better listener than you are now. Listen carefully to your clients and those who can advise and teach you, but also listen particularly closely to those who know you best and love you most.

4. Keep learning. Much of what you have learned in law school—and what you think you know—is or will soon be obsolete.

5. Be involved in all of those things that are important to you as soon and as often as you can. Little League ball games, piano recitals, and the like are inconvenient, but they may never come around again, and your presence or absence will likely never be forgotten. Likewise, don't delay too long in being involved in your communities, churches, and professional organizations. You run some of the same risks that physicians face. Many years ago, Milton Mayer made a somewhat humorous but true observation when he said: "One of the things the average doctor doesn't have time to do is catch up with the things he didn't learn in school, and one of the things he didn't learn in school is the nature of human society, its purpose, its history, and its needs. . . . If medicine is necessarily a mystery to the average man, nearly everything else is necessarily a mystery to the average doctor." Be glad this doesn't apply to lawyers!

6. Watch out for each other. No one else, no matter how concerned, really understands what your life and responsibilities are like and may not see what you see. With the tremendous privileges that are accorded to you, there are also commensurate risks you face with respect to the abuse of drugs, alcohol, client resources, and even your privileges.

7. Be loyal to your profession by doing your part to see that you follow the same standards privately that you espouse publicly.

8. Always be thinking and watching for better ways to do things. This applies not only to the technical aspects of your work but also to your human touch.

9. Take care of yourself. As strong, vigorous, accomplished, and important as you are, you still need appropriate rest, exercise, nutrition, recreation, and rejuvenation. Wise leaders have counseled that we should not run faster or farther than we have strength and means.

10. Lastly, whatever you do and wherever you do it, always make a conscious effort to leave the world a better place than you found it.

This address was President Samuelson's first public speech since the announcement on March 18, 2003, that he would become the 12th president of Brigham Young University on May 1, 2003. It was given to the Salt Lake Chapter of the J. Reuben Clark Law Society at the Joseph Smith Memorial Building in Salt Lake City on April 7, 2003. Reprinted from the Clark Memorandum, *fall 2004, 12–19.*

Cecil O. Samuelson Jr. received his MD *from the University of Utah in 1970. He was a professor of medicine 1973–1990, dean of the School of Medicine 1985–1988, and vice president of health sciences at the University of Utah 1988–1990. He has served as a member of the First Quorum of the Seventy since 1994 and as a member of the Presidency of the Seventy 2001–2003. He is currently president of Brigham Young University in Provo, Utah.*

Three Assumptions Lawyers Must Never Make

Brett G. Scharffs[1]

I. Introduction

"You did what!?" my Uncle bellowed.

"I assumed you saw me pass you," I said defensively.

My Uncle Dick, no children of his own, had brought 13-year-old me along on one of his epic bicycle treks down the California coast near Carmel. Inevitably he ended up waiting for me to catch up, and when I finally did, he was ready to hop back on his bicycle and begin peddling again. For once, when I caught up, he was deep in conversation with another cyclist on the side of the road. I waved and hurried on, savoring the prospect of choosing my spot to rest and wait for him for a change. Finally, I stopped and rested. So this is what it feels like to be out front, I thought.

But when 30 minutes passed, I got nervous enough to climb on my bike and pedal back. When I got to the spot where I had passed my uncle, he was no longer there. Now I was concerned, and I decided I had better continue retracing my trail, although I couldn't be sure that he hadn't passed me at some point during my rest. By the time I met up with him, he must have been pretty worried, but all I saw was anger.

"You what?" he repeated.

"I assumed you . . ."

"You assumed?" he said sarcastically. "Spell it."

I meekly complied. "A-s-s . . ."

"Stop. What does that spell?"

"Ass?" I answered doubtfully.

"Continue," he ordered.

"...u-m-e."

"What does that spell?" he demanded.

I hesitated. "u ... m-e?"

"That's what assuming does," he declared. "Makes an 'ass' out of 'you' and 'me.'"

"Don't ever assume," he ordered, and to his credit my Uncle Dick communicated the message with a directness and clarity that makes the experience as vivid today as it was over 25 years ago.

II. Assumptions and Presumptions

Lawyers make assumptions many times every day. We may wish to think that we are all about evidence and proof—Just the facts, ma'am—but in reality, making assumptions is the bread and butter of our professional lives. An assumption involves believing something to be true without sufficient grounds for knowing it to be true. When we assume, we take something for granted without proof.[2] As lawyers we routinely make assumptions, sometimes formally,[3] as when we write an opinion letter,[4] sometimes informally,[5] as when we engage in stereotyping or attempt to exploit the suspected prejudices of others.[6]

Closely related to assumptions are presumptions. A presumption relieves a party in whose favor the presumption runs of the burden of proof. "Legal presumptions ... are not a 'means of proof' ... [but rather] a dispensation of the need to furnish proof."[7] For example, we presume that someone is "legally dead" when they have been absent for a given length of time without evidence that they have been seen or heard.[8] The most famous presumption in the law is the presumption of innocence,[9] but our criminal system is based upon even deeper assumptions about individual responsibility for one's actions.[10] Some presumptions are rebuttable, such as when we presume that a child of a certain age is not capable of committing a crime.[11]

As lawyers we often have to make snap judgments, sometimes in rapid-fire succession, which often are built on an undergirding of assumptions. We also make assumptions when we form a hypothesis and develop evidence to prove our "theory of the case." But while making assumptions is a necessary and natural part of our professional lives, making assumptions can also get us into trouble. Making assumptions may reflect laziness or pride: laziness when we trust our impressions without doing the hard work of verification, and pride when we close our eyes to evidence contrary to our favored presuppositions. I want to suggest that lawyers are particularly prone to mistakes that arise from making assumptions. Let me explain.

III. Three Perilous Assumptions

While it would be quite easy to compile a long list of assumptions that lawyers are prone to make and that routinely cause lawyers grief,[12] there are three assumptions that pose particular peril to lawyers. It would hardly be an exaggeration to say that these are three assumptions that a lawyer must never make.

1. First, don't assume you are the good guy.[13] You probably are not.

2. Second, don't assume you understand the other guy. You almost certainly do not.

3. Third, don't assume you are right. You are most likely wrong.

Now, please do not misunderstand me. It is as important for me to avoid making these assumptions as it is for you. And, while you are probably not the good guy, you might well not be the bad guy either. You very well may understand the other guy, in a partial and limited way. And you are probably not entirely wrong. Although your spouse and I are certain that you are not entirely right.

Unfortunately, avoiding these assumptions requires a large dose of self-doubt, empathy, and humility, and there is precious little in our professional education or practice that helps us cultivate this particular set of habits or traits of character. Indeed, our professional lives are organized and structured in a way that almost compels us to make these particular assumptions.

IV. The Organization and Structure of Our Professional Lives

What is it about the professional lives of lawyers that makes us particularly prone to assuming that we are the good guy, that we understand the other guy, and that we are right? Three features of the legal profession are of particular significance, each of which is closely related to one of these three assumptions.

A. The Adversarial System

First and most obviously, ours is an adversarial profession, and this means we take sides. There are two important implications of this rather pedestrian observation. First, we tend to identify with the side we are on. As we identify with our cause, we tend increasingly to think of it as being good, or right, or just. Naturally, we come to think of ourselves as the good guys. Second, we tend to caricaturize, villainize, or in extreme cases even dehumanize our opponents. This tendency is a well-documented feature of rivalries, feuds, and war.[14] While this tendency is hopefully less severe in the law than when facing a mortal enemy, there is still a strong propensity to think of the other side as the bad guys. The reality, of course, is likely much more complex, and in most situations there will be good and bad, right and wrong, as well as the potential for abuse on both sides. As Isaiah Berlin said, quoting Immanuel Kant, "Out of timber so crooked as that from which man is made nothing entirely straight can be built."[15]

This risk of assuming you are the good guy is particularly acute for prosecutors, who quite naturally view themselves as being on the side of truth and justice. But prosecutors are in a uniquely powerful position and face a particular proclivity to abuse the weapons at their disposal. For example, I have an acquaintance who was indicted nine years ago for securities fraud. For nearly a decade he was bullied and hounded by prosecutors who never quite got around to pursuing or resolving his case. From time to time he was threatened with a lengthy prison sentence, and the government attorneys tried to cajole him into being a witness against his father, who had been in business with him. Over this period of almost 10 years, he spent more than a hundred thousand dollars on lawyers' bills. Finally, on the eve of trial, the government offered him a deal. He pled guilty to one misdemeanor. The negotiated description of his alleged misconduct was so technical that even as a professor who teaches securities law it was difficult to discern exactly what he had done wrong. Nevertheless, this criminal indictment hung over his head for nearly 10 years, caused many sleepless nights, and took a toll on his marriage, not to mention his relationship with his father, which has been all but destroyed.

I suspect the prosecutors in this case have little or no idea the ordeal they put this man through. Indeed, they probably think they showed statesmanship and restraint in allowing him to plead to a lesser offense and avoid prison. They probably assume they were the good guys and that they let him off easy.

B. Stereotyping

A second reason we make unwarranted assumptions relates to the ways in which we rely upon stereotypes. As lawyers we are in the business of making quick assessments. We often deal with people or situations that seem quite familiar, and we become adept at noting patterns and similarities. After years of practice we lawyers may come to believe that there is nothing we haven't seen before.

One of my mentors, Dean Anthony Kronman, has argued that legal training, especially the case method, cultivates in students an attitude of "moral cosmopolitanism that is best expressed, perhaps, by the old Roman motto *nihil humanorum alienum meum est*, 'nothing human is foreign to me.'"[16] Lawyers are less likely to be gullible than they were before beginning their legal training, but they are also less likely to be trusting, and are unlikely to be surprised by human selfishness and perfidiousness. Having seen so much so many times, it becomes easy for lawyers to mistakenly think they know exactly what is going on when they encounter a situation that looks very familiar.

We assume we understand the other guy because we have become expert in assessing situations and people. This can lead us to making confident, and often inaccurate, assumptions about people or situations based upon a paucity of real evidence. Thus, one of the most common quips about lawyers is "Often wrong, never in doubt." We may jump to conclusions too quickly. For example, we are all familiar with how biases and prejudices of various types tend to become more hardened and extreme as we grow older.

C. Passing Judgment

Closely related to assumptions made when stereotyping are assumptions made when passing judgment. As lawyers we are constantly passing judgment on others: Are they telling the truth? Can they be trusted? Are they virtuous or vicious? Over time we get better at making snap judgments. The tendency to pass judgment emphatically and confidently grows stronger as we gain experience and expertise—indeed, simply as a facet of growing older. As we age, our mode of problem solving gradually changes from one based upon analysis and calculation to one based upon pattern recognition. In his book *The Wisdom Paradox,* neuroscientist Elkhonon Goldberg describes this process:

> Frequently, when I am faced with what would appear from the outside to be a challenging problem, the grinding mental computation is somehow circumvented, rendered, as if by magic, unnecessary. The solution comes effortlessly, seamlessly, seemingly by itself. What I have lost with age in my capacity for hard mental work, I seem to have gained in my capacity for instantaneous, almost unfairly easy insight.[17]

Today some people urge us to believe that the immediate judgments we make in a blink of an eye are more accurate and reliable than the decisions we make when we engage in a lengthy process of investigation, thought, and deliberation. For example, in his book *Blink,* Malcolm Gladwell describes an experiment involving student evaluations of teachers. A psychologist gave students "three ten-second videotapes of a teacher—with the sound turned off—and found they had no difficulty at all coming up with a rating of the teacher's effectiveness."[18] When the clips were cut back to five seconds, "the ratings were the same." These ratings were "remarkably consistent even when she showed the students just *two* seconds of videotape." When these snap judgments were compared with evaluations made by students after a full semester in a professor's class, the outcomes were essentially the same. "A person watching a silent two-second video clip of a teacher he or she has never met will reach conclusions about how good that teacher is that are very similar to those of a student who has sat in the teacher's class for an entire semester. That's the power of our adaptive unconscious."[19]

But our instantaneous judgments and snap assessments are almost certainly incomplete and quite probably wrong. Why?

For one thing, our stereotypes and judgments often rest upon prejudices that we don't even suspect we possess. For example, in the past 30 years since putting up screens between musicians auditioning for orchestra jobs and the committees evaluating them has become commonplace, "the number of women in the top u.s. orchestras has increased fivefold."[20]

Another cause of our proclivity to judge imperfectly is the human capacity for self-deception, which is surely one of our most highly developed capacities. Consider the hypocrite who beheld the mote (a small particle or speck of dust) in his brother's eye, but failed to consider the beam (a large piece of timber or metal that is long in proportion to its thickness) that was in his own eye.[21] Why is it that we have such a keen eye for spotting self-deception in others, but a big blind spot for recognizing it in ourselves? Part of the reason, I suspect, is that we tend to judge ourselves based upon our intentions, whereas we judge other based upon their actions.

V. Corrective Actions

I would like to suggest several concrete steps we can take to counteract the tendency to make unwarranted assumptions, including the assumption that we are the good guy, the assumption that we understand the other guy, and the assumption that we are right.

A. Keep an open mind

First, when trying to counter these powerful assumptions, it is important to keep our minds open to contrary evidence. Myson of Chen, one of the Seven Sages, advised, "We should not investigate facts by the light of arguments, but arguments by the light of facts."[22]

Judge Learned Hand is often considered the most influential American judge who was never on the Supreme Court. Judge Hand was famous for the painstaking and evenhanded approach he took to the law. Justice Felix Frankfurter occasionally referred to Hand as the "modern Hamlet," and Hand's biographer, Gerald Gunther, noted that Hand "was uncertain about the proper result in most cases, even after decades of judicial experience."[23] Hand believed that every judge should first and foremost entertain the possibility that he or she might be mistaken. Hand said:

> Of those qualities on which civilization depends, next after courage, it seems to me, comes an open mind, and, indeed, the highest courage is, as Holmes

used to say, to stake your all upon a conclusion which you are aware tomorrow may prove false.[24]

The truth is we may not be the good guy and we almost certainly do not understand the other guy. This is not only because we have not walked the proverbial mile in his moccasins, we often lack the imagination and empathy to even consider what such a journey might look and feel like. A few years ago I wanted to learn more about the word "empathy," so I looked it up in my 13-volume *Oxford English Dictionary*. Imagine my surprise when the word "empathy" was nowhere to be found in the "E" volume.[25] Upon reflecting on my treatment at the hands of my tutors as a student at Oxford, it seemed to me quite fitting that this was a concept that was not even a linguistic possibility at Oxford.[26]

One reason why we sometimes trust our assumptions more than we should is that we mistake having our assumptions *vindicated* with having them *justified*. Consider prejudice and stereotyping. Perhaps I believe that Mormon men are narrow-minded and sexist, even though I haven't really ever known any Mormon men. I have heard this about Mormons and have no reason to doubt that it is true. I meet a Mormon man and he behaves in a way that I view as being narrow-minded and sexist. My assumption about Mormon men has been vindicated. I saw what I was expecting to see. I can say emphatically that every Mormon man I have met is narrow-minded and sexist. With this firsthand experience, my assumption about Mormon men will likely become even stronger, and my sense that my assumption is valid will be stronger, too. Indeed, after a few more verifying experiences, I probably won't even view this as an assumption, but rather a fact.

But the fact that one of our assumptions has been vindicated does not mean that it is or was justified. Justification involves having a sufficient basis in reason for believing something to be true. A belief that Mormon men are narrow-minded and sexist is only justified if, based upon a broad array of evidence and proof, a general rule can be inferred from a large number of cases. Even then, a justified belief will probably be qualified by a variety of caveats and limitations that have emerged from our observation of numerous examples of the phenomena in question to account for exceptions and variations.

It is easy to mistake vindication as justification, especially given our tendency to give more weight to evidence that confirms our presuppositions and to discount evidence that calls our assumptions into doubt. Perhaps this explains why many members of minority groups are so sensitive to portrayals of members of their groups that reflect stereotypes. The American writer Jessamyn West once observed, "We want the facts to fit the preconceptions. When they don't, it is easier to ignore the facts than to change the preconceptions."[27] This tendency to ignore facts that do not fit our preconceptions, while problematic for everyone, can be even more problematic for the lawyer. As La Rochefoucauld memorably said, "There is nothing more horrible than the murder of a beautiful theory by a brutal gang of facts."[28] Many a courtroom lawyer has witnessed the massacre of their beautiful theories.

B. Be a Skeptic, Not a Cynic

A second protective measure against making unwarranted assumptions lies in the distinction between being a skeptic and a cynic. When I was a student, Dean Guido Calabresi repeated like a mantra, "For a lawyer skepticism is necessary, cynicism devastating." What is the difference between being skeptical and being cynical, and why is it important that a lawyer be one, but dangerous if he or she is the other? I had thought of the two terms as more or less synonymous. In time, however, I began to understand what Dean Calabresi may have meant by this distinction.

A lawyer must be skeptical. We see people acting at their self-interested worst. Clients do not always tell the truth, even to their lawyers. Memories tend to be selective and self-serving. Opposing counsel often engage in grandstanding and gamesmanship. A lawyer cannot afford to take things at face value; the unexpected and improbable must be foreseen and planned for. How things will look in litigation must be anticipated at a time when partners seem to see eye to eye. Lawyers encounter human beings treating each other with almost inconceivable indifference and brutality. Lawyers know too much to be completely trusting.

But a lawyer must not be cynical. The *Oxford English Dictionary* defines a cynic as "one who shows a disposition to disbelieve in the sincerity or goodness of human motives and actions, and is wont to express this by sneers and sarcasms."[29] The cynic exhibits contempt rather than compassion. Believing the worst of others serves as grounds for treating them with disregard.

To be skeptical is to doubt whether someone is telling the truth; to be cynical is to doubt whether there is such a thing as truth, or whether being truthful matters at all. To be skeptical is to be unsurprised by human selfishness; to be cynical is to maintain that there is no such thing as selflessness. To be skeptical is to realize that people sometimes behave in ways that are insincere or deliberately hurtful; to be cynical is to disbelieve in the human capacity for sincerity or goodness. To be skeptical is to recognize that we are each capable of evil; to be cynical is to believe only the worst about each other. To be skeptical is to recognize that matching means to ends can be difficult and controversial; to be cynical is to believe that one's ends always justify one's means. One can be doubtful, wary, and watchful without being contemptuous, sneering, and sarcastic.

A skillful, cynical legal technician is dangerous, the more dangerous for being the more skilled. In your practice as lawyers, there will be times when it will prove more difficult than you can possibly imagine to keep your skepticism from degenerating into cynicism. Especially at moments of extremity, it is useful to ask ourselves whether we have crossed the line from skepticism to cynicism. If we have, or if we cannot say for certain that we have not, we should be alarmed—not only out of concern for the damage we may work but also out of concern for the welfare of our own souls.

C. Doubt Thyself

A third way in which we can avoid some of the pitfalls of unwarranted assumptions lies in having a measured tentativeness about our own opinions, even those we hold strongly. In 1958, at age 87, Judge Hand delivered the Oliver Wendell Holmes Lectures at Harvard Law School. To the dismay of many in the audience, he expressed doubt about the correctness of the recent school desegregation cases. But, quoting Benjamin Franklin, Hand acknowledged his doubts about his own conclusions:

> Having lived long, I have experienced many instances of being obliged by better information or fuller consideration to change opinions even on important subjects, which I once thought right, but found to be otherwise. It is therefore that the older I grow, the more apt I am to doubt my own judgment, and to pay more respect to the judgment of others.[30]

Unfortunately, this attitude does not seem to be characteristic of most of us as we grow older. The more common tendency is to become more set in our ways, more committed to our previous viewpoints, and more unwilling to reassess honestly our prior conclusions. Charles Alan Wright suggests that "[i]n spite of being a modern Hamlet—or, more likely, because of it—Learned Hand is firmly enshrined in the small group of judges who universally are regarded as great."[31] Simply being unsure or indecisive is not what made Hand great; rather, it was his open mind, his willingness to entertain opposing possibilities and to characterize each in its best possible light, and his capacity to understand and feel the independent force exerted by each side of an argument.

In cautioning us about the perils of passing judgment, I am not making a postmodernist observation about the impossibility of differentiating between good and evil. There is a difference between right and wrong, good and bad, light and dark, and we can know it.[32] But most truths are partial, and all human perceptions are imperfect. Too often we draw a stark dichotomy between objectivity and subjectivity, when in reality our perceptions are objective, subjective, and relative—objective due to the character and traits of the thing being perceived, subjective due to the character and traits of the person doing the perceiving, and relative due to outside factors such as the color and frequency of light. For example, when I conclude that you acted courageously, it is partly based upon something you did, partly based upon my own values and perceptions, and party based upon the contingencies of the situation.

VI. Conclusion

My purpose has not been to denounce all assumptions. To the contrary, I have suggested that our work as lawyers requires us to make assumptions. Rather, my purpose has been to highlight certain assumptions that pose particular peril for lawyers, not only because they can lead us astray, but because they engender a kind of professional arrogance and hubris for which lawyers are all too famous.

Whereas the adversarial system drives us to think of ourselves as the good guy, if we try to keep an open mind and strive to develop empathy, if we remain willing to alter our preconceptions when facts are contrary to our suppositions, then we will be more open to the possibility that we may not be completely in the right. Whereas the necessity of making snap judgments and our increasing capacity to recognize patterns creates a strong tendency for us to assume that we understand the other guy, if we subject our stereotypes to verification, if we temper our skepticism before it degenerates into cynicism, if we genuinely strive to develop empathy, then we may retain the capacity for reassessment and correction. And whereas we may get better at exercising judgment as we grow in expertise and even wisdom over years of deliberate practice, if, like 87-year-old Judge Learned Hand, we can retain a healthy measure of self-doubt, then our judgments may be tempered by a measure of humility and open-mindedness that may enable us to transcend our natural inclinations and limitations, in life as well as in the law.

This Spirit of the Law address was given at BYU Law School on March 9, 2005. Reprinted from the Clark Memorandum, *fall 2005, 10–19.*

Brett G. Scharffs was a Rhodes scholar at Oxford University in 1989 and received his JD from Yale University in 1992. He clerked for Judge David B. Sentelle of the U.S. Court of Appeals for the D.C. Circuit 1992–93. He is currently Francis R. Kirkham Professor of Law and associate director of the International Center for Law and Religion Studies at J. Reuben Clark Law School.

Notes

1. I am grateful to Danny Walker and the Spirit of the Law Board for the invitation to speak today. I wish to thank Marjorie Fonnesbeck Layne for her kind and capable research assistance. This article is dedicated to the richly wrathful Richard Wrathall, my wonderful Uncle Dick. I love you. Copyright © 2005 Brett G. Scharffs.

2. There are numerous related definitions of the term "assumption" that illustrate additional dimensions of the phenomena, including pretending to possess, as to "assume a virtue, if you have it not"; or taking something as one's own, to appropriate, or usurp, as in to "assume an honor." Synonyms include, to "put on, counterfeit, sham, affect, pretend, simulate, feign." Making assumptions is more related to appearance than to reality. *See* MERRIAM-WEBSTER'S COLLEGIATE DICTIONARY 70 (10th ed. 1994).

3. An example of a formal assumption in the law is the policy of inferring that someone who is engaged in obfuscation is trying to hide something. For example, the law assumes that someone who pays child support is hiding something when he resists discovery of detailed financial information. *See* Philip G. Seastrom & Michelle L. Kusmider, *Family Law Corner: Child Support and the High Income Earner*, 41 ORANGE COUNTY LAWYER 40, 41 (1999).

4. I once heard a lawyer brag that when he gave a validity opinion in connection with a securities offering, it was so filled with qualifications and disclaimers that a careful reading would reveal that he had actually said nothing that was not either based upon a stated assumption or a declaration in an officers certificate upon which he explicitly relied.

5. One of the most problematic examples of informal assumptions in the law is racial profiling. *See* Frank Rudy Cooper, *The Un-balanced Fourth Amendment: Cultural Study of the Drug War, Racial Profiling and Arvizu*, 47 VILL. L. REV. 851 (2002). Cooper explains:

> Racial profiling does not provide information; it collapses all potential information around the assumption about behavior derived from the stereotype about one characteristic. Whereas a description of a suspect simplifies merely for purposes of proper identification, a racial profile takes very broadly defined characteristics and associates any individual owning those characteristics with bad behavior.

Id. at 872.

6. To gain advantages for their clients, attorneys often exploit the suspected prejudices of jury members. In an attempt to combat the effect of jury prejudice in a case involving an altercation between a black student and a white student in Anchorage, Alaska, the defense lawyers for the black student proposed a jury instruction that required the jury to engage in a "race-switching exercise" to assure they were not relying on racial-stereotype thinking. *See* James McComas & Cynthia Strout, *Combating the Effects of Racial Stereotyping in Criminal Cases*, 23 CHAMPION 22 (1999). A portion of the proposed jury instructions describing the "race-switching exercise" is as follows:

> To ensure that you have not made any unfair assessments based on racial stereotypes, you should apply a race-switching exercise to test whether stereotypes have affected your evaluation of the case. "Race-switching" involves imagining the same events, the same circumstances, the same people, but switching the races of

the parties and witnesses. For example, if the accused is African-American and the accuser is White, you should imagine a White accused and an African-American accuser. If your evaluation of the case is different after engaging in race-switching, this suggests a subconscious reliance on stereotypes. You must then reevaluate the case from a neutral, unbiased perspective.

Id. at 24.

7. Geoffrey J. Orr, *Toward a Workable Civil Presumptions Rule in Louisiana,* 53 LA. L. REV. 1625, 1629 (1993).

8. The Uniform Probate Code provides that an individual is presumed dead if he or she is "absent for a continuous period of 5 years, during which he (or she) has not been heard from, and whose absence is not satisfactorily explained after diligent search or inquiry." U.P.C. § 1-107(5) (1990).

9. *See* Cathy Lynne Bosworth, *Pretrial Detainment: The Fruitless Search for the Presumption of Innocence,* 47 OHIO ST. L.J. 277 (1986) (documenting the history of the presumption of innocence and how the presumption has evolved in recent times).

10. *See* Matthew Jones, *Overcoming the Myth of Free Will in Criminal Law: The True Impact of the Genetic Revolution,* 52 DUKE L.J. 1031 (2003). Jones asserts that the theoretical justification for criminal punishment in the American criminal justice system is based on the idea that "offenders have made a voluntary choice to break the law, thus validating the imposition of a societal sanction." *Id.* at 1031.

11. *See* Andrew Walkover, *The Infancy Defense in the New Juvenile Court,* 31 UCLA L. REV. 503 (1984). Walkover explains:

> The common law's resolution of this basic tension between culpability and juvenile status was lodged in the infancy defense. This defense constituted a series of presumptions that embodied largely intuitive judgments concerning a child's capacity to take responsibility for individual acts. These presumptions had the effect of screening out the non-culpable from treatment as adult offenders. Children under the age of seven were conclusively presumed to be incapable of taking responsibility for their acts and thus were precluded from criminal adjudication. Children over the age of fourteen were regarded as adults and thus were presumed capable of committing crimes. Between these two ages the common law created a rebuttable presumption of incapacity.

Id. at 511. The U.S. Supreme Court created a strong presumption when it held last week in *Roper v. Simmons,* 543 U.S. 551 (2005), that it is cruel and unusual punishment to execute an individual who was under the age of 18 at the time he committed the crime.

12. Consider the following classics: "It doesn't matter." "No one will find out." "No one will be hurt." "I'm sure this case is still good law." "These partners will be friends forever." "I can handle this matter." "I've still got time." The list is virtually endless.

13. No gender implication is intended by the use of the informal term "guy," and hopefully none will be inferred.

14. *See* John M. Kang, *Deconstructing the Ideology of White Aesthetics,* 2 MICH. J. RACE & L. 283 (1997). Kang reports that during World War II, when American sentiment toward the Japanese was strongly negative, the *Los Angeles Times* published the following: "A viper is nonetheless a viper wherever the egg is hatched—so a Japanese American, born of Japanese parents—grows up to be Japanese, not an

American." *Id.* at 329. In addition, U.S. World War II propaganda often depicted Japanese soldiers with "buck teeth, slanted eyes and with thick glasses." *Id.*

15. Isaiah Berlin, The Crooked Timber of Humanity xi (Henry Hardy ed., 1991) (quoting Immanuel Kant, *Idee zu einer allgemeinen Geschichte in weltbürgerlicher Absicht* [1784]).

16. Anthony T. Kronman, The Lost Lawyer 159 (1993).

17. Elkhonon Goldberg, The Wisdom Paradox: How Your Mind Can Grow Stronger as Your Brain Grows Older 9 (2005). Dr. Goldberg observes, "With age, the number of real-life cognitive tasks requiring a painfully effortful, deliberate creation of new mental constructs seems to be diminishing. Instead, problem-solving (in the broadest sense) takes increasingly the form of pattern recognition." *Id.* at 20.

18. *See, e.g.,* Malcolm Gladwell, Blink: The Power of Thinking Without Thinking 12 (2005).

19. *Id.* at 12–13.

20. *Id.* at 250. Gladwell adds, "What the classical musical world realized was that what they had thought was a pure and powerful first impression—listening to someone play—was in fact hopelessly corrupted." *Id.* at 250–51.

21. "Or how wilt thou say to thy brother, Let me pull out the mote out of thine eye; and, behold, a beam is in thine own eye? Thou hypocrite, first cast out the beam out of thine own eye; and then shalt thou see clearly to cast out the mote out of thy brother's eye." Matthew 7:4–5 (King James Version).

22. Quoted in Burton Stevenson, Home Book of Proverbs, Maxims and Familiar Phrases (1948).

23. Justice Frankfurter's characterization of Judge Hand as the "modern Hamlet" can be found in a letter from Felix Frankfurter to Charles C. Burlington (Jan. 1933) (Burlington Papers, Harvard Law School). Gunther's observation that Hand was uncertain about the proper result in most cases can be found in Gerald Gunther, Learned Hand: The Man and the Judge 136, 289 (1994).

24. Learned Hand, *The Bill of Rights, in* The Oliver Wendell Holmes Lectures 1958, 75 (1962).

25. In volume III (D–E) of the 1933 edition of the *Oxford English Dictionary,* the word "empasma" is followed by the word "empatron." 3E The Oxford English Dictionary 125 (1st ed. 1933).

26. You will be relieved to learn that the first supplement to the 1933 edition of the OED includes the following definition of "empathy": "The power of entering into the experience of or understanding objects or emotions outside ourselves." The Oxford English Dictionary 329 (1st ed. Supp. 1933).

27. Jessamyn West, The Quaker Reader 2 (The Viking Press ed. 1962).

28. Francois Duc De La Rochefoucauld, Reflections, or Sentences and Moral Maxims (1678).

29. The Oxford English Dictionary 1304 (1st ed. 1933).

30. Learned Hand, *The Bill of Rights, in* The Oliver Wendell Holmes Lectures 1958, 75 (1962).

31. Charles Alan Wright, *A Modern Hamlet in the Judicial Pantheon,* 93 Mich. L. Rev. 1841, 1841 (1995).

32. And so can the postmodernist, as is evidenced all too frequently by her passionate devotion to the correctness of her own point of view. As a theoretical

matter, it may be the case that all truth is relative and that objectivity is impossible, but one cannot coherently assert these propositions, since doing so involves what philosophers have called operational self-refutation—the making of the assertion belies one's belief in its truth.

Packing Your Briefcase

Deanell Reece Tacha

Thank you so much, Dean Worthen. It's a great privilege to be here at one of my favorite law schools in the country, the J. Reuben Clark Law School at Brigham Young University. It is a particular privilege to celebrate with you, the graduates of 2007, who follow in a long line of great lawyers who have either taught at this school, graduated from this school, or been instrumental in its founding. Dallin Oaks and Rex Lee have left a broad swath, indeed, across the legal profession and throughout this nation.

The human experience rewards each of us with a few days in our lives that stand out as days of reflection, days of celebration, and days of renewed commitment to the ideals that brought us to this place in our journey. Well, today is such a day. So I congratulate you and all those who have supported you thus far. Although you the graduates richly deserve every appellation, every praise, every congratulatory greeting, I remind you that in many ways it is not only your efforts that have brought you to this day. Instead, you are the beneficiaries of a great legacy. You learned this in Wills and Trusts: "A legacy is that which you inherit but do not earn and do not deserve." It is what was left to you from other generations: a nation where the promise of freedom is a daily reality unlike most of the rest of the world; a tradition of religious pluralism that has fostered the growth of this great university; and a long, long line of those who came before you and settled these beautiful western lands. On a day like this, we owe them a great debt of gratitude. Thus it is that today marks another important milestone in your lives, for this is the day that you begin to leave a legacy for those who come after you. Remember what you have inherited, and add luster to that legacy after this day is long lost in history.

Now, to you, the Law School graduates of 2007: Today is the day that you begin to pack your briefcases. Many of you, I suspect, on this day have received a new briefcase as a gift. Perhaps it's one of those beautiful leather ones or more likely the more hip canvas variety that crowds the overhead bins of the airlines of our nation. A briefcase is the lawyer's most constant companion. You will be with that briefcase more than you will be with any person or other thing in your life. Now I considered whether calling it a briefcase marks my age and whether or not it might be the holder of the laptop. But don't think it is an outdated relic of the age of paper communication, for even the name is drawn from the professional calling of the lawyer, though everyone else has adopted its use.

I am the mother of four children, and when they were very young my briefcase was their favorite toy. I would dump it in the front hall, run off to get ready for dinner or take somebody to Scouts, and inevitably by the time I got back to ready my briefs or finish some little part of an opinion, the papers and briefs would be scattered, the scissors would have transformed some important document into a paper doll, and the pockets would be stuffed with a cornucopia of treasures. In those days it might have been a Star Wars figure, a dirty little sock, a bug, and almost always a note tucked somewhere that contained a very lopsided heart inscribed, "I love you, Mom." On more than one occasion I would open my briefcase somewhere far from home and find a Cheerio or the remains of an Oreo sifting onto the bench. They were a bit of a nuisance, but those treasures became for me a symbol of the bits and pieces of our lawyer lives that inhabit our briefcases and speak volumes about who we are. They speak of professional commitment—of moving from desk to courthouse to corporate office, meeting with clients, and visiting the sites of great new developments, scenes of accidents, homes of foster children, and the host of places where lawyers and their briefcases go together to carry out their professional responsibilities.

Those briefcases speak of hard work and constantly learning about new issues and new areas of the law. You will have in that briefcase all the equipment of the lawyer, and it will constantly change with clients, court decisions, the will of the body politic, and especially the needs of society—for the law requires you to take a veritable moveable feast with you in those briefcases. The law that you enter is never static. The tools of your work and the substance of what you do will constantly change. So you, too, must be opening and closing and opening and closing that briefcase as rapidly as that change.

For you, the Law School graduates of 2007, I have a packing list for your briefcase, a list of those things I hope you'll include as you go about your lives as lawyers, a list of symbols that will come tumbling out of your briefcase along with the briefs, books, and paperclips.

First and foremost, keep a treasured memento of your loved ones affixed to the top of the upper compartment of that briefcase in a place where it will always be in plain view. It might not be a Star Wars figure, and it won't be the CD of all my husband's favorite music that I have kept my whole career and play from time to time and even in far corners dance to myself, but make sure it speaks instantly and always to you about the treasure of human commitments and friendships. Make sure that it evokes powerful reminders that we lawyers are also loving and passionate people who although deeply engaged professionally place the highest priority in every respect on our human ties and human commitments. So frequently I have seen lawyers lose their way and become so preoccupied with the case of the day or the bill of the hour that they don't hear the chatter of their children or the longing or even loneliness of spouses or aging parents. Keep something right there in your briefcase that will remind you of those human ties of incalculable worth.

Second, but related to the first, tuck into that front corner an old dishrag or a torn piece of a kitchen towel to remind you that the good lawyer is also the helping family member, roommate, friend, and community volunteer. Your responsibilities span a far wider range than those that come under the technical definition of lawyer. The law can be an all-consuming passion, but do not let it become so. You will be truer to yourself, more empathetic with those around you, and ultimately represent your clients with more understanding if you see each day, each and every day, as including both professional and personal responsibilities, purposefully keeping in equal poles the measure of yourself that you devote to each. So whether it is to pick up that dishrag and clean the kitchen, set the mousetraps in the garage, or ladle soup in a homeless meal site, be a caring, down-and-dirty working member of your household and community. It will pay rich rewards far beyond those that are represented by your billable hours.

Third, place conspicuously in that briefcase some symbol of your faith commitment. You at BYU have a long and rich legacy of those faith symbols. For some of you they will be the symbols you are accustomed to here. For others they will be a Star of David, a crescent, or a simple set of philosophical guideposts. But remind yourselves constantly that your behavior as a lawyer, as a citizen, and as a person must be guided by a set of ethical, moral, or religious principles that rise far above the letter of the law. For remember always that the law and its codes of conduct are the lowest common denominator of conduct. They are the minimum thresholds upon which we can all agree. But each of us individually is called as a lawyer from whatever religious and ethical groups we come from to pattern our behavior far above the minimal requirements of the various laws and codes that govern us. It is tragically evident in the world around us that when people attempt the minimal ethical standard of the letter of the law—to say nothing of the societal consequences—they often fail and then suffer the personal and legal consequences of inaccurate line drawing. A good lawyer is guided by a set of standards far above the letter of the law. So keep those symbols in front of you. I could not be here on this day and not mention that I am also national president of the American Inns of Court and that the American Inns of Court were founded right here in this state by my good colleague the late Judge A. Sherman Christensen along with Chief Justice Warren E. Burger. The American Inns of Court are committed to the higher ideals of professionalism, civility, ethics, and legal excellence. This is my commercial message: Everyone, join the Inns.

Fourth, tuck into that briefcase a kite, a harmonica, a Frisbee, or a paintbrush. Never forget to play. Never forget the common language of music and the arts so beautifully demonstrated here today. It is in these shared expressions of our human interests and talents that we can bridge the gap between cultures, communities, and chasms of misunderstanding. When we humbly and joyfully embrace the parts of us that connect us to every other human being, we become world players on a level playing field. We discover new dimensions of our personalities and join hands with the rest of the human race in shared experience. Much too often lawyers are too busy, too distracted, and, yes, even too arrogant to sing the same songs, dance the same dances, or fly the same kites on that rich playground of life. If we do not play or paint with our neighbors, why would they trust us to settle their controversies or determine their liberties? Keep your kites and paintbrushes close.

Fifth, throw in there a pair of handcuffs and a dirty nail or two, so they rattle around and bother you a bit every time you carry that briefcase. Why? To remind you of and propel you toward the important responsibility of every lawyer: to contribute your time and professional expertise to providing high-quality legal services for those among us who cannot pay. This responsibility is an important part of what gives us the right to call ourselves professionals. To the extent that we see our work only in terms of billable hours, we have no right to the badge of honor of a professional even though we have paid a handsome price for our law degree. Many distinguished lawyers and judges before us have made the difference in perpetuating the legacy of a free nation where there is equal justice under the law. Your generation perhaps more than any other generation carries on that essential legacy. Many among us and on every street and byway in America feel forgotten by the system. They feel powerless. They do not think the law and legal system either apply to them or belong to them. You, all of you, must be part of changing these perceptions. Whether you are the representative for criminal defendants, build houses for Habitat for Humanity, or teach schoolchildren about the legal system, you must be out there among the people spreading the message that the rule of law is essential to a free people, and it is equally available to all. So let the clanking of the handcuffs and those nails draw you to representation for the greater good.

Sixth, put a little magnetic board somewhere in your briefcase, and get those little magnetic words to describe your opponents, the judges, other lawyers, and all those with whom you interact as you go about your work.

Now, listen carefully as they say those words, and describe those essential players in the system. Do you speak in respectful and professional tones, or do you allow yourself to be seduced into the rhetoric of the day that is so derisive and so harsh? The language of the law is the language of civilized people. Learn to carry out conflict, to settle our differences under the law, in a civilized discourse and not in shouting at each other. To a great extent lawyers have brought upon themselves the culture of lawyer jokes and serious mistrust because they have allowed the ethos of media showcasing to replace respectful professional interaction.

Seventh, embellish your briefcase with a leaf, a pine bow, or just handfuls of dirt. These emblems of our natural world serve several purposes. They can be simple reminders of the joy of the natural world that requires you to look up from your desk and briefcase and absorb this gift of beauty. But they can also be conscience prickers reminding us that lawyers have an important role to play in preserving and revitalizing the natural treasures of the earth. Here in the West we have a job to do. We do not have enough water. We have all kinds of issues with the quality of our air, natural resources, and endangered species. The list goes on and on. Most certainly these emblems of the natural world will keep you and your work grounded in a commitment that this earth and its bounty and beauty will last, God willing, long after we are gone, for we are but a single organism in the rich procession of a living, constantly changing, ever-adapting universe.

Eighth, inevitably your briefcase will be packed with law books, cases, and all of those equivalents; but remember your common law heritage. It is linked in no small way to the optimistic but historical perspective that we build upon the past to add to our collective understanding of the world and its human institutions and alter its course to meet the needs of changing times. Lawyers have the potential and the training to be essential agents of both stability and change if we will but force ourselves to look at the big picture. Are we illuminating or advancing the course of history? Or do we see our work only as a series of cases and clients? If so, we will have missed our brief opportunity to be stewards for another generation.

The only book I recommend you keep in your briefcase is a little pamphlet I keep. It contains the full text of the Constitution of the United States. Although you will live and work in a global society, never forget that this nation stands as a beacon of freedom for the rest of the world. Well over two centuries ago, a ragged bunch of revolutionaries practiced not a code of law but a short and stunningly idealistic set of principles that would stand the test of time and constant challenges to lead us to this time and place. It was in large measure the lawyers who guided the orderly change and progress for this nation. Their briefcases were packed with patriotic fervor, a sense of purpose, and a commitment to preserving those freedoms for future generations. Their briefcases contained no paralyzing cynicism. Today, join that long and distinguished line of the guardians of our national and professional heritage.

Pack your briefcases carefully. Let them be symbols of who you are and what you stand for. I hope very much that out of your briefcases will come tumbling a Cheerio, a diaper, or a crumbled Oreo to remind you that another generation depends on you for the right to someday realize the dream and the privilege that are yours today.

This J. Reuben Clark Law School convocation address was given at the Provo Tabernacle on April 27, 2007. Reprinted from the Clark Memorandum, *fall 2007, 2–9.*

Deanell Reece Tacha received her JD *from the University of Michigan Law School in 1971. She served as law professor at the University of Kansas School of Law 1974–85, member of the* U.S. *Sentencing Commission 1994–98, and chief judge of the* U.S. *Court of Appeals for the Tenth Circuit 2001–2007. She began her current service in 1985 as judge on the* U.S. *Court of Appeals for the Tenth Circuit in Denver, Colorado.*

And with All Thy Mind

John W. Welch

President Samuelson, brothers and sisters: I am humbled to address you. For almost 40 years my wife and I have been blessed by the full life of the mind offered by Brigham Young University—first as students, where we met in the library, and now as we both serve on the faculty. For 23 years I have taught in the Law School and worked in various campus assignments. We are grateful to all who have worked to make BYU so intellectually inspiring. I hope my words will in some small way repay the many to whom I am deeply indebted.

And thanks to each of you for coming and bringing the Holy Ghost with you. Brigham Young's instruction to the BYU faculty was that they "ought not to teach even the alphabet or the multiplication tables without the Spirit of God" (in Reinhard Maeser, *Karl G. Maeser: A Biography* [Provo: Brigham Young University, 1928], 79). I would state a corollary to that: As students, you should not *learn* even the multiplication tables without the Holy Ghost. It does little good for someone to *teach* with the Holy Ghost if you aren't ready to *receive* with the Holy Ghost.

Today I would ask: What does it mean to you to love God with all your mind? We *feel* what it means to love Him with our heart, but what does it mean to love Him with our mind? I have asked many people this question. I get many different answers. What would your answer be?

At the outset, let me turn to a passage in Mark 12, which I find terribly important. A highly educated scribe (their equivalent of a college graduate) who had overhead Jesus reasoning with some Sadducees, asked the Savior, "Which commandment is the first of all?"

Jesus answered: "Thou shalt love the Lord thy God with all thy heart, and with all thy soul, and with all thy mind, and with all thy strength."

"And," Jesus added, "this is the second: Love thy neighbor as thyself."

To this the scholar responded, "Teacher, you speak very well and in truth, for to love God with all one's heart and all one's understanding and all one's strength, and to love one's neighbor as oneself is more advantageous than all burnt offerings and sacrifice."

Seeing that this person spoke with keen intelligence, Jesus declared, "You are not far from the kingdom of God." (See Mark 12:28–34; author's translation in part.)

This brief encounter is deeply interesting to me. Since Jesus was dealing with a craftsman of words, let me mention some notable vocabulary in their conversation. When Jesus stated the prime commandment, He carefully included the mind. The Greek word used for *mind* is *dianoia,* meaning with all your "way of thinking" or your "perception of things." In his response the scholarly scribe used an even more dynamic word, *synesis,* meaning "understanding, getting things all together, comprehensive comprehension, synthesis, and insight." And then, escalating a third step, Jesus told this man that he was not far from the kingdom because he spoke *nounechos,* literally "having *nous,*" the highest term in some philosophical pantheons for true, even divine, intelligence. These three words regard the mind highly, the last being especially strong.

How many lessons can we draw from this inspiring exchange between the Savior and this educated individual? Let us not pass lightly over this stunning scripture; divine declarations often come without much elaboration yet are laden with profound implications. I would speak today of seven dimensions of loving God with our all our mind, drawn from words in this account.

It Is *Possible*

First, we learn with assurance that it is *possible* to get near to the kingdom of God while having intelligence. This smart man was close to the mark, and Jesus congratulated him for it.

Likewise, we on the faculty congratulate and welcome you. At this university and in this religion, you don't need to check your brains at the door. To be a gospel scholar, you'll need all the brilliance you can muster, for we have the double challenge of knowing not only the ways of the world but also the ways of the Lord—and then, getting the two together. In this sense the world actually has the lighter assignment. Of course, in another sense, our task is the easier. Because of modern scriptures and the temple, we have more pieces in life's puzzle, as well as the picture on the box.

I hope you are excited and humbled to be at Brigham Young University, where we boldly affirm that "the glory of God is intelligence" and that "to be learned is good," so long as we avoid the vainness, the frailties, and the foolishness of men and also "hearken unto the counsels of God" (D&C 93:36; 2 Nephi 9:29). Ancient and modern prophets offer role models of highly intelligent people who have loved the Lord with their minds. Until only recently, President Hinckley has enjoyed reading the classics in Latin and Greek, which he learned in college. Isaiah was a brilliant writer, and Paul was amazingly articulate. Alma went head-to-head against the stubborn issues of his day. As Limhi promised his people, "If ye will turn to the Lord with full purpose of heart, and put your trust in him, and serve him *with all diligence of mind* . . . , he will . . . deliver you" (Mosiah 7:33; emphasis added). Thus it is indeed possible to get near to the kingdom of God with intelligence.

It Is *Commanded*

Second, Jesus makes it clear that we are *commanded* to love God with our mind. Pondering this, I realized that I should approach this commandment as a responsibility, not just as an opportunity or privilege. I wondered: Do you think of this commandment when you partake of the sacrament or when you answer the recommend question about striving to keep the Lord's commandments?

Like keeping any commandment, keeping this one will surely take conscious effort. We don't keep the Word of Wisdom by accident. We don't keep the Sabbath day without planning and devotion. So what do you do to keep this commandment deliberately? Do you earnestly strive to love God with all your mind? I doubt that a flimsy "Well, I guess so," is going to be good enough. Speaking to the pure in heart in the city of Nephi, Jacob exhorted them to "look unto God with firmness of mind" (Jacob 3:1). And Alma made it clear that God will give people knowledge of His mysteries only "according to the heed and diligence which they give unto him" (Alma 12:9). There is a direct connection between answers obtained and our effort in keeping this commandment.

I know that God will help us keep this commandment, for He will give no commandment save He shall prepare a way for us that we can keep it (see 1 Nephi 3:7).

With *All* Thy Mind

Third, the word *all* is all important here. It appears seven times in this scripture—itself a symbolic number of completion, often associated with sacrifice in Leviticus. Keeping this commandment requires genuine, dedicated completeness. You are commanded to love God with *all* thy heart, *all* thy might, and *all* thy mind. We have a word *wholeheartedly*. Maybe we should coin a word *wholemindedly*.

The gospel is not a cafeteria plan. We can't just pick and choose the parts we like.

Elder Neal A. Maxwell has spoken often about discipleship, submissiveness, and consecration, especially in intellectual settings. He has sensitized us to the dangers of what he calls "holding back," of not loving God with all the mind that we could. He said in a talk at a banquet for the Foundation for Ancient Research and Mormon Studies (FARMS) on September 27, 1991:

> Whatever our particular fields of scholarship, the real test is individual discipleship, not scholarship. . . .
> . . . We usually tend to think of consecration in terms of property. . . . But there are so many ways of keeping back part and so many things we can withhold a portion of besides property. All things [including our minds] really ought to be put on the altar. ["Discipleship and Scholarship," BYU Studies 32, no. 3 (summer 1992): 7]

Minds must bend, as well as knees.

An idea is often the last thing we are willing to let go of. Our pet ideas are often the beginning of our undoing. A wise drama teacher once said, "Forget your best idea." Clinging to it will often block the flow of even greater creativity and more expansive inspiration.

Fortunately, each of us has been blessed with definite mental talents, with plenty to give forth. And remember, in the world of the New Testament, even one talent of gold or silver was an enormous sum, worth several million dollars in today's markets. It is true that some minds work better in one mode than in another, but that's irrelevant: we can and must love God with our weakest mental abilities, as well as by playing to our strengths. Surely God cares less about what we give Him than if we have brought all of our best, whatever that may be.

Many Ways to *Love*

Fourth, this all has to do with *love.* Sister Welch and I have a pillow on our bed. On it are words of Elizabeth Barrett Browning: "How do I love thee? Let me count the ways." With similar fervor, let us count the ways we love God with our minds and love Him "to the depth and breadth and height / My [mind] can reach, when feeling out of sight / For the ends of Being and [eternal] Grace . . . to the level of everyday's / Most quiet need, . . . freely, . . . purely, . . . with the passion put to use, . . . and, if God choose, [even] better after death" (*Sonnets from the Portuguese* [1850], no. 43).

We love Him with our minds by being observant of the things He has created—by appreciating the amazing things that He has given us in the worlds of chemistry or geology, scriptures or linguistics. If you love a person, you notice and admire the fantastic things he or she has done. President Hunter once said, "He loves God with all his mind who . . . sees God in all things and acknowledges him in all ways" (*Conference Report,*

April 1965, 58; also "'And God Spake All These Words,'" *Improvement Era* 68, no. 6 [June 1965]: 512).

We love God with our mind by caring about the problems He cares about. We love God with our mind by embracing His work, giving it the best of our planning, research, and problem solving. Figuring out what you can do as a home teacher to motivate someone to repent is truly a challenging intellectual task, and learning the names of everyone in your ward is another way to love God with your mind.

When we love God, we want to be like Him—and remember, He knows everyone's name. It takes careful thought to internalize all that we can know of Him.

It takes mental effort to forgive other people as He does, for that begins by thinking nonjudgmental thoughts about them and seeing them as He does.

Loving God also means loving His words. I love the scriptures, although admittedly some chapters are harder to love than others. We love God with our mind by memorizing scriptures. The conversation between Jesus and the scribe was possible because both of them knew that scripture by heart. We rely too much on our books, notes, and hard drives. Your mind can actually retain far more than you imagine. One of the best things I ever did was to take a challenge from my leader in the MTC to memorize all of the Sermon on the Mount. In an honors Book of Mormon class, I had my students memorize most of King Benjamin's speech. One student recalled: "When we first got the assignment, it was overwhelming; but it was probably the most rewarding assignment I've ever had at BYU."

We love God with our mind by skillful analysis of problems; it is often said that "God is in the details." But don't forget also to love God by skillful synthesis as well, seeing things as one great whole. When I go to the temple, I give attention to its tiniest details and carefully presented words; at the same time, my mind sees the temple as a huge pattern and cosmic road map that tells me where I am and where I need to go.

We love God with our mind by asking good and righteous questions. There is nothing wrong with asking. In fact, we are commanded to ask, seek, and knock (see Matthew 7:7). Our scribe in Mark asked Jesus a good question, much better in fact than the unlikely hypothetical one posed by the Sadducees about a supposed seven-time widow who had remarried six of her husband's brothers (see Mark 12:18–27). We need to spend more time discerning between good questions and bad ones. It won't do to be knocking on the wrong door. For examples of good questions, look at the 50 questions Alma asked in Alma 5 (see John W. Welch and J. Gregory Welch, *Charting the Book of Mormon: Visual Aids for Personal Study and Teaching* [Provo: FARMS, 1999], charts 61–65). Or look at the many questions Jesus asked people in the New Testament gospels, and then go and do

likewise (see John W. Welch and John F. Hall, *Charting the New Testament* [Provo: FARMS, 2002], chart 9-16).

We love God by listening better to Him and to those who speak for Him. A good measure of people who love each other is how well they listen to each other. Listening is a mental process. It involves attentively processing what we hear. Notice that the scribe repeated back (a good communication strategy) what Jesus said, and thoughtfully commented on its implication.

How do we love God? Let us count the many ways. It is here at BYU, more than at any other place, that you can specialize in learning how to love God with all your mind and as an integrated soul.

It is here that we see no irreconcilable conflict between the heart and the mind. The restored gospel of Jesus Christ exquisitely harmonizes the traditional paradoxes of life, embracing both study and faith, reason and revelation, truth and goodness, thought and action, spirit and mind. The one is not without the other in the Lord. The gospel strives, above all, for the fullness of eternal life, not just either half of it. An incomplete view is partial in more ways than one.

Getting the heart and the mind together is a joyous experience. It is not easy to describe the collaborative workings of the two, but analogies can help. Getting the spirit and intellect together is like seeing with two eyes, allowing depth perception lacking through a single lens. It is like playing a violin that requires two hands, each performing its own function to produce a harmonious melody (see John W. Welch, "The Power of Evidence in the Nurturing of Faith," in *Echoes and Evidences of the Book of Mormon,* ed. Donald W. Parry, Daniel C. Peterson, and John W. Welch [Provo: FARMS, 2002], 17–53). Or, as a student suggested, it's like chocolate and milk: they taste fine alone, but better together.

With All Thy *Mind*

Fifth, I learn from the conversation in Mark that Jesus cares very much about our *minds*. He carefully noticed that the scribe answered with great intelligence. This means that He notices and cares what we think, write, and teach. I know that God watches over our intellectual endeavors. The surgical testimony of Elder Nelson shows that God will help things happen that far exceed human ability (see Russell M. Nelson, "Sweet Power of Prayer," *Ensign,* May 2003, 7–9). Have miracles ceased? No. In fact, Mormon says that miracles are ministered "unto them of strong faith *and a firm mind* in every form of godliness" (Moroni 7:30; emphasis added).

I have asked for and have received His support in many academic pursuits, often through the unimaginable help of other people. One day, with no appointment, a person walked into my office with the precise skill set I had been praying for, only to tell me she didn't know why she had come but that she had decided not to stay with another job and wondered if I needed any help.

Last Christmas, facing a crucial year-end deadline after months of work, my staff finally downloaded a huge collection of scanned Church historical documents onto 74 DVD production masters; with those master disks safely in hand, they watched as our linked hard drives crashed irrecoverably only a few hours later.

I cannot believe that these things were mere coincidences.

I know that God will support us as we strive to love Him with our minds. My colleagues and I have attended and presented papers at many academic conferences. Not infrequently, results have been transformational in ways that we gladly attribute to the Spirit of the Lord.

I know that God inspires us, but most often only after we have studied things out in our minds (see D&C 9:8) and have paid the price of thorough research directed by the light of faith. Many LDS scholars and regular members as well can tell of sacred experiences they have had in discovering things through study and faith that they never would have found on their own.

I myself treasure several such discoveries. I remember searching for an answer to a recurring criticism of the Book of Mormon about the resurrected Savior's use of the Sermon on the Mount in 3 Nephi. As I dug into the task, confident that there must be an answer, the apparent problem turned into a strength as the temple and covenant settings of both texts distilled upon me as the dews from heaven (see John W. Welch, *Illuminating the Sermon at the Temple and Sermon on the Mount: An Approach to 3 Nephi 11–18 and Matthew 5–7* [Provo: FARMS, 1999]).

I also remember one early missionary morning in Germany when the significant literary feature of chiasmus in the Book of Mormon amazingly unfolded to my view. Outside study and spiritual promptings had set the stage, but a mind firmly and tenaciously pursuing the implications of my testimony of the Book of Mormon caused that discovery actually to happen (see John W. Welch, "Chiasmus in the Book of Mormon," BYU *Studies* 10, no. 1 [autumn 1969]: 69–84).

My testimony does not depend on finding such things; rather, my mind looks with confidence for such things precisely because I know the Book of Mormon and the gospel are true. Faith precedes the miracle of insightful understanding. As President Packer has cautioned and encouraged, we should not say, "I know the gospel is true, however . . ." Rather, say, "I know the gospel is true, therefore . . ." And for me, that has made all the difference. (See Boyd K. Packer, "The Mantle Is Far, Far Greater Than the Intellect," BYU *Studies* 21, no. 3 [summer 1981]: 270; also *Let Not Your Heart Be Troubled* [Salt Lake City: Bookcraft, 1991], 113.)

I also know that God rewards us after long hours of service. Some of my favorite scriptural insights—making intellectual sense and dissolving spiritual challenges throughout my life—have come at weary hours of the night during my service as a bishop. Ironically, my most productive years as a scholar have been the years when I have been busiest as a bishop.

It Is the *First* Commandment

Sixth, what of the fact that this is part of the *first* commandment? Loving God is the prime commandment because all else follows from it. Loving God is the wellspring of all righteousness. Loving Him with all our mind is the taproot of true intelligence. Loving Him with all of the integrated faculties of our whole being echoes the integrated harmony of the Godhead and godhood itself.

John 14:15 can also be translated "If you love me, you *will* keep my commandments." When you love God with all your mind, you will mind Him and mind all His precepts. And by minding Him always, by obeying Him always, you remember Him always. In Hebrew, the same word, *zakhor,* means "to remember" as well as "to obey" (see "'O Man, Remember, and Perish Not,'" chapter 35 in John W. Welch, ed., *Reexploring the Book of Mormon: The FARMS Updates* [Salt Lake City: Deseret Book; Provo: FARMS, 1992], 127–29).

If you love God, you will think of Him often. You will want to share with Him your whole day, every day and every night, Fridays as well as Sundays, everything you have thought, said, and done. You miss Him and hope to see Him again.

You will think kind and loving things about Him. In the face of any type of inconclusive uncertainty, love gives the benefit of the doubt.

You will also think correct things about Him. Although you cannot talk yourself into loving God or anyone else, it is possible to talk yourself out of love, so give heed to what you think.

Loving God leads to all else that is of the divine nature.

It Is Possible to Break This Commandment

Finally, we must also acknowledge that it is possible to disobey this commandment. How do we break the commandment to love God with all our mind, and, if we have transgressed, what must we do?

We break this commandment when we think contrary to the degree of knowledge we have received, when we know better.

We break this commandment when we promote ideas that injure other people, for with knowledge comes power, and with any power comes duty and accountability.

We break this commandment when we harbor in our mind errors or excuses that deny the existence, love, power, or knowledge of God. As a bishop, I've heard people say: "Everyone is doing it." "I couldn't stop." "It's my life, I can do what I want with it." "Every point of view is equally valid." "I have no friends." "No one will notice." But where do these mental mistakes leave God? Is God doing it? Couldn't God help you stop? Is it really your life? Does God's view count? Isn't He your friend? Doesn't God know and notice everything, including your thoughts?

We break this commandment whenever we believe Satan, the enemy of all righteousness. Beware: Satan is the father of lies. And he's a good liar. Take the lie of pornography. Satan tells us we will find satisfaction by staring at pornography. This is simply a lie. Can we love God with *all* our mind if even part of our mind is filled with this pollution? When I came to BYU in the sixties, we were just beginning to worry about environmental pollution. Previous generations had foolishly believed that the oceans could absorb an endless amount of garbage and waste. We learned that pollution doesn't just go away.

I wonder if people aren't just as naïve today. They foolishly think that the human mind can absorb an endless amount of filth and violence and that somehow we can just push a delete key in our brain and erase all that. You have been blessed with an amazing brain, with incredible retentive powers. Whether or not you can recall that information during a test, it's all still there. Old folks often find that their brains retain things they haven't thought of for decades. Mental pollution sticks; there are no Teflon brains. Just as it is true that "whatever principle of intelligence we attain unto in this life, it will rise with us in the resurrection" (D&C 130:18), so, too, whatever degree of unrepented smut or cynicism we attain unto, it will rise with us as well.

Thus, Moroni says, "Come unto Christ, and be perfected in him, and deny yourselves of all ungodliness; . . . and love God with all your might, mind and strength" (Moroni 10:32). He says, "Be perfected *in him*." We cannot perfect our minds without His help. We know the effects of the Fall on our bodies, but our minds are also in a fallen state. Our minds must also be redeemed. This happens by repenting of our bad or erroneous thoughts and submitting to the mind and will of Christ.

We must repent of our academic pride. Pride is the main occupational hazard for scholars, who too quickly suppose "they know of themselves" (2 Nephi 9:28). Being right is part, but only part, of being righteous.

We must overcome our rebellious thoughts every bit as much as our disobedient actions. We must pray "and lead us not into *intellectual* temptation" as much as any other kind of temptation (see Matthew 6:13). Satan knows a lot of truth, but that's not enough, for he still rebels.

We must feel godly sorrow for our mental sins. Like Zeezrom, we must suffer spiritual migraines over our intellectual mistakes (see Alma 15:3, 5). In many ways, their effects on ourselves and on others are the hardest to undo, but through the Atonement, the human intellect can be transformed into an instrument for loving God.

So the question becomes: Has your mind been sanctified by the atoning blood of Christ? (see Welch, *Echoes and Evidences*, 44–47). As described in Mosiah 3:19, has your mind "yield[ed] to the enticings of the Holy Spirit"? Or, as stated in Mosiah 5:2, have you "no more disposition" to think evil? Has the finger of the Lord touched our inert cerebral stones and turned them into light-giving gems? To use the words of Paul in Romans 12:2, have you been "transformed by the renewing of your mind [your *nous*]"?

If so, the Lord will light up your mind, as He did King Lamoni's (see Alma 19:6). He will cause your mind to expand, as Alma promised (see Alma 32:34). He will write His covenants upon your mind, as Jeremiah guaranteed (quoted in Hebrews 8:10; see Jeremiah 31:33). He will bless your heart and mind with peace that passes all understanding, as Paul assured (see Philippians 4:7–9).

And in the end, if you love God with all your mind, you will be fit for the *kingdom*. What a promise! At byu we are playing for keeps, "for as [a man] thinketh in his heart, so is he" (Proverbs 23:7), and in the day of judgment, our unrepented thoughts will weigh against us (see Alma 12:14). But if you "worship him with all your . . . mind," the scriptures say, "ye shall in nowise be cast out" (2 Nephi 25:29) and "the hope of his glory and of eternal life [shall] rest in your mind forever" (Moroni 9:25).

A Final Blessing

In conclusion, as a bishop and teacher, may I offer a prayer in your behalf?

May you not just pass through byu, but may the spirit of this university pass through you.

May you know it is possible to love God with all your mind.

May you love Him with invigorating questions.

May you perceptively discern between truth and error.

May your intellect be keen and sharp but never harm even the least intelligent of the children of God.

In your academic freedom, may you intellectually "choose liberty and eternal life, through the great Mediator of all men," not "captivity and death" (2 Nephi 2:27).

May you pray over your books, as you would bless food for thought.

May you pray as you go to class, and not just as you enter the Testing Center.

May your love of God give harmony, value, and joy to all that you think and do, that you may become perfected in Christ.

And in all of this may God find you, too, not far from His kingdom.

In the name of Jesus Christ, amen.

This devotional address was given to the BYU *student body on September 30, 2003. Reprinted from* Brigham Young University Speeches 2003–2004, *105–112 and the* Clark Memorandum, *spring 2004, 16–23.*

John W. Welch was a Woodrow Wilson Fellow at Oxford University 1970–72 and received his JD *from Duke University in 1975. He was founder of the Foundation for Ancient Research and Mormon Studies in 1979, served on the board of editors for the* Encyclopedia of Mormonism *(1992), and has served as editor in chief of* BYU Studies *since 1991. He is currently Robert K. Thomas University Professor of Law at J. Reuben Clark Law School.*

Avoiding Pitfalls

Dale A. Whitman

My dear friends, I am happy to be with you on this joyous occasion. I have a great love for this law school and for many of its students in past years. I regret that I haven't had the opportunity to get to know you, the graduates of 2003, but I am sure you have received a first-rate legal education. I know most of your faculty as close friends, and I have the highest regard for them. They combine faith with the best of professional accomplishment. The J. Reuben Clark Law School is highly thought of among legal educators. I began law teaching in 1967—a mere 36 years ago—and this law school opened its doors six years later, in 1973. I am reluctant to give credence to the *u.s. News* rankings of law schools, which are deeply flawed in many ways. But in general those rankings are quite accurately reflective of the reputations of law schools. Of all the law schools that have opened during my professional lifetime—and it is a large number of schools—none has a higher *u.s. News* ranking than BYU. I think it fair to say that none is better on the merits.

There are several standard law school commencement speeches. You can guess what they are: the "lifetime of learning" speech, the "let's restore civility to the profession" speech, the "balance your professional life and your personal and family life" speech, and one of my favorites, the "why you should give money to your alma mater" speech. These are all grand speeches, but I have decided to take my remarks in a different direction today. I want to talk about how lawyers get into trouble and how you can avoid doing so.

I know that none of you expect to get into professional trouble. You think of yourselves as ethical and moral people, and you have all taken a class called "professional responsibility." You know the rules, and you expect to live by them. Nonetheless, you are at risk of getting into trouble—typically in ways that have little to do with the subject matter of your professional responsibility course.

The key to staying out of trouble is to act professionally. This means something much more than simply staying within the bounds of the technical rules. At its core it means that you—and only you—must make decisions on how you will practice law and that you must sometimes make decisions that are difficult, painful, and at least in the short run, contrary to your economic self-interest.

The challenges you will face in this area will depend a great deal on whether you practice on your own or in a small firm on the one hand, or in a large, highly structured firm on the other. In many ways, these situations are as different as night and day, even though they both involve the practice of law. Let me begin with the small firm or solo practice situation. The principles for staying out of trouble here are quite simple. There are three of them:

1. Don't accept work you can't handle.
2. Communicate constantly with your clients.
3. Don't touch their money for your personal use.

These three principles are connected: they all involve money. If you are a solo practitioner or in a firm with one or two other lawyers, your biggest concern will be paying the bills and making a living. For a good while, economic security will seem out of your reach. As a result, every potential client who walks into your office will seem to have a slightly green tinge and to have a large dollar sign emblazoned on his or her forehead! Clients represent income, and as a result it is almost impossible to turn a client away. Unfortunately, this means that you will be tempted to accept clients whose ethics are far from your own and who intend to use you to accomplish their unworthy goals. You will be tempted to take on matters in which you have no expertise and no time to develop it. Above all, you will be tempted to take work that you simply don't have time to do.

The right response to all of these situations is simply to say no, even though saying yes will seem to have the potential for making money. It is easy to identify a lawyer who is inundated with work that she or he doesn't know how to do and doesn't have time to do. Just look on the desk for that stack of unanswered telephone messages. Lawyers in this situation practice what the psychologists call "avoidance behavior." They don't return calls from clients because then they would have to admit that a client's pleading isn't filed or a client's contract isn't drafted or a client's deposition isn't scheduled.

This desire for more money sometimes manifests itself in an even worse and more reprehensible way—the lawyer who holds the client's funds and decides that it would be permissible to "borrow" them, just for a little while, to pay some pending expenses, without mentioning the "loan" to the client.

Sadly, this is the pathway to bar discipline and attorney malpractice actions. State bar journals are full of cases in which all of these things occurred, and someone lost his or her license to practice law as a result. You simply must temper your desire for a good income with your desire to be a good lawyer. Sometimes the need for income must take second place. Again, the rules are simple:

1. Don't accept work you can't handle.
2. Communicate constantly with your clients.
3. Don't touch their money for your personal use.

Now let me turn to the big-firm lawyer. Oddly enough, the same considerations of time and money get these lawyers into trouble, but usually through a far different route. Young associates in big firms are unlikely to take their clients' funds, and they are largely protected by the firm's structure from undertaking work they can't perform. But often they are caught up in the desire to make the partners happy in order to keep a job that pays well. Let me illustrate their dilemma with three little vignettes.

Illustration 1 Your firm represents the plaintiffs in a complex construction litigation case. Discovery, which seems to have taken forever, has now been completed and the trial is only two weeks away. One day the partner to whom you report comes bouncing into the office and says enthusiastically, "I just found a terrific expert witness. This guy has impeccable credentials, and he will make mincemeat out of the defense's experts. I talked to him on the phone last night, and he is happy to appear at trial. I want you to fly to Cleveland tomorrow to meet with him and prep his testimony."

"Fine," you say. "I'll just phone defense counsel and let them know about this new witness."

"Wait a minute," says the partner. "The time for exchanging witness lists has long since passed us by. There's no need to tell the other side. If we do, they will just want to take another deposition, and that could throw the whole trial schedule off. They can just deal with him at trial."

Illustration 2 Your firm represents a high-profile criminal defendant accused of homicide. There are no eyewitnesses, and the evidence is entirely circumstantial. One day as you return from visiting the client in jail, the partner in charge of the case asks you, "Have you prepped the testimony of the alibi witnesses—you know, the ones who say our client was at their house watching a football game when the crime took place?"

"Well, we have a problem with that," you say. "The client just confessed to me this morning. I didn't even ask him; he just blurted out that he did the killing and that it was bothering his conscience terribly. Under the circumstances, we can't use those alibi witnesses."

"Wait a minute," says the partner. "You may say that you know he did it, but I don't know that. I didn't hear him say it, and I'm not bound by his statement. Now get busy with those alibi witnesses. We're going to put them on the stand and get our guy an acquittal."

Illustration 3   One morning as you are rushing out the door for the office, your spouse says, "Dear, did you remember the church breakfast on Saturday? Our daughter is counting on your being there."

"Oh, gosh," you reply, "I forgot to tell you. I'm taking depositions in Atlanta on Friday, Saturday, and Sunday. I guess I'll have to miss it. By the way, would you call Brother Archer in the Sunday School presidency and let him know that I won't be able to teach my class this week? Oh, and honey, I'll be late again tonight. We're going over all the testimony in the Perkins case, since we have the pretrial conference tomorrow. I probably won't be home until after 10."

What's happening in these three cases? One might say that it is an excess of obedience. Now obedience to the right people and the right principles is a wonderful thing. We might paraphrase Nephi: "To be obedient is good if you hearken to the counsels of God" (see 1 Nephi 1:29). But a lawyer is a professional, and professionals must be obedient to the principles of the profession to which they belong, not to other people—even the ones who sign their paychecks. These are principles that have been worked out over years—indeed, centuries—to protect the public and the integrity of the legal system. They may interfere with an attorney's short-term gain, but they will protect his or her long-term ability to serve the public.

So what is a young lawyer to do when faced with a conflict between obedience to professional standards and obedience to a senior partner? Is it conceivable that a partner in a highly regarded law firm could actually ask a young associate to do something unethical? It is not only conceivable but fairly predictable. Some of you are going to have that experience.

Your natural reaction will be twofold: First, you'll respond, "I'm new around here, and I don't know much about how things are done. Maybe those professional responsibility principles that I studied in law school aren't really followed here. I don't have much standing to give advice about ethics to this partner, who has been practicing for 30 years." Second, you'll say, "If I raise a fuss about this, I'll quickly become known as a trouble-maker. At best, I will not be well thought of when it's time to make partner. At worst, it's goodbye to my job."

The very essence of being a professional is that you—not a partner, not a client, not anyone else—must decide what is right. You and only you are in charge of your professional life. "The partner made me do it" is not a viable defense. Yes, there are risks in doing the right thing, but when you do, you will have the satisfaction of knowing that you cannot be bought or bullied, that you stand for something valuable and right.

Perhaps the worst toll taken on young lawyers by big firms is the firm's total domination of their personal lives. If you bill 2,400 hours a year, you will essentially have no life outside the firm. Do you really want to be burned out for $150,000 per year? Do you want to know that your children are growing up without you and that your spouse is, in effect, a single parent? Do you want the relationship with your spouse—a relationship that you prize and honor, and that in many of your marriages has the blessing of eternal duration—to dwindle and atrophy while you make large sums of money? The answer, once again, is that you must do what is right, even if the firm tells you differently and even if you must risk your income and your job to do so.

These decisions are not easy ones, and they call for the blessings of the Spirit to help you make them. It is my hope and prayer that, whether in a small firm or a big one, you will have the strength and wisdom to do what is right. In the name of Jesus Christ, amen.

This J. Reuben Clark Law School convocation address was given at the Provo Tabernacle on April 24, 2003. Reprinted from the Clark Memorandum, *fall 2003, 20–23.*

Dale A. Whitman received his LLB *from Duke University in 1966. He served as a law professor 1973–78, visiting professor 1979–80 and 1989, and Guy Anderson Professor of Law 1992–98 at J. Reuben Clark Law School. He served as law dean 1982–88 and James E. Campbell Missouri Endowed Professor of Law at the University of Missouri in Columbia 1998–2007. He served as co-reporter of the American Law Institute's Restatement Third of Property 1991–97 and president of the American Association of Law Schools 2002. He has been a visiting law professor at various schools, with the most recent as D&L Strauss Distinguished Visiting Professor of Law at Pepperdine University in Malibu, California, in 2009.*

In Search of Atticus Finch

Lance B. Wickman

The journey that brought me to the profession of law was more odyssey than freeway. From the time that I was a young boy, my mother wanted me to be a lawyer, which was interesting because we had no other family members on any branch of the family tree who were lawyers.

Unlike some others present here, I had no father or uncle who took me to his law office as a child. I don't recall ever hefting a law book until my first day as a law student. There were no Socratic discussions at the dinner table of my youth. All I can recall is my mother's counsel: Go into law.

For one thing, having come of age in the Great Depression, she saw an occupational independence in the legal profession. "You can always hang out your shingle as a lawyer," she would say. But there was much more than that behind her admiration for the profession. She saw law, and those who follow its profession, as a force for good. In her mind there was a nobility associated with it. She saw it as a worthy calling and thought she saw in me the "right stuff" for such a calling.

But I was unpersuaded. As an undergraduate I flirted somewhat with the possibility of going to law school after graduation. But in that season of life, I was drawn more to the prospect of becoming a soldier. So, when a commission in the regular army was offered upon graduation, I accepted it. Thus began a turbulent five years. One tour of duty in Vietnam followed another. And somewhere in the midst of the turbulence the idea of becoming a lawyer reemerged in my mind. My mother's counsel of years before began to resonate. I decided that I wanted to become a lawyer when the war was over. But swept along as I was by the overpowering currents of the Vietnam War, I felt like a man caught in a riptide. The goal seemed far off, unreachable. I felt like events were sweeping me farther and farther away. There were times when

I wondered if I would ever return, if this newly realized dream would ever happen.

But, at last, it did happen. I still remember vividly purchasing my case-books at the Stanford Bookstore before the first day of class. I was so grate-ful to be there. Really, it felt like Christmas! For many of my classmates, starting law school was just another year of school. But for me it was a time of gratitude, of answered prayers. I can honestly say that I enjoyed law school. Oh, sure, by my third year I was anxious to move on from school to actual law practice, but I thoroughly enjoyed the law school experience. I enjoyed my years of law practice with a fine law firm. For more than a decade now, I have felt privileged to serve as the general counsel of the Church.

But in all of my years of affiliation with the profession of law, I have had many occasions to ponder wherein lies the nobility that my mother thought she saw in it so many years ago. Wherein lies the deep—but often elusive—satisfaction that can and ought to come to those who are asso-ciated with the profession? With cascading reports of disenchantment, or "burn out," as it is now called, within the ranks of those who have come to the bar, it would seem that finding that nobility—and the accompanying satisfaction—is anything but a unique or simple quest.

So, I should like to say something this evening about that quest. I should like to say something tonight about finding *the profession* in the profession of law. To that end I have entitled my remarks "In Search of Atticus Finch."

After preparing these remarks, I learned quite by chance that my selection of title is not new! In fact, I have discovered that there is an excellent book of the same title on the subject of lawyer ethics by Mike Papantonio.[1] So much for originality! However, I can assure you that the ideas expressed in these remarks are all mine, and I alone am responsible for them.

Tom Robinson was guilty. That was the popular verdict in Maycomb County, Alabama, even before he went on trial. There wasn't really any question about it. Miss Mayella Ewell had been assaulted. Her father, Bob Ewell, claimed to have returned home just in time to see Tom disappear-ing out the door of their cabin with Mayella screaming. Perhaps more to the point, Tom Robinson was black. Mayella Ewell was white. And in Maycomb in 1932 that color scheme added up to guilt—an open-and-shut case. Some even wondered why it was necessary to have a trial at all. Just string Tom Robinson up from the water tower and be done with it.

Enter Atticus Finch. Having descended from the "founding fathers" of Maycomb County, Atticus' birthright made him one of the county's lead-ing citizens. He had "read law" in Montgomery, obtained his law license, married, saw two children born—a boy and a girl—and, while they were yet small, lost his wife to a heart attack. Atticus Finch hung out his shingle in a tiny office at the Maycomb County courthouse. His first two clients, the Haverford boys, were hanged for murdering the local blacksmith in the presence of witnesses in a dispute over a horse. Atticus had urged them to accept the county's offer of a plea to second-degree murder and a prison sentence. But the Haverfords, who were never accused of having the sense Providence had bestowed upon a goose, refused—insisting instead on placing their fate in the "he-had-it-coming" defense. So, Atticus' only meaningful service in that case had turned out to be attendance at the hanging ceremony.

The whole experience had left him with a strong distaste for criminal law. Atticus preferred helping common people resolve the common problems of life, often taking payment of his fee in kind, such as a bag of hickory nuts or some such thing. He was not wealthy by any means, but he provided a roof and meals and other necessities for his family. He was satisfied.

So, when the trial judge approached him and asked him to defend Tom Robinson as a public service, Atticus was not enthusiastic. But Atticus Finch was above all else a man of principle. He believed that law exists to serve the interests of the people, who created it in the first place. As an officer of the court, he believed that a lawyer's first duty is to assist in the administration of justice. He believed that in a real sense the rights of the Tom Robinsons of the world are the rights of everyman. If Tom could not be assured a vigorous defense, no one else could either. So, Atticus Finch— lawyer—took the case.

By now, many of you will have recognized this recitation as a creature of fiction. In one sense Atticus Finch and Tom Robinson live only in the pages of Harper Lee's Pulitzer Prize–winning masterpiece, *To Kill a Mockingbird,* and in the classic motion picture by the same title, starring the late, great Gregory Peck as Atticus Finch. But in another, more important, sense Atticus Finch lives! He must live! Should the day ever come that he ceases to exist, the *profession* of law also would cease to exist, because Atticus Finch is the embodiment of what it means to be a *professional* in law.

How so? What is a "professional" anyway? In our 21st-century vernacular, the word is seen as synonymous with competence. In one dimension it means possessing a particularized set of skills beyond those commonly found in the general populace. Often it means advanced education, qualifying examinations, and certification. "Know how." "Board certified." "Admitted to the bar." "MD." "CPA." "NFL." "NBA." "The National Academy." These are all words, initials, and phrases commonly found in the context of any reference to a professional.

But in law, especially, there is another dimension. Being a professional is more, much more, than possessing a set of skills, a license, or the initials JD. Being a lawyer means more than being a skilled advocate, more than a legal technician, or more than an architect of business transactions. The lawyer has taken an oath—a solemn oath, administered by a judicial officer—to uphold the Constitution and the principles, rights, and privileges enshrined in the laws of his state and nation. He is, above all else, an *officer of the court*—a servant and preserver of the law. No less than the judge who sits upon the bench, the lawyer who stands at bar has pledged his talents, his knowledge, his experience, and his very life to advance and defend the cause of "justice for all." If he is also able to provide a living for his family, all the better. This is the ideal embodied in Atticus Finch.

One can only wonder what Atticus would think if, like Rip Van Winkle, he should awaken from a long nap and find himself not in the Maycomb County of 1932, but in the courtrooms, board rooms, and law office suites of the 21st century. "Billed hours," "bottom lines," "originations and proliferations," "partner tracks," and other law business buzz words and phrases doubtless would be mystifying to a man who was happy to take his modest fee in a sack of hickory nuts. More mystifying still would be the go-ahead-make-my-day lawsuit craze and the overzealous and take-no-prisoners litigation strategies that infect and threaten to overwhelm our courthouses. In an age when the phrase "officer of the court" has become quaint and lawyers are too often known more for their extravagant lifestyles than for their service to the people and the cause of justice, Atticus Finch would indeed stand bewildered.

Some years ago I served on the Stanford Law School board of visitors. We met annually at the law school for two or three days of meetings with faculty and students. One year the Friday evening event was a dinner of the board with the first-year law school class. The guest of honor was Justice Stephen Breyer of the United States Supreme Court. He was, of course, the featured speaker at the dinner. Justice Breyer gave a marvelous address (seemingly off-the-cuff, although I am quite sure it had been carefully prepared) on the subject of a lawyer's professional obligation to serve the best interests of the people. His theme was that there must be much more to law practice than billing hours and collecting fees. There must be time to give back to the community in professional service. He asked the rhetorical question as to why public esteem for lawyers is low (and why the public esteem for Congress is even lower!). He noted that, by contrast, public regard for the *army* is quite high.

Justice Breyer said, "I asked Derek Bok (who was the president of Harvard University) why this was the case. He didn't know either but expressed the view that the army is seen as not being in it for itself." What he meant was that those who serve in the armed forces are devoted in their service to their country. There is no evident greed or self-promotion as they perform their duties. This is a thought-provoking idea!

Certainly it is true that professional soldiers are not in it for themselves, and yet even they may not be highly regarded or even considered much in the public square until the war trumpet sounds. This phenome-non was captured lyrically in Rudyard Kipling's immortal poem "Tommy,"[2] which was a tribute to the selfless service of the British soldier of the 19th century. Here are just two stanzas that capture the flavor of the sentiment:

> I went into a public-'ouse to get a pint o' beer,
> The publican 'e up an' sez, "We serve no red-coats here."
> The girls be'ind the bar they laughed an' giggled fit to die,
> I outs into the street again an' to myself sez I:
>
> O it's Tommy this, an' Tommy that, an' "Tommy, go away";
> But it's "Thank you, Mister Atkins," when the band begins to play,
> The band begins to play, my boys, the band begins to play,
> O it's "Thank you, Mister Atkins," when the band begins to play.
>
> Yes, makin' mock o' uniforms that guard you while you sleep
> Is cheaper than them uniforms, an' they're starvation cheap;
> An' hustlin' drunken soldiers when they're goin' large a bit
> Is five times better business than paradin' in full kit.
>
> Then it's Tommy this, an' Tommy that, an' "Tommy, 'ow's yer soul?"
> But it's "Thin red line of 'eroes" when the drums begin to roll,
> The drums begin to roll, my boys, the drums begin to roll,
> O it's "Thin red line of 'eroes" when the drums begin to roll.

We in the United States have witnessed this same phenomenon in recent years, as young men and women in uniform—professionals as well as "citizen soldiers"—have found themselves in places like Iraq and Afghanistan. Often unappreciated in peacetime, their devotion to a higher duty than themselves in wartime has earned them the overwhelming appreciation of the nation.

But even the army struggles to maintain its tradition of selfless profes-sionalism in this egocentric society of the 21st century. In an insightful and thought-provoking essay entitled *Army Professionalism, the Military Ethic, and Officership in the 21st Century,*[3] published in 1999, three professors at West Point express their views about what they contend is an ascendancy within the army of a so-called "force protection" ethic—an academic euphemism for an inclination on the part of soldiers to exalt the preser-vation of their own lives over the army's traditional "mission first" ethic. A number of factors explaining this alleged phenomenon are addressed in the essay. But of some relevance to us in the legal profession is this observation about our contemporary "postmodern" society:

> What many call "post modernism" is best thought of as a complex collection
> of beliefs and theories that, in essence, reject the idea that there is any such
> thing as objective truth, ethical or otherwise. Without an objective standard,
> "truth" is then left to the individual or group to decide and thus becomes rela-
> tive to their desires and beliefs. This has undermined the earlier consensus
> among Americans that any particular belief can actually be wrong.

Of course, not all Americans embrace such relativism, but often what arises in its place is an unreflective egoism, which is best characterized as the belief that what is morally good is "what is best for me." Rather than the relative standard that post modernism offers, egoism is an objective standard against which to measure conduct. Its basic premise is everyone should do those things, and only those things, that they perceive are good for them.[4]

Whatever pertinence that observation about postmodernism and egoism may have in the profession of arms, it seems to me that it is profoundly applicable in the legal profession. Lawyers, too, can empathize with the "Tommy" of Kipling's poetry. We, too, endure the so-called "lawyer jokes" and snide comments—sometimes good-natured, sometimes not. But well might we ask how far the parallel to "Tommy" extends. In the public's mind, after the humor is there ever an occasion for gratitude, even redemption, for those following the profession of law? Do we ever have our "thin red line of 'eroes"? If not, why not? Could there be, if we in the profession devoted ourselves more to actually *being* professional? President James E. Faust—himself a very distinguished lawyer during an earlier season of his life—once humorously remarked to me in a private moment: "Lance, you and I can't laugh at the lawyer jokes, because we know that most of them are true!"

True or not, is not this humor based to some degree on those same postmodern and egoistic trends within the legal profession that may be infecting other social institutions, like the army? Is there not a justifiable public perception, as Justice Breyer noted, that lawyers are seen as "in it" for themselves? Is it not true that too many of our brothers and sisters in the law—and perhaps even we ourselves—measure our sworn duty as officers of the court against the "what-is-best-for-me" standard? *Where, indeed, is Atticus Finch in the 21st century?*

My own view is that *Atticus lives!* We—each of us—just need to coax him out of the shadows. As Justice Breyer put it to us in his remarks at Stanford, "Why not five days of billings and one for service?" I look into the faces of those assembled here in the conference center. I try to imagine those of you gathered at other locations, participating by satellite. I see some of the finest people ever to walk the earth. The *crème de la crème!* The best of the best! Here is a gathering of men and women at law with spouses and friends who, as Latter-day Saints, are already committed to the principle of service after the manner of the Savior. In the priesthood quorums, auxiliaries, stakes, wards, and branches of the Church, those here assembled represent hundreds of thousands of hours of service in the kingdom of God. Do we not also have within us a few hours to give as officers of the court, as true *professionals* in the profession of law?

Opportunities abound. For one thing, there are genuine pro bono service opportunities just waiting to be filled. I have been gratified to learn that a growing number of chapters of the J. Reuben Clark Law Society are seeking out such opportunities. To you I say bravo! Additionally, many law firms have developed programs allowing their members and associates to devote professional time in public service. Bravo, again!

But I think there are other opportunities for true professional service that go beyond such organized efforts to render legal services to the poor and the indigent. I refer to what could be called, in the spirit of Atticus Finch, "sack-of-hickory-nuts" service—that is, providing some services for those who can pay something, but not the stratospheric fees that are becoming the norm rather than the exception in the law business. There is a large segment of our society, neither rich nor poor, which often goes unrepresented (or at least underrepresented) at bar. These are the proverbial "just plain folk," who work hard, struggle on modest means to raise their children and provide for their own old age. These are they who simply do not have a waiting financial reserve when the unexpected encounter with the legal system occurs, but neither do they stand destitute at the doorway of the courthouse and thus eligible for free services. They also need the services of a professional—a lawyer. What about them?

In my experience, at least, the biggest challenge to the spirit of public service that in the Atticus Finch tradition is the very essence of the legal profession is the egoistic "what's-in-it-for-me" attitude that often stalks the hallways and conference rooms of profit-mesmerized law offices and firms. Billing rates continue to rise to match the sense of financial entitlement held by too many lawyers—and their families! And—can I say this without using an overly broad tar brush?—some law firm pro bono programs may be motivated as much by a desire to be "seen of men" as by a genuine desire to render "alms" in the form of legal services. Those who practice law solely for the money or the acclaim, in the words of the Master, "have their reward."[5]

So, without in any way condemning any selfless professional service rendered to anyone in need, may I just point out that there are some real opportunities for sack-of-hickory-nuts service among the ranks of the great middle class of society. I speak to those of you in the great, institutional law firms, as well as those in smaller firms and sole proprietorships. A will expertly drawn for an elderly widow who has not much money, but who can bake the best apple pie on the planet! Accepting a hundred dollars as full payment from an anguished father and mother whose teenage son has gotten on the wrong side of the law in some adolescent miscreance. Receiving a modest line of credit as payment from a struggling tradesman or small merchant for helping him solve a commercial dispute. Such charity from a legal professional is in the highest tradition of what it means to be an officer of the court. It is service that would resonate with Atticus Finch.

But there is yet another, even more fundamental, dimension to lawyer professionalism. I have struggled to encapsulate it in a single phrase with only limited success. The best I can do without circumscribing too narrowly what I am referring to is simply this: *Standing for goodness. Doing the right thing.* Not because it is profitable, not because it looks good, not even because the bar association has included it in a code of conduct or set of ethical standards; but doing the right thing simply because it is *the right thing!* On my office desk is a framed quotation attributable to President Harry S. Truman. It states simply: "When in doubt, do what's right." That, I believe, is the spirit of Atticus Finch.

"Standing for goodness"—"doing the right thing"—is a personal philosophy that covers a multitude of virtues. It begins at the everyday level with just common courtesy and pleasantness. Recently, I read a number of codes of "professionalism" promulgated by various states. Universally, they include something like this: "Lawyers should exhibit courtesy, candor, and cooperation in dealing with the public and participating in the legal system." Or, "Lawyers should avoid hostile, demeaning, or humiliating words in written and oral communications with adversaries." I shook my head sadly—not at these declarations, which are commendable in sentiment, but at the notion that a "sandbox" or Sunday School lesson, like treating others decently, needs any mention at all in a professional code of those sworn to serve the public interest. For you and me—for men and women at law who weekly covenant to take upon ourselves the name of Jesus Christ, to keep His commandments, and to always remember Him— such codes should be unnecessary. Standing for goodness is something that should just be part of who we are. Like Atticus Finch.

This matter of standing for goodness as reflected in one's civility towards others is not mere idealism. It is also practical and, in my experience at least, one of the very first evidences of a true professional. A number of years ago while practicing law in San Diego, I was invited to participate in a bar association committee that was drafting one of these codes of conduct. The association also decided that it wanted to establish an annual award for the lawyer whose skill and integrity best exemplified the maxim "His word is his bond." The first such award was given to a good friend of mine who I regarded as perhaps the finest civil trial lawyer in San Diego.

I attended the bar association dinner in his honor where the award was to be presented. Numerous fine tributes were paid to this able and good man by lawyers who were his partners and by those who had been his opponents. Finally, it was his turn for a response. He said this: "When I was a new lawyer, just starting out, I went to Judge Louis Welch [who had been one of the deans of the Superior Court bench] and asked for his advice. He answered with five words. 'The decided are always gentle.'" What a lesson! *The decided are always gentle!* Gentility. Cordiality. Understatement. Honesty. These are all evidences of a gentleman or woman. They are the marks of integrity in one committed to standing for goodness. And, in my experience at least, they are invariably the marks of an opponent to be reckoned with! They are the very first signs of a true professional in law.

Sometimes, standing for goodness is not easy—as Atticus Finch knew. Sometimes it means standing up for justice—for doing the right thing— even when it is difficult.

The news in July 1942 was bleak on every hand. Only six months earlier, air and naval forces of the Empire of Japan had left the u.s. Pacific Fleet a smoking ruin at Pearl Harbor. A seemingly invincible Japanese juggernaut had advanced the boundaries of the Japanese empire through- out Asia and the islands of the Pacific and was literally knocking at Australia's door. In Europe the invincible Nazi war machine had advanced hundreds of miles into the Russian heartland, seizing Stalingrad on the Volga River. Except for a brilliant naval victory at Midway in June, the United States had hardly gotten into the game. And in New York City, Anthony Cramer, a former German national, was charged with high trea- son for allegedly aiding a group of Nazi saboteurs. Public sentiment cried out for Cramer's prompt conviction.

Into that grim situation stepped Harold R. Medina, one of New York's best-known trial lawyers. A federal judge asked Medina to represent Cramer. As Medina later recalled, "He told me that Cramer was wholly without means to hire any lawyer, that it was important to demonstrate to the American people and to the world that, under our system of American justice, the poor man is just as much entitled to the advice of competent counsel as is a man with plenty of money. He explained that he wanted me to defend the accused as a patriotic duty."[6] Without hesitation, Medina accepted the unpaid assignment.

It was a delicate and courageous endeavor. Many in the public, even some friends, thought he was giving aid and comfort to the enemy. Others thought he was just in it for the money. But burning deeply in Harold Medina's heart was the principle embodied in the Sixth Amendment that assures every accused the able assistance of legal counsel. So devoted was Harold Medina to this, and all other, provisions of the Constitution that he refused to say or do anything to betray doubt in his client's cause, even refusing to acknowledge that he was a court-appointed attorney. Years later he said:

> I had made up my mind from the beginning that not one word should come from my lips to give the jury the impression that I was anything other than a lawyer retained by Cramer to defend him. He was entitled to the best defense we could give him. He was entitled to the full advantage of everything which went with the fact that I was standing by his side as his lawyer. Nor did I want the jury to think for even one moment that perhaps I thought Cramer was guilty but was defending him only because I had been assigned by the court to do it.[7]

On May 15, 1947, President Truman nominated Harold R. Medina as a federal district judge. Four years later he presided at the marathon trial of 11 top-ranking American Communists accused of advocating the violent overthrow of that same Constitution. Eventually, he succeeded the eminent Judge Learned Hand as a judge of the Second U.S. Circuit Court of Appeals.

The cover of *Time* magazine for October 24, 1949, carried the picture of Judge Harold Medina. The caption read, "A certain calm and peace of mind." Truly, the decided are always gentle.

Atticus Finch's decision to defend Tom Robinson was anything but popular. Some accused him, in less elegant tones than these, of being a "lover" of the black race. There was even an attempt on the lives of his two children. But Atticus Finch was a true professional. His love of law was more than a mere flirtation, more than an occasional dalliance, certainly more than a marriage of convenience. His was a deep and profound devotion to the idea of justice and to the bedrock principle of charity and the worth of each soul underlying it. Tom Robinson was a man. As such, in his earnest protestations of innocence, he deserved to be taken seriously. As was the right of any man—rich or poor, white or black or brown, honored or despised—Tom Robinson was entitled to the full requirement of the law that the government's case against him be established beyond a reasonable doubt.

And there was plenty of doubt. Evidence at the trial revealed that Tom Robinson had a withered arm, making it highly unlikely, if not altogether impossible, that he could have committed the alleged crime. And Tom's own compelling testimony was that he had been lured into the Ewell cabin by a seductive Mayella on the pretense of performing a small chore for her—a seduction, like that of Joseph in Egypt, that he had firmly resisted.

Atticus' closing argument was even more compelling—marshaling the facts convincingly, showing that Mayella was likely under the abusive influence of Bob Ewell (who turned out to be the real aggressor), and ultimately dragging into the sunlight the racism that lurked in the shadows of Maycomb County. It was magnificent.

But in Maycomb in 1932, it was not enough. Tom Robinson was convicted. Unable to face the prospect of a lifetime in jail, Tom fled while being transported to jail and was shot dead in the attempt. What possible good was served by Atticus Finch's taking that case? In the end Tom Robinson was dead anyway. Atticus' own relationship with some in the white community was strained. His children barely escaped the attempt on their lives. And Atticus certainly was not any richer; he had represented Tom Robinson for free—as a public service. For those who measure value according to the egoistic "what's-in-it-for-me" standard, nothing good came from that ill-fated representation.

But there is another standard of valuation, a nobler, deeper, richer, infinitely more satisfying standard, a standard that only the true professional, the genuine officer of the court, can appreciate. It is profoundly portrayed in the film version of the story about Atticus Finch and Tom Robinson. During the trial the black community of Maycomb had been present—not on the main floor of the courtroom, but in the steaming balcony and outside at the windows.

Now, picture this: The verdict has been announced, the defendant led away. The judge, the lawyers for the county, and the white audience have all departed. Only Atticus Finch remains in the courtroom proper, slowly putting papers into his briefcase. But in the balcony the black audience remains, silent and still. Atticus' two children are with them. As Atticus Finch rises and slowly walks from the courtroom, the entire black population, as though on signal from an unseen hand, arises to its feet in quiet reverence and gratitude, gratitude to a great and good man—an ordinary man perhaps, but a great one. A professional. Says the black preacher to the two Finch children at his side, "Stand up, children. Your father is passing."

This satellite fireside address was given to the J. Reuben Clark Law Society at the Conference Center in Salt Lake City on February 10, 2006. Reprinted from the Clark Memorandum, *spring 2006, 2–11.*

Lance B. Wickman received his JD *from Stanford University in 1972. He served as a member of the Second Quorum of the Seventy 1994–2000. He is currently general counsel for The Church of Jesus Christ of Latter-day Saints and a member of the First Quorum of the Seventy.*

Notes

1. Mike Papantonio, *In Search of Atticus Finch: A Motivational Book for Lawyers* (Pensacola, Florida: Seville Publishing, 1996).

2. Rudyard Kipling, "Tommy," *Ballads and Barrack Room Ballads* (1892, 1893), stanzas 1, 2, 5, 6.

3. Don M. Snider, John A. Nagl, & Tony Pfaff, *Army Professionalism, The Military Ethic, and Officership in the 21st Century* (Carlisle, PA: Strategic Studies Institute, U.S. Army War College, 1999).

4. *Id.* at 7.

5. Matthew 6:2.

6. William M. Kunstler, *The Case for Courage* (New York: William Morrow & Co., 1962).

7. *Id.*

BE SERVANTS

On the Wings of My Fathers

Larry EchoHawk

Echo Hawk: that is the English translation of the name given to my great-grandfather, a Pawnee Indian who did not speak English. He was born in the mid-1800s in what is now called Nebraska. Among the Pawnee, the hawk is a symbol of a warrior. My great-grandfather was known for his bravery, but he was also known as a quiet man who did not speak of his own deeds. As members of his tribe spoke of his good deeds, it was like an "echo" from one side of the village to the other. Thus he was named Echo Hawk.

According to accounts of the first white men who encountered the Pawnee people, the Pawnee were estimated to number about 20,000. Under the laws of the United States they had the right to occupy 23 million acres of land on the plains of Nebraska. When my great-grandfather was 19 years of age, the Pawnee people were forced to give up their homeland along the Platte River to make way for white settlers. In the winter of 1874 the Pawnee people were marched several hundred miles to a small reservation located near the Cimarron River in the Oklahoma Indian Territory.

Like so many other tribes before them, the Pawnee had their own Trail of Tears. Tears on that trail from the Platte to the Cimarron were shed for loss of a homeland, loss of the great buffalo herds slaughtered for their tongues and hides, and loss of a way of life. After arriving at that small Oklahoma reservation, the Pawnee people did not number 20,000. They did not number 5,000. Not even 1,000. Less than 700 Pawnee people survived.

That is a painful history. But the pain was not limited to one generation. In his childhood my father was taken from his parents by the federal government and sent to a boarding school far distant from his home. There he was physically beaten if he spoke the Pawnee language or in any way practiced his native culture or religion. In my generation my oldest sister was sent home from a public school because her skin was the wrong color. I remember sitting in a public school classroom and hearing the teacher describe Indians as "savage, bloodthirsty, heathen renegades." And, as I look back through past years, perhaps the most painful thought is the realization that in my childhood my family had no expectation of achieving a higher education and becoming doctors, lawyers, or engineers. A college education seemed beyond our reach.

But out of that pain was born promise. Of the six children born to my parents, all six of us went to college. Four of us graduated from Brigham Young University. Three of us became lawyers. We have received the best this country has to offer—the full promise of America.

The most vivid realization of that promise for me came in 1990. That year I ran for the office of attorney general of Idaho. I knew I faced a daunting task because there had not been a member of my political party elected as attorney general in 20 years. There had not been a person from my county elected to any statewide office in 38 years. And, in all the history of the United States, there had never been an American Indian elected to any statewide, state constitutional office (such as governor, lieutenant governor, secretary of state, or attorney general).

Furthermore, right after I filed my declaration of candidacy with the secretary of state, a political writer for the largest newspaper in the state wrote an article saying I had no chance to win the race for attorney general. He said: "Larry EchoHawk starts with three strikes against him: he is a Mormon, Indian, Democrat." In response to this challenge, I just went out and worked as hard as I could on that campaign.

On election night I was at a hotel where voting results were being reported. Late that night I received a call from my opponent conceding the election. I remember hanging up the phone and thinking about what I should say to a large group of news reporters who were waiting for me to comment on that historic election. After a few moments of reflection, I walked out to meet the news media and made a statement. I did not have a written speech. I did not need one. I simply spoke from my heart, repeating words I had heard when I was 15 years old. They were spoken by a black civil rights leader on the steps of the Lincoln Memorial:

> I . . . have a dream. It is a dream deeply rooted in the American dream that one day this nation will rise up and live out the true meaning of its creed: "We hold these truths to be self-evident, that all men are created equal." . . .
>
> I have a dream that my . . . children will one day live in a nation where they will not be judged by the color of their skin but by the content of their character. [Martin Luther King Jr., "I Have a Dream," speech at the Lincoln Memorial, Washington, D.C., 28 August 1963]

That night I felt the power of those words and the realization of that dream. I felt the full promise of America.

For me life began to change at the age of 14, when two missionaries from The Church of Jesus Christ of Latter-day Saints, Lee Pearson and Boyd Camphuysen, came into my home and presented the missionary lessons. Up until that time I knew very little about Christian religion and had seldom attended any church. When the time came for the missionaries to challenge our family to be baptized, they first challenged my dad, then my mother, and then the children, starting from the oldest child and descending to the youngest. By the time they got to me, the second youngest in the family, everyone else had said yes. When they asked me, I remember looking at my dad. He had this stern look on his face, and I knew what my answer should be.

I was baptized, but I did not have a testimony of the truthfulness of the Restoration of the gospel of Jesus Christ through the Prophet Joseph Smith. I was, however, glad that my family had been baptized. Prior to joining the Church I had doubts about whether my family would stay together because my father had a drinking problem, and this had led to problems within our home. After we were baptized, my father quit drinking and family life was much better. However, I continued to live much the same as I had before I was baptized.

Fortunately my parents made me go to church every Sunday, and I had the benefit of listening to Sunday school teachers, priesthood leaders, and sacrament meeting speakers. I paid attention, but church attendance was not influencing my life.

Things began to change between my junior and senior years of high school when Richard Boren became my priests quorum advisor. I felt like he took a special interest in me. He was a successful lawyer, and I admired him very much. He told me repeatedly, "You can do anything you want. You can go to college, get a good education, and do wonderful things with your life." He pulled me aside and said, "If you really want to do well in sports, you have to work at it. You have to set goals and develop yourself."

At this point I was not a particularly good football player. Although I wasn't a bad athlete, I wasn't anything special. With Brother Boren's encouragement and guidance, I set my goal to become a good football player. We set up a program of weight lifting, running, and skills development.

I was small in size. To become a good football player I had to gain weight. Weight lifting would help, but I had to do more. I began mixing up a special weight-gaining formula to drink. It consisted of raw eggs, powdered milk, peanut butter, and other fattening things. I always put a little vanilla in it to make it taste better. It still tasted awful.

In one year I gained 20 pounds. When I showed up for football practice at the beginning of my senior year of high school, my football coaches could hardly believe their eyes. I thought I was going to be a defensive back, but when practices started, the coaches had me listed as a quarterback. This was disappointing because the captain of the football team was the starting quarterback. I feared that I would again be on the bench. But I was prepared to compete, and I gave it everything I had on the practice field. After a few days of practice, I came into the locker room and saw my name listed as the first-team quarterback. I had beaten out the captain of the football team!

A life-changing moment occurred during two-a-day practices before the first game of the season. Between practice sessions I was playing with my brother and two friends. Someone threw a ball. I turned around at the wrong time, and the ball hit me squarely in the eye. It was a serious and painful injury. I was taken to the emergency room at the hospital. My eye was swollen shut. I couldn't see a thing out of that injured eye. The doctor told me and my parents that it was too early to tell, but I might lose the sight in that eye. He bandaged both eyes and sent me home.

I had to lie in bed for a week. You can imagine how devastating this injury was to me because I had worked so hard and the first game of the season was just a week away. I kept saying to myself, "How could this happen? Why me? How unfair."

But this was a turning point in my life because, as I lay there in bed, for the first time I started to seriously think about the other things Brother Boren had talked about. He had talked about the gospel of Jesus Christ, the teachings of the Book of Mormon, and the power of prayer.

I remember slipping out of bed to my knees. It was the first time in my life that I had ever prayed intently. There I was, with bandages on my eyes, alone in my bedroom, praying for help. I remember saying, "Heavenly Father, please, if you are there, listen to my prayer and help me not lose the sight in my eye." I said, "I promise, if I can just keep the vision in my eye, I will read the Book of Mormon as Brother Boren has challenged me to do."

When the bandages came off, at first I could not see out of the injured eye. But gradually, day by day, my sight came back to near-perfect vision within a week.

My Farmington High School football team had played their first game, and the season was underway. Soon the doctor cleared me to practice with the team. I was able to travel with the team to the next game in Grand Junction, Colorado, but I didn't think I was going to play in the game.

That night our team fell behind by two touchdowns in the first half. Just before halftime my coach approached me and asked me if I wanted to play. I said yes. During halftime in the locker room the coach came to me and said my doctor and parents had cleared me to play. He said to be ready because I might get a chance to play in the second half of the game. Our team did not play well at the start of the second half. Finally the coach came to me and said, "The next time we get the ball, you are going in to play quarterback." I remember being on the sideline and kneeling on one knee, like football players sometimes do to rest and watch the game. I just dropped my head and said a prayer. I whispered that prayer "with real intent" (Moroni 10:4) because I was about to face my biggest challenge on an athletic field. This would be my chance.

The coach called me over, told me the first play to run, and sent me into the game. The play was a bootleg, pass-run option. I was supposed to fake a handoff to the halfback, hide the football on my hip, and roll out around the end. If the field was clear, I was supposed to run with the ball. If the field was not clear, I was supposed to try to throw the football to a receiver. I took the snap, faked the handoff, and rolled out around the end. I could tell after just a few strides that I wouldn't be able to run the ball for a gain. The other team had the play well-defended. A defensive end was rapidly pursuing me and was about to tackle me for a loss. At the last second I saw one of my teammates downfield. I planted my foot, and—this is where the weight lifting paid off—I threw the football as far as I could. As soon as I turned the ball loose, I was clobbered. I was on my back when I heard a loud roar in the stadium. I remember thinking, "I don't know whether they are cheering for my side or the other side." I jumped up and looked downfield. I saw my teammate with the ball 68 yards down the field in the end zone. It was a touchdown! That was the greatest moment of my teenage life. To me, it was an answer to my prayer.

I played the rest of the game. I passed for another touchdown and ran for two more. That night my team, the Farmington Scorpions, came from behind to beat the Grand Junction Tigers. The next day my name was in the headlines of our local newspaper.

I had another eventful football game that year in Albuquerque. We played the state championship team harder than they had been played in any other game that year. After the game ended, one of the football coaches from the University of New Mexico came into our dressing room. He introduced himself to me and said, "We like what we saw tonight." He shook my hand and told me that he would be watching me the rest of the year.

When I recovered my sight after the accident, I had immediately started reading the Book of Mormon. I had not been a good student through junior high and high school. I struggled because my mind was not focused on school. I loved sports but not academics. The Book of Mormon would be the first large book that I had ever read from cover to cover.

As Brother Boren had suggested, I planned to read 10 pages every night. I never missed a nightly reading. When I finished the entire book, I knelt down and prayed. At that moment I had my first very strong spiritual experience. I knew then the Book of Mormon was true. I had received my most important answer to prayer. Up until that moment I had not realized that Heavenly Father had been watching over me and giving me answers to all my prayers for healing and for a witness of truth.

It seemed to me that the Book of Mormon was about my Pawnee Indian ancestors. The Book of Mormon talks about the Lamanites, a people who would be scattered, smitten, and nearly destroyed. But in the end they would be blessed if they followed the Savior. That is exactly what I saw in my own family's history. When I read the Book of Mormon, it gave me very positive feelings about who I am, knowledge that Heavenly Father had something for me to accomplish in life, and instruction in how I could be an instrument in His hands in serving the needs of other people.

After I had finished reading the Book of Mormon and football season had ended, I was sitting in a class one day when a student messenger passed me a note. It said I was to go see the football coach. I went down to his office. The door was closed. I knocked, and he said to come in. I opened the door and looked across the room. The head football coach of the University of New Mexico was sitting there. I remember that moment vividly because as soon as I saw him I knew I was going to college.

Brigham Young University also recruited me, but I wasn't sure if BYU would offer me a scholarship. I remember the meeting with Tommy Hudspeth, the head football coach. He asked me if I had any other scholarship offers. I said, "Yes, I have a full-ride scholarship to the University of New Mexico." I happened to have the scholarship offer from New Mexico in the notebook I was carrying. I handed him the letter, and he read it. He folded it up, handed it back, and said, "You have a full scholarship at BYU if you want it." My hard work, encouraged by Brother Boren, had paid off, opening a door to a college education. But, more important, a seemingly freak accident had opened a spiritual door through which celestial blessings have continued to pour on me and my family. Reading the Book of Mormon and receiving a testimony of it gave me an unexpected but welcome gift in my life.

Being a student-athlete at BYU for four years was a remarkable spiritual experience for me. I associated with many great men and women and learned important lessons in life under their tutelage. I became a product of the BYU experience. My testimony of the gospel of Jesus Christ grew, and I solidified my vision of what I should do with my life.

There was a companion spiritual influence in my youth: Spencer W. Kimball. He was one of my greatest mentors. At church in New Mexico, people talked about the apostle who had a great love for Indian people. The name of Spencer W. Kimball was revered. Prior to coming to BYU I met him at an Indian youth conference in Kirtland, New Mexico, a largely LDS community about 10 miles outside of Farmington. I remember standing out on a softball field with several other Indian youths, waiting for this apostle to come. There was a lot of anticipation. A car pulled up. Men in dark suits got out and started walking across the field toward all these young Indians waiting for the apostle. As the men approached, I stood there thinking, "Which one is he?" Finally he stepped forward. He started talking to us in a raspy voice. My thought was, "Is this him?" The wonderful thing about him was that he befriended us all very quickly. This was a real feat because it is not easy to get close to Indian youths.

Later, when I was a student at BYU, I heard him speak several times. Like Brother Boren, he provided a blueprint for my life. When I was a BYU student he gave a speech entitled "This Is My Vision." In this talk he related a dream: "I woke up and I'd had this dream about you—about the Lamanites. I wrote it down. It may be a dream. It may be a vision. But this is what I saw you doing." In one part of the speech he said, "I saw you as lawyers. I saw you looking after your people. I saw you as heads of cities and of states and in elective office" (for a more detailed description of the 1946 dream, see Dell Van Orden, "Emotional Farewell in Mexico," *Church News,* 19 February 1977, 3). To me it was like a patriarchal blessing and a challenge from a prophet of God: "Get an education. Be a lawyer. Use your education to help your people." That is what I wanted to do. I carried an excerpt from that talk in my scriptures. At a certain point in my life I read the passage where he said we could become leaders of cities and states, and it was as if it were directed specifically to me. Even though I had never envisioned running for elective office, I knew that I could and should do it.

I loved President Kimball. The day he passed away, I cried. I was overcome because I had felt his love for me. I had seen so much of the good that he had accomplished for all people. But I was especially grateful for what he had done to lift Native Americans.

When I graduated from BYU, I decided to become a lawyer for one reason: to help Indian people. After graduating from law school I spent nine years working as the attorney for Idaho's largest Indian tribe, the Shoshone-Bannock Tribes, located at the Fort Hall Indian Reservation. I saw a marvelous awakening under laws that now help Native Americans to become self-sufficient and economically strong. I have always thought it no accident that Indians were able to survive as a separate, identifiable people. I don't know how the Lord is going to use such people in His ultimate plan, but I see many Native Americans who have been able to earn a college education and do the same kinds of things I have done. There has been a very definite positive cumulative impact.

During the Vietnam War I volunteered for service in the United States Marine Corps. Soon after I arrived in Quantico, Virginia, for boot camp, I found myself standing at attention in front of my bunk in our barracks along with 54 other Marine Corps recruits. I met my drill instructor when he kicked open the door to the barracks and entered while yelling words laced with profanity. He was a tough, battle-hardened veteran who had been previously wounded in Vietnam. He started at one end of the barracks and confronted each recruit one by one. Without exception, the drill instructor methodically found something about each recruit to ridicule with vulgar language. I dreaded that it would soon be my turn. When it was my turn, the drill instructor grabbed my duffle bag and dumped my personal belongings onto my bunk. I could not see what he was doing because I had my back to my bunk, and we had been instructed to stand at attention with our eyes looking straight ahead. When we spoke to the drill instructor we had to call him "Sergeant Instructor" and yell out our words. The drill instructor looked through my things and grabbed my Book of Mormon. He then walked up to me, and I braced myself for his attack. I expected that he would yell at me as he had done with all the other recruits. Instead, he stood close to me and whispered, "Are you a Mormon?"

As instructed, I yelled, "Yes, Sergeant Instructor!"

Again, I expected he would then rip into me and my religion. He paused, raised his hand holding my Book of Mormon, and then, in a very quiet voice, said, "Do you believe in this book?"

Again I yelled out, "Yes, Sergeant Instructor!"

At this point I was sure he would yell out disparaging words about Mormons and the Book of Mormon. But he just stood there in silence. Finally he walked back to where he had dumped my personal things and gently laid my Book of Mormon down. He then proceeded to walk right by me without stopping and went on to the next recruit, who he ridiculed and disparaged with vile language. He thereafter did the same with every other recruit.

I have often wondered why that tough Marine Corps drill instructor spared me that day. But I am glad I was able to say without hesitation that I am a Mormon and that I know the Book of Mormon is true. That testimony is a precious gift given to me with the help of two missionaries, a priests quorum leader, and a prophet of God. For this I am very grateful.

I bear my testimony of the truthfulness of the gospel of Jesus Christ as contained in the Book of Mormon, and I do so in the name of Jesus Christ, amen.

This devotional address was given to the BYU *student body on August 7, 2007. Reprinted from "An Unexpected Gift,"* Brigham Young University Speeches 2007–2008, *97–107 and the* Clark Memorandum, *spring 2008, 8–13.*

Larry EchoHawk received his JD *from the University of Utah in 1973, was elected Idaho state attorney general 1990–94, and served as a law professor at J. Reuben Clark Law School 1995–2009. He is currently serving as assistant secretary for Indian Affairs in the* U.S. *Department of Interior in Washington,* D.C.

With Charity for All

Matthew S. Holland

At the invitation of Associate Dean Scott Cameron, I am here to talk to you about some things that I've recently published in a book called *Bonds of Affection: Civic Charity and the Making of America*. I'm coming at this as a political scientist—in particular, a political theorist—but there are lots of interesting connections, I believe, to the study of law. I want to talk about an important moment in the development of American political life and culture in Lincoln's second inaugural speech—one of his last and, I believe, very best speeches. To appreciate what he has to say here, though, we must first consider one of his very first speeches.

Lincoln's speech to the Young Men's Lyceum on January 27, 1838, is one of his earliest published speeches, given just after he moved to Springfield, Illinois, to open what would become a very successful law practice. In the heart of this speech, he said:

> Let reverence for the laws be breathed by every American mother . . . ; let it be taught in schools, in seminaries, and in colleges; let it be written in primers, spelling books, and in almanacs; let it be preached from the pulpit, proclaimed in legislative halls, and enforced in courts of justice. And, in short, let it become the political religion of the nation.

Lincoln greatly admired and loved the law. He thought it was absolutely essential that the rule of law prevail, even to the point of declaring that we must obey bad laws, or unjust laws, because to just choose which laws we will live will exacerbate tendencies to mob rule. Accordingly, he urged that America adopt a "political religion." By this he meant that the country should collectively work at giving reverence to the law, preaching all over the land—in churches and schools and homes—how critical it is for everyone to obey the law at all times. This political religion was a kind of extra resource he thought was needed to preserve democratic order and freedom.

In Lincoln's view, political religion was not dependent upon a robust view of the god of the Bible or upon any of the other doctrines found in scripture. The fact is that most evidence suggests Lincoln was not much of a Christian believer in his youth. Political religion was purely about bringing a sense of sacredness to the law and fostering a religious commitment to it. He thought it necessary because of a tendency of what he called "our baser passions" to get the best of us. We are given to hatred, and we are given to revenge, and these passions, if not kept in check, will overwhelm the system. They will cause us to skirt the law or carry out our hatred upon another person. And if that happens, he said, we will lose our affections for government and the law and we will be ripe for tyranny. Lincoln began his speech saying that the only way we could lose our liberty in America is internally. We'll always be strong enough and protected enough through our geography, through our natural resources, and through our latent sense of patriotism to rebuff an outside attack. But we could become vulnerable to tyranny if we become detached from a fervent commitment to due process and the substance of duly passed law.

This was the early Lincoln. But then a remarkable change came over him. By the time of the Civil War, Lincoln had gone through a religious transformation. He never joined a particular church or confessed Jesus as his savior, but by the end of his presidency, he had developed what could only be considered a robust biblical sense and faith. And this newfound faith caused him to urge a kind of political religion. For Lincoln, America was in critical need of a civic faith that not only would foster reverence for law but would more actively encourage a Christlike spirit of love, concern, and forgiveness.

Now, let me say a word about the Bible and charity and the Civil War. One of the key influences leading the North into the Civil War was a piece of literature: *Uncle Tom's Cabin,* by Harriet Beecher Stowe. It was the single most important political novel that had ever been written. The first year it was published, the only book to outsell it was the Bible. It was a blockbuster; there had been nothing like it before in the history of the country. Why did this book have such a profound effect? In my book I argue that it was the nature of the chief protagonist, Uncle Tom.

In our culture *Uncle Tom* is a pejorative term. It conjures up an image of a shuffling, self-loathing, subservient soul who is trying to cater to his white master in order to get ahead within plantation life. That's a very different view than you get if you read the novel itself. There, Uncle Tom is a strong, powerful character who repeatedly makes great efforts of self-sacrifice to protect his family and other slaves on the plantation, finally giving up his own life and emerging as what can only be read as a Christ figure. This had a dramatic effect on northern Protestants who read about this slave figure from a population that heretofore had not been considered on a par with fellow whites. The readers saw this black slave practicing Christian charity with a kind of Christlike quality superior to anything they saw among themselves, and they said, "How is it that this man could do that in slavery and be treated in this way?" So, at some level then, I argue that it was distinct ideals of charity and Christianity that took us into the Civil War. Such ideals, triggered by this powerful move, were critical to prompt Northern determination to end the grossly uncharitable and unjust practice of slavery. Thus, when Harriet Beecher Stowe came to the White House and Lincoln purportedly said, "So here's the little lady that started this Great War," he was not exaggerating too much.

Now let's turn to Lincoln's second inaugural speech at the end of the Civil War. I want to share some assessments of the speech and then explain why I think it is the most remarkable speech ever given in American political life.

First of all, Alfred Kazin, a noted public intellectual on the left, calls this speech the most remarkable address in our history and the only one that has reflected literary genius. And George Will, from the right, calls it "the only presidential inaugural that merits a place in the nation's literature." You can, I think, read the second inaugural like you would read a classic piece of literature; it operates on that profound level of depth and wisdom.

The speech opened in an unexpected way. Lincoln began by saying that this was not the occasion for a long speech, like his first inaugural. For that speech, Lincoln noted, there was good reason and real need to lay out a detailed argument concerning what the country was facing and where it should go. Consequently the speech was a finely tuned piece of jurisprudence, a careful reading of the constitutional prerogatives Lincoln thought he had as president. In short, it was a clear and crisp summary of the constitutional limits on what he thought the North could and couldn't do vis-à-vis slavery, and it was also a constitutional argument about what the Southern states could and couldn't do vis-à-vis succession. At the time of the second inaugural, Lincoln suggested there just was not as much to say. After four years of war, the war was still going. And while he stressed that victory depended on the progress of arms and that things seemed to be going in a reasonably satisfactory way, he gave no ultimate prediction of what would happen. Now this was just remarkable. Why? It had something to do with the setting. At the moment he was speaking, Lee was pinned at Richmond, the capital of the Confederacy. Grant was dug in to the west; Lee obviously couldn't go into the North; and Sherman was marching through the South with his swathe of destruction in an unstoppable fashion. So the biggest army, the best general, and the capital of the Confederacy were right there in the clutches of the North, and everybody knew it. Four years of the costliest war we had ever fought and the enemy was within our clutches, and Lincoln refused to predict victory and say anything in concrete terms about what the country would need to do after victory.

How many politicians do you know who would not take every opportunity possible to claim credit and predict victory, especially in such a costly cause at what appeared to be such a triumphant moment? But Lincoln wouldn't even say it looked like they were going to win. He made no prediction; he just didn't speak about it. Why not? Well, I think this odd start has something to do with the unprecedented ending of his speech. What was that unprecedented ending? Why was it unprecedented? Well, again, let me build this up a little bit more. Let's talk about the costs of the war. These are statistics I've pulled from the federal archives put out from the Department of Defense about casualties associated with each of our wars up until the most recent one.

The Civil War had 364,000 casualties. You've probably heard all your life that there were more people killed in the Civil War than all other wars put together, but these statistics do not bear that out. What is going on here?

Student: It's a proportional figure.

We can say something even stronger than that.

Student: It's only soldiers?

Okay, you're getting warmer.

Student: It's just the Union forces.

Yes, it is just the Union forces. The Confederate soldiers did not fight for the U.S. Army, so their deaths are not counted. So what you have to do is take that number and double it. Then, if you extend the analysis out a year or two and count soldiers who died after the war from disease or amputation, you get about a million deaths. So there truly were more people killed in this war than all other wars put together. Proportionately it's astounding, but even in raw numbers alone it's astounding. And that's just the death figures; that's not the number wounded and that's not say-ing anything about the women and children who were left behind to fend for themselves. It's not saying anything about the damage done, especially in the South after Sherman's marches: the farms that were ripped up, the railroads that were destroyed, the homes that were blown up, the economy ruined. So many people's lives were ruined. It's just hard to calculate and fathom the price we paid as a country for these four years of war.

So that was going on at the moment when Lincoln stood up to give this address. I also want to personalize it a little more and talk about the war's cost not just to the country but to Lincoln himself. Lincoln was savaged in the press—not just the Southern press but also the European press and even the Northern press. In one cartoon he was made out to be a vampire figure hovering over the pure figure of Columbia representing America. In another cartoon he was personified as death itself, but death attired in a

Caesarean wreath as a Roman dictator, depicting that the bloodshed and war were from Lincoln's evil ambitions for power and domination. On the other hand, there were images that captured the view many people had that Lincoln was not a commanding figure at all, showing him as a pathetic middle-of-the road character, a cross between a baboon and a hellish imp. These depictions were what he saw when he picked up the paper in the morning even as he was doing everything in his power to hold this country together and eliminate the great injustice of slavery.

The toll all of this took on Lincoln was vividly captured in Lincoln's own face. Compare the photograph of him taken just a few months before he became president with one of the last known photos we have of him taken just four or five years later. You can see what this experience did to him physically, adding deep subcutaneous lines of worry. He looks 20 years older, if not more. That is the Lincoln I want you to have in mind: that war-weary, melancholy, devastated Lincoln who led this country through this incomprehensibly costly war. And now finally the South was in the country's grasp. If ever there was a moment to gloat or to speak out in tones of vindication and revenge not only against the South but also against his own political allies—including cabinet members, several of whom had been disloyal to him and publicly ridiculed him—this was it. Yet what did he say? He looked out at that audience and said:

> With malice toward none, with charity for all, with firmness in the right as God gives us to see the right, let us strive on to finish the work we are in, to bind up the nation's wounds, to care for him who shall have borne the battle and for his widow and his orphan, to do all which may achieve and cherish a just and lasting peace.

I have read a fair amount of American and world history. And nowhere in that reading have I come across anything like this. There Lincoln was, standing not just as the president or leader of a country but as a military leader leading a country in the middle of civil war. And there, in the middle of all the bloodshed and personal abuse, Lincoln stood up and said, "With malice toward none, with charity for all." It was just an absolutely breathtaking, unprecedented moment in human history to have a military leader stand up and say something like that. Where on earth did he find the power, the strength, and the direction to do this?

Let me just boil it down to two things. One comes from what I would call his anthropology, his view of human nature. All through his life Lincoln saw people as the same. He saw that human nature was relatively consistent wherever you were. If you saw significant differences in behavior, you should chalk things up primarily to the environment people were in and thus be quite generous in your assessments of others. All through his life he effectively said to the North: "Don't get on your moral high horse. If you lived in the South, you would probably be proslavery too. There are such strong incentives financially; there is such a strong culture and tradition of it; be a little bit careful about being morally self-righteous." Lincoln efficiently emphasized this sense of human sameness and unity in his extensive use of pronouns throughout the second inaugural address. First there was the repeated theme of "all." Speaking of the war, Lincoln indicated that *all* thoughts were anxiously directed toward it. *All* dreaded the war. *All* sought to avert it. *All* deprecated war. *All* thought the interest of slavery was somehow the cause of war. This theme of "all" was followed by repeated references to "neither," "each," and "both." Neither party expected the war to last as long as it did. Neither anticipated that slavery would end before the war would. Each looked for an easier triumph. Both read the same Bible. Each invoked God's aid. The prayers of both could not be answered; neither side's had been answered fully. Again and again Lincoln put the North and the South on the same moral footing. But this alone fails to explain the depth and power of Lincoln's sense of mercy and forgiveness.

The second and most critical key here comes from Lincoln's religious transformation. This was the mature Lincoln, the believing Lincoln, the biblical Lincoln who got to the point of charity in part because of his relatively new biblical outlook. Here Lincoln advocated a kind of political religion that went well beyond a simple, sacred reverence for law. What he came to see and teach for purposes of political and national well being was that there was a God with His own purposes, and if God punished people according to injustice, which the Bible said that He did, then those who introduced and brought about those injustices had better watch out. And it seemed to Lincoln very likely that slavery was one of those offenses, and thus the North and the South should be expecting retribution. Why? Why could Lincoln say that God gave this awful war to both the North and the South if most of the North, at the time, had eliminated slavery? In part it was because Northern economic interests still depended upon and did business with Southern, slave-owning powers. Furthermore, the North, even if mostly free of slavery at the time, had practiced slavery for a long time. Lincoln wasn't just talking about the payment for slavery now but for 250 years of slavery. For more than two centuries many of the Northern states had practiced slavery. If there was a God of justice—and every drop of blood drawn with the lash of a slave master had to be paid for with another drawn by the sword of the soldier—then God was still just. Thus Lincoln concluded that God was likely giving this war to both the North and the South.

Now this, I argue, helps explain not only the remarkable, charitable ending but also the unprecedented start of this speech. Lincoln couldn't predict the end of the war, even though all signs were pointing toward it. Why? Because it was not his war; it was God's war. God was in charge. God had His own purposes. They were not always fully fathomable— rarely are they fathomable to the human mind. God was doing something here, and so we had to be patient and let it unfold. That was the kind of faith Lincoln came to by the end of the war. And, by seeing both the North and the South responsible for the war and the war as a matter of God's judgments against both sides, he took away from the North a moral high ground from which to seek revenge on the South for starting and sustaining the war, and he took from the South the low ground of resentment and retaliation against the North for the brutal, bulldog tactics finally required to end the war. What Lincoln accomplished in this masterpiece of literature and political thinking was to take away the impetus for both of these hateful impulses so that both the North and the South had to come together, forgive each other, and move forward in unity. To say all of this while still effectively leading the troops in battle, was, again, a kind of unmatched moment in political and military history. Also, it bears repeating that, as in his address to the Young Men's Lyceum, Lincoln was still concerned in the second inaugural address with the threats that human hatred posed for democratic health and survival. The big difference now was that he went beyond just making human law sacred as a way to minimize the effects of human hatred. Rather, he employed a recognizably Judeo-Christian worldview and ethic to try to root out hatred itself.

What Lincoln tried to do in the second inaugural address—heal a nation through notions of mercy and love—was cut short by his assassination a month later. But in some ways, at least in the long term, Lincoln's untimely death only added to the power of his second inaugural message. Within hours of his death there developed around Lincoln what I call a Christological myth. This myth used to be a lot better known in our American culture than it is today. Frederick Douglass, a noted black abolitionist, was the first one to foster this notion. When called upon extemporaneously to say some words at a hastily called memorial for Lincoln, he said that while Christ's blood atoned for our sins, perhaps Lincoln's blood was required to atone for the sin of slavery in this nation.

There are some remarkable similarities between Christ and Lincoln. Christ was born in a manger; Lincoln, a log cabin. Both had rustic beginnings in life. We know there are traditions of Christ's saintly mother; Lincoln famously speaks of his "angel" mother as the most important influence in his life. Christ grew up in Nazareth; Lincoln, on the American frontier. Christ was a man of sorrows; in that last picture of Lincoln you can see the heaviness and the burdens he suffered regularly from depression. Christ made a triumphant entry into Jerusalem a week before He was crucified; Lincoln made a triumphant entry into Richmond exactly one week before he was killed.

Lincoln was in Richmond with his son Tad. He came off a boat unannounced, slipping down without fanfare. Slave populations now freed gathered around him and started to call him "Messiah," started to kneel down before him. Lincoln said, "Don't kneel to me. Save that for your

Maker, who made you free. That is not me." But their impulse was to see him as their savior and to worship him. Christ was crucified; Lincoln was shot. Lincoln was shot on Good Friday, the day the traditional Christian world recognizes as the crucifixion day of Christ. He didn't die immediately. It was a long, slow, painful death just like crucifixion was. The bullet went into the back of his head and lodged behind his eye. He was in immense pain. He was attended to through the night while his wife and various figures of government kept watch. He moaned and labored and breathed through the night and didn't die till seven o'clock the next morning.

At the turn of the century the most famous man in the world was a man of letters, author of some of the world's finest novels. Among his words, Leo Tolstoy wrote, "Lincoln was . . . bigger than his country— bigger than all the Presidents together. Why? Because he loved his enemies as himself. . . . He was a Christ in miniature."

The image of Lincoln as a second Christ is a two-edged sword for Latter-day Saints. On one hand we have to remind ourselves that there is one God and we are to have no other gods before Him. Lincoln was not a god. He did not atone for the sins of America. That was done by somebody else long ago and in an infinite way that Lincoln never could. We must not fall into the trap of revering him as a kind of deity or a god that he wasn't or worshipping him in a way that would be blasphemous. On the other hand, to do as so many people have done and try to make Lincoln just a man, an ordinary politician driven by shameless self-interest and self-advancement, is to miss this great figure who is great because he saw something powerful in the life and teachings of Jesus Christ.

As citizens of this great country, we must learn from Lincoln. In moments of dissension and difficulty—moments you will face as you practice law—you must, even as you fight with a "firmness in the right" as Lincoln did, remember that your highest and holiest obligation is to love your enemies as yourself. And the greatest exemplar and teacher of that is Christ, of whom I testify, in the name of Jesus Christ, amen.

This Law and Literature class lecture was given at BYU *Law School on April 3, 2008. Reprinted from the* Clark Memorandum, *fall 2008, 18–26.*

Matthew S. Holland received his PHD *in political science from Duke University in 2001. He was an associate professor of political science at Brigham Young University 2001–09, a James Madison Fellow at Princeton University 2006, and author of* Bonds of Affection: Civic Charity and the Making of America—Winthrop, Jefferson, and Lincoln *(2007). He is currently president of Utah Valley University in Orem, Utah.*

Unto This Very Purpose

Neal A. Maxwell

President Faust—my mentor of many years—President Samuelson, Dean Hansen, ladies and gentlemen, brothers and sisters all: While anticipating this occasion, my reflections have turned in special gratitude to President Marion G. Romney for his personal role in founding the J. Reuben Clark Law School. Likewise, appreciation goes to Elder Dallin Oaks, President Rex Lee, and all who were, and now are, a part of that initial and continuing achievement, including Dean Reese Hansen and the current faculty. While I cannot speak to you from shared professional experience, almost all of us share a certain theology. The scriptures contain so many jewels over which we pass too lightly, especially some stunning one-liners. The compressed truth in these terse verses defies our full comprehension. Moreover, such divine declarations come without detailed explanations but are laden with so many implications. One such cluster, as you well know, has to do with the unique founding of this American nation. Therein, the Lord revealed that He established our Constitution "by the hands of wise men whom [He] raised up *unto this very purpose*" (D&C 101:80; emphasis added). I know of no parallel declaration with regard to the Constitution of any other nation, ours being the first written constitution. Given in 1833 in Ohio, these verses were part of the Kirtland cascade of revelations. Moreover, revealed words, such as "unto this very purpose," clearly remind us that God's hand is in the details of such things—sometimes obviously, sometimes subtly (see D&C 59:21).

Granted, we noddingly accept these revealed words, but we seldom stretch our minds to explore their implications. However, if pondered—both as to its substance and the miraculous process of its coming forth—the Constitution is deserving of our prolonged, spiritual applause.

Think of all that the Lord had to oversee, including the shaping events that occurred long before the Constitution was *written, ratified,* and *implemented. First,* it was necessary for God to cause a handful of highly talented and wise individuals to be raised up. *Second,* they needed to live in one geographic area on this planet. *Third,* this contiguity also had to occur in a short time frame. *Fourth,* a citizenry had to be prepared who wanted and would then implement and sustain self-governance. This latter incubation was as important as the later ratification. Thus, the words "raised up" involve multiple and concurrent conditions. Without similar incubation, it is no wonder that establishing modern republics and democracies is not easy. Founders require foundational building blocks. Otherwise, holding elections can be cathartic but not consequential.

The late historian Barbara Tuchman has noted how our Founding Fathers have been called "the most remarkable generation of public men in the history of the United States or perhaps of any other nation" (Barbara W. Tuchman, *The March of Folly* [New York: Alfred A. Knopf, 1984], p. 381). Tuchman observed, "It would be invaluable if we could know what produced this burst of talent from a base of only two and a half million inhabitants" (Tuchman, p. 383).

The Constitution not only needed to be written but also ratified, and there were some dramatic moments and narrow margins of approval. The Massachusetts vote was "one hundred and eighty-seven [in favor] to one hundred and sixty-eight [unfavorable]"; Virginia was "eighty-nine to seventy-nine"; New York, "thirty to twenty-seven" (Catherine Drinker Bowen, *Miracle at Philadelphia* [Boston: Atlantic Monthly Press Book, 1966], pp. 290, 304, 306).

In one instance, extraordinary measures were used:

> Early on Saturday morning [in Philadelphia], September twenty-ninth, a mob . . . seized two assemblymen and carried them, fighting, to the State House, where they were thrust down in their seats, with clothes torn and faces— said one account—"white with rage." A quorum being thus achieved, it was decided, amidst approval from the gallery, that seated members who had answered to their names were a legitimate part of the House, no matter how they got there. [*Id.*, p. 274]

Thus, not only was a special parchment produced, but so were a sufficient number of approving and sustaining people.

One who fought for freedom in the War for Independence was asked why he fought. Was it the Stamp Act? The Tea Party? Or reading Locke? He replied in the negative, saying, "Young man, what we meant in going for those Redcoats was this: we always had governed ourselves and we always meant to. They didn't mean we should" (David Hackett Fischer, *Paul Revere's Ride* [New York: Oxford Press, 1994], p. 164).

President Wilford Woodruff boldly declared in general conference, April 1898:

I am going to bear my testimony to this assembly, if I never do it again in my life, that those men who laid the foundation of this American government and signed the Declaration of Independence were the best spirits the God of heaven could find on the face of the earth. They were choice spirits, not wicked men. General Washington and all the men that labored for the purpose were inspired of the Lord. [*Conference Report,* April 1898, p. 89]

This nation was blessed not only with Washington's wisdom and prestige but also by his superb character. One of his biographers wrote:

In all history few men who possessed unassailable power have used that power so gently and self-effacingly for what their best instincts told them was the welfare of their neighbors and all mankind. [James Thomas Flexner, *Washington: The Indispensable Man* (New York: Plume, 1984), p. xvi]

Washington was the rare man who would not be king!

The cumulative contribution came from such varied personalities. As Franklin's most recent biographer, Walter Isaacson, wrote,

Benjamin Franklin is the founding father who winks at us. George Washington's colleagues found it hard to imagine touching the austere general on the shoulder, and we would find it even more so today. Jefferson and Adams are just as intimidating. But Ben Franklin, that ambitious urban entrepreneur, seems made of flesh rather than of marble, addressable by nickname, and he turns to us from history's stage with eyes that twinkle from behind those newfangled spectacles. [Walter Isaacson, *Benjamin Franklin: An American Life* (New York: Simon and Schuster, 2003), p. 2]

God raised up not only these founders but the necessary supporting cast. Involved, therefore, were not only the obvious luminaries—Washington, Adams, Jefferson, Madison, Franklin, etc., and with Abigail Adams as an added measure of influence—but also, for example, John Marshall, who his biographer, Jean Edward Smith, calls the "definer of a nation" (Jean Edward Smith, *John Marshall: Definer of a Nation* [New York: Henry Holt & Co., 1996], subtitle).

As you would know better than I, Marshall and colleagues did their defining superbly, requiring successive and often unanimous Marshall Courts spanning many years. Even the replacement appointees were vital contributors. Presidents who differed with John Marshall nevertheless appointed justices who were, like Marshall, nation builders. Such was Jefferson's appointment of William Johnson, and Jackson's of John McLean.

Such individuals helped the Constitution to become firmly established in the difficult cases that faced the Supreme Court. Nevertheless, times of deep discouragement were experienced. Marshall's biographer, Smith, wrote:

> As the states rights rhetoric escalated that autumn, Marshall's spirits sagged. In late September he wrote to Story in an even more despondent mood. "I yield slowly and reluctantly to the conviction that the Constitution cannot last. The Union has been prolonged thus far by miracles. I fear they cannot continue."
>
> But a miracle of sorts was in the offing. Jackson was swept back into office in November and immediately moved to suppress the impending states rights revolt. . . . Jackson said the Supreme Court was the ultimate arbiter of the constitutionality of the nation's laws and that if the Court held a statute to be constitutional, it must be obeyed. [*Id.*, p. 519]

Such history should be borne in mind when, from time to time, we may wince—or more—over particular decisions by the ultimate arbiter.

Human history makes abundantly and sadly clear that not all mortals use power wisely. Unsurprisingly, therefore, certain of the Constitution's central features—such as the vital separation of powers and the precious First Amendment, as conceived and intended—were and are needed to foster moral agency (see D&C 121:39). This later condition is central to God's plan of salvation for all mortals. Back in the founding days, however, these and other key concepts needed "cleats" that would take hold early in the history of the American nation. Otherwise, things could have come apart soon after the birth of a nation.

Dean Rex Lee observed of such central features:

> In some ways the free-exercise-of-religion guarantee bears closer marks of kinship to the free-expression provisions of the First Amendment than to its sister religion clause. Like the speech, press, and assembly guarantees, the free-exercise-of-religion clause deals directly with the protection of individual liberties, whereas the establishment clause is a structural provision, regulating institutional relationships between church and state.
>
> Moreover, speech and assembly are central to most religious activity. [Rex E. Lee, *A Lawyer Looks at the Constitution* (Provo: Brigham Young University Press, 1981), p. 135]

One cannot resist reflecting on the foliage of the First Amendment. I read somewhere of the contrast between a banyan tree and a Lombardy poplar that is a relevant metaphor. The latter, though a thing of beauty and symmetry, does not really offer much shade from the heat of the day or shelter from the storm, whereas a banyan tree is thick with foliage and has sturdy, wide branches. How ironical, therefore, for some to neglect to nourish certain branches of that First Amendment tree and then seek its shelter later on. Likewise, a persistent preoccupation with freedom of speech to the neglect of other freedoms can diminish the shelter available for religion and eventually for other precious freedoms. The intense twinings of all our freedoms is greater than we realize.

Having pondered the miracle of the Constitution's emergence and just how God manages to be in so many details, while at the same time honoring our individual agency, I confess not to fully comprehend it all

(D&C 59:21). Only God can strike the divine balance. Such was, never-theless, the case with the inspired American Constitution. Clearly, God cares too deeply about our moral agency to force things—even things He desires. Clearly, too, God cares about how power is handled and not only in His kingdom. It is likewise clear that He also desires to protect all mortals by means of certain rights and principles:

> According to the laws and constitution of the people, which I have suffered to be established, and should be maintained for the rights and protection of all flesh, according to just and holy principles. [D&C 101:77]

Elder James E. Talmage believed that our Constitution "is the pattern after which the organic laws of other nations shall be framed" (*Conference Report*, October 1919, p. 98). President George Albert Smith said in the dedicatory prayer of the Idaho Falls Temple that the Constitution was to be emulated by other governments in fulfillment of Isaiah's words about how "out of Zion shall go forth the law" (Isa. 2:3; see *Improvement Era* 48 [October 1945], p. 564). Years later, President Harold B. Lee recalled and endorsed President Smith's words (see "The Way to Eternal Life," *Ensign* [November 1971], p. 15).

The ongoing tug-of-war over power and over the preeminence of contending values continues, but does so within the context of a modern condition too little noted. Zbigniew Brzezinski described how "the politi-cal structure of the state guarantees the relativism of all values through constitutional protections." Brzezinski also noted how "the traditional socializing institutions—the family, the school, and the church—[when] fully intact . . . provided a moral grounding, a counterbalance to the indulgent propaganda of the mass media" (Zbigniew Brzezinski, "Weak Ramparts of the Permissive West," *At Century's End* [ed. Nathan P. Gardels, ALTI Publishing, 1995], p. 56).

But will the counterbalances check relativism, as was once the case? The heightened emphasis in our time on individuality, often at the expense of community, needs no elaboration with this audience. In my opinion, the big challenge for Christians is maintaining a moral grounding amid surg-ing secularism, and, sometimes, amid arrogant irreligion. Operationally, except for thoughtful and genuine pluralists, irreligion may become, *defacto*, the established state religion with its own rituals, orthodoxy, and various tests for prospective office holders.

Yet, even given such relativism and secularism, many will still deeply honor what was handed down from Sinai centuries ago while, of necessity, being mindful of what is handed down from the marble steps of state or national capitols.

Significantly, regarding the fundamental doctrine of moral agency (D&C 101:78), the Lord conjoins individual accountability and constitu-tional freedoms:

> And that law of the land which is constitutional, supporting that principle of freedom in maintaining rights and privileges, *belongs to all mankind,* and is justifiable before me. [D&C 98:5; emphasis added]

Why is all this so vital?

> That every man may act in doctrine and principle pertaining to futurity, according to the moral agency which I have given unto him, that every man may be accountable for his own sins in the day of judgment. [D&C 101:78]

Whatever the persistence of secular permissiveness, the eventual and sobering reality of individual accountability lies ahead.

A quarter of a century ago, I ventured to write:

> Hopefully, governments will use the test of "by their fruits ye shall know them," and hopefully those officials who cannot thereby distinguish between a peach tree and a pyracantha will put away their pruning shears! First Amendment freedoms, tested before, will surely be tested again. Irreligion, protected by these same freedoms, will surely seek to snuff out real religion. [Neal A. Maxwell, *All These Things Shall Give Thee Experience* (Salt Lake City: Deseret Book Co., 1979), 116]

Almost tucked away in the same 1833 revelation are these words: "Therefore, it is not right that any man should be in bondage one to another" (D&C 101:79). Do we appreciate these revealed and discomfiting words, especially in view of their obvious relevance to so many human situations involving bondage of one form or another?

Given the obvious time span being covered by these remarks, as is by now apparent, I speak not of particular cases. Rather, I am spurred on by the sweep of history with the ebb and flow of Constitutional concerns mirrored therein. Surely the bestowal of such divine attention on a few mere colonies located on one planet is especially reassuring, given God's governance among "worlds without number," thus only adding to our wonderment (see Moses 1:33, 35).

A few words about you and the law. As alumni, what you *are* is more important than what you *know* about the law. The long-term influence of your character is more significant than legal expertise, though how commendable when both are combined! Hence, adequate emphasis on character at J. Reuben Clark Law School is as vital as the curriculum.

Therefore, as you help to manage conflict, you should always practice advocacy without acrimony and without animosity. Be eloquent, not only before the bench but also in your life's example. You need your own checks and balances, including at times the constraining influence of the Spirit.

The Lord expresses general confidence in the voice of the people; but a slack citizenry and cunning devices can, over time, corrupt even a constitutional system (Alma 10:13, 15, 19, 27). Lawyers can first shape and then exploit the voice of the people, which, if done amiss, can bring the judgments of God (see Mosiah 29:27 and Alma 10:19, 26.) Sixty-two years *after* King Benjamin's warning, we read:

> For as their laws and their governments were established by the voice of the people, and they who chose evil were more numerous than they who chose good, therefore they were ripening for destruction, for the laws had become corrupted. [Helaman 5:2 (30 B.C.)]

The precepts of men can give ascendancy to that which is more fashionable than it is constitutional (D&C 45:29).

The living Constitution remains a most remarkable document. Nevertheless, the various interpretations of the Constitution are finally more reflective of the moral status of America's citizenry, its lawyers, and its judges than we may care to acknowledge. A people, for instance, can actually lose the capacity for genuine self-governance by losing one of its precious prerequisites: "Obedience to the Unenforceable." Lord Moulton, the originator of that perceptive phrase, focused on an individual's obedience to that "which he cannot be forced to obey," which, significantly, Moulton, nearly 80 years ago, linked to free choice (The Right Honorable Lord Moulton, "Law and Manners," *The Atlantic Monthly* 134:1 [July 1924], p. 1).

Secular churning can lead to a heedless democratization of values and truths, which, after all, are not equal—hence, the hunger for a more proportional and a genuine hierarchy among competing values. For instance, would we approve all else that characterized ancient Sodom and Gomorrah if only assured that they balanced their budgets? It may be true, for instance, that the people of Sodom and Gomorrah had absolute free speech, but did they have anything worth saying? Those surfeited in sensualism may produce sounds all right, but scarcely the enlivening and enriching speech that John Stuart Mill and our Founding Fathers had in mind.

Virtue must reside in the people as well as in leaders. John Adams cautioned, "Our constitution was made only for a moral and religious people. It is wholly inadequate to the government of any other" (John R. Howe Jr., *The Changing Political Thought of John Adams* [Princeton: Princeton University Press, 1966], p. 195).

No wonder Michael Novak was moved to write his timely book *On Two Wings,* lest we forget how America's becoming "airborne" reflected a spiritual wing, too, noting that this "one wing of the American eagle . . . has been quietly forgotten" (Michael Novak, *On Two Wings* [San Francisco: Encounter Books, 2002], preface, p. 1).

Elder Dallin H. Oaks has written perceptively:

> The citizens who founded this nation understood the relationship between self-government and citizen responsibilities. Their writings are replete with references to public or civic virtue—meaning the willingness of individual

citizens to sacrifice their private interests for the well-being of the nation. . . . For example, in *The Federalist Papers*, James Madison makes pointed reference to the fact that self-government presupposes the existence of virtue among its citizens in a higher degree than any other form of government. [Dallin H. Oaks, "Rights and Responsibilities," *Mercer Law Review* 36 (1985): 434]

Therefore, while we cannot fully fathom all that was done in order to raise up wise individuals, I nevertheless praise God for the miracle that came forth, disjointed and discouraging as some events must have been back then.

As you know, the Prophet Joseph Smith praised the Constitution as:

A glorious standard; it is founded in the wisdom of God. It is a heavenly banner; it is to all those who are privileged with the sweets of its liberty, like the cooling shades and refreshing waters of a great rock in a thirsty and weary land. It is like a great tree under whose branches men from every clime can be shielded from the burnings rays of the sun. [*History of the Church*, Vol. III, p. 304]

Note his metaphor of "a great tree" and also the constituency of "men from every clime" (see D&C 98:5; 101:77).

Joseph noted, however, that the Constitution had

but this one fault. Under its provision, a man or a people who are able to protect themselves can get along well enough; but those who have the misfortune to be weak or unpopular are left to the merciless rage of popular fury. [*Teachings of the Prophet Joseph Smith*, p. 326]

After the Civil War, of course, came the 14th Amendment, prescribing equal protection for citizens.

Having attempted, at least briefly, to demonstrate a particularized divine detail with one powerful example—the American Constitution—God willing, I hope to speak sometime soon of even more strategic revelations and stunners so fundamental to the grand mosaic of God's master plan. Ironically, young Joseph Smith went into the grove merely wanting to know which Church to join, where there began to unfold a supernal serendipity of stunners.

These revelations, as with the one discussed tonight, likewise belong to all mankind (see D&C 98:5).

Paul's words of commendation about Abraham are an applicable caution to us. Given the stretching and reassuring promises made about his posterity, yet Abraham staggered not in disbelief (see Romans 4:20). There is a risk that we might stagger in the face of such stunning truths.

If Joseph Smith had taught only one of the Restoration's major revelations, it would be, standing alone, sufficient to insure his prophetic greatness, to say nothing of the cumulative cascade of revelations that came through him. We may smile at Joseph's occasional imperfect spelling, but instead we ought to be breathless over the gospel restored through him. Besides, Joseph said, "I never told you I was perfect—but there is no error in the revelations which I have taught" (Andrew F. Ehat and Lyndon W. Cook, *Words of Joseph Smith* [Provo: Brigham Young University, 1980], p. 369).

Some of us have grown too content with the largesse of mere gum-ball machines and are scarcely prepared for the promised deluge, when the windows of heaven are opened and God gives to the faithful "all that [he] hath" (See D&C 84:38). Oh, the poverty of our *perceptions!*

God bless you all, in the name of Jesus Christ, amen.

This Founders Day address was given to the J. Reuben Clark Law Society at Little America Hotel in Salt Lake City on September 4, 2003. Reprinted from the Clark Memorandum, *spring 2004, 2–9.*

Neal A. Maxwell (1926–2004) received his MA in political science from the University of Utah in 1961, six honorary degrees (including honorary Doctor of Laws degrees from the University of Utah in 1969 and from Brigham Young University in 1976), and the Liberty Bell Award for public service from the Utah State Bar in 1967. He served as the commissioner of education for the Church Educational System 1970–1976, as a General Authority 1974–2004, and as a member of the Quorum of Twelve Apostles 1981–2004.

The Beginning and the
End of a Lawyer

Dallin H. Oaks

Thank you, President Samuelson, for that gracious introduction. Thank you, thank you for this undeserved but deeply appreciated honor you have paid me this evening. I feel humbled by the presence of so many in this audience who I esteem as treasured friends and role models, and I express my personal affection and appreciation for each of the persons on the stand this evening—each a treasured, personal friend.

My dear brothers and sisters in the law: I appreciate this invitation to address you in person and electronically in more than 100 locations. At the outset I express my gratitude for that generous introduction and pray that I will be able to fulfill the challenge it poses.

Your invitation has given me cause to reminisce. This is one of the privileges of age, and I am getting to the point when I feel impressed to claim that privilege. I pray that these recollections will be sufficiently tied to general principles that their recital will be helpful to lawyers who are 20 to 50 years my junior.

I was admitted to the bar of the state of Illinois 48 years ago this summer. Next month it will be 34 years since the Board of Trustees of Brigham Young University announced the founding of J. Reuben Clark Law School—two months after which I was announced as president of BYU. I immediately undertook the planning of the Law School: the appointment of a dean, the recruitment of faculty, the assembling of a library, and the construction of suitable quarters. So much has happened in all of our lives since that time!

I have titled my remarks "The Beginning and the End of a Lawyer." For "the beginning" I will reminisce about my own foundations in the law.

For "the end" I will review some of the things lawyers face as they reach the conclusion of their formal service in the profession.

I. Fathers in the Law

In the beginning every lawyer has some fathers or mothers in the law—persons whose teaching and example has a profound influence on their initial thinking and development in the profession. I have had many influential teachers and mentors in my life, but when it comes to my initial thinking and development in the legal profession, four men stand out above all the rest. I want to tell you about each of these fathers in the law and what I credit them with teaching me. I will mention them in the order in which they came into my life.

1. Dean Edward H. Levi

Most of you will remember Edward H. Levi as the United States attorney general whose stature and wisdom restored integrity to a Department of Justice badly bruised by the Watergate scandal.

Much earlier, Edward Levi was the dean of the University of Chicago Law School when I enrolled there in 1954. He was my teacher in various courses and circumstances. As dean he recruited me to the faculty in 1961. When he went to the university administration the following year, he appointed me acting dean of the law school and tutored me in those responsibilities. Still later he was the wise academic leader who spoke at my inauguration as president of Brigham Young University in 1971. The influence in my life of this great Jewish legal scholar and leader was prolonged and powerful.

In my first year Levi's writings introduced me to the way of precedent and reasoning in the law (see Levi, *Introduction to Legal Reasoning* [1948]). As a teacher he was brilliant, thorough, and extremely rigorous. All of us remember being terrorized in classrooms by law teachers whose high expectations and threat of public humiliation drove us to exhaustive preparation and gave us the scar tissue and thick skin we would need to survive in an adversary profession. I will never forget the day Dean Levi called on me in his antitrust course. He directed me to state a particular case and to explain how it differed from another case. Being poorly prepared that day, I hesitated slightly. Reading the circumstance and wanting to teach a lesson to me and everyone else, he cut me off with, "Oh, never mind, Mr. Oaks. You have to be *good* to do that." Years later I could laugh about that put-down, but the scar tissue and the motivation for preparation have never left me.

Levi taught that the law is a learned profession, so law study should be much more than preparation for the practice of law. The law requires intellect as well as craftsmanship, and its obligations include improvement of the system of justice for the common good of mankind. "The problem for the lawyer," he once said, "is not just to know the law, but how to create within it. It is a world of artistry and craftsmanship and change" (see Edward H. Levi, "An Approach to Law," *Occasional Papers,* University of Chicago Law School, 13 [1976]; also see Edward H. Levi, *4 Talks on Legal Education,* University of Chicago Law School [1952]).

President James E. Faust has said that his law school dean "constantly impressed upon us that his primary mission was not to teach us the law, for the law would change; rather, his primary mission was to teach us to think straight, based upon sound principles" (James E. Faust, "The Doctrine and Covenants and Modern Revelation," *The Doctrine and Covenants* [Craig K. Manschill, ed. (2004)], 1). Dean Levi did the same for me.

Levi also gave his students assurance of the natural goodness of the law and the legal profession, showing how they are ideally founded on what is right and good and workable. The practice of law is not just a way to earn a living or to secure a position of power. Levi's paramount interest was making the law what it ought to be for the good of the people and the country and teaching his students and associates to do the same. He never seemed to have any personal interest. I saw him as a man without self-promotion or concern with political correctness who was fundamentally grounded in what he believed to be right. To me his leadership and his wisdom illustrated our doctrinal teaching that "the Spirit of Christ is given to every man, that he may know good from evil" (Moro. 7:16).

When I was a new law teacher, Dean and President Levi taught me the workings of higher education. This served me well as a faculty member, as an acting dean, and much later as a university president. For example, Levi was a master at honoring and leading his faculty. His faculty meetings were always routine, because he had already thoroughly analyzed every difficult matter, worked out the needed compromises, and done the advocacy with key individuals before the meeting was held. He avoided contention.

Levi also taught me the meaning of a university and the respective roles of faculty, students, administration, and board. These teachings were tested in 1969 in the crucible of a massive student demonstration that seized the University of Chicago's administration building and held it for 15 days. As president of the university, Levi received enormous pressure to call in the police to forcibly evict and prosecute the trespassers. Instead, he announced that the university would govern itself. He appointed a disciplinary committee of nine faculty members from different fields. I was the chairman and the only lawyer on the committee.

Levi said later:

> The University has sought throughout this period . . . to exemplify the values for which it stands. . . . In a world of considerable violence, and one

in which violence begets violence, it has emphasized the persuasive power of ideas. It has sought—and the unique response of faculty and students has made this possible—to handle its own affairs in a way consistent with its ideals. [Public statement, 14 February 1969]

That is a great lesson for every organization, especially those involved in teaching. Do your own work, and don't ask the law or other organizations to do it for you.

After two months of individual hearings on 150 students summoned to university discipline, our faculty committee concluded its assigned task and the university continued its work, all without outside intervention.

This was a time of great disruption on campuses throughout the country. When the political desire to punish student demonstrators produced proposals for federal legislation, I was asked to write my recommendations to Arthur F. Burns, a counselor to President Richard M. Nixon. I was merely following the teaching and leadership of Edward Levi when I wrote:

My advice is for the federal government and federal officials to stay out of this controversy. Spare us the spectacle of federal prosecutions of university students for campus-related activities. . . . Let the response to student disorders be local. Let universities, in cooperation with local law enforcement agencies if necessary, handle the problem. . . . [B]y all means stay off the campus, and don't make university administrators and faculty look like federal policemen. [Letter of 15 May 1969]

I am happy to recall that no federal legislation was enacted. As Levi was fond of saying, the law is a crude instrument. He taught that we should only use the law when we have to.

Two years later I left the University of Chicago to become president of BYU. President Levi gave me a brief but insightful send-off with this letter: "As I have told you, we are proud of you and sorry to lose you, but we bow, as we must, to this calling." As usual, he had it right.

2. President John K. Edmunds

John K. Edmunds was my stake president during my law studies, law practice, and early law teaching in Chicago. A giant in Church leadership, he served for over 20 years as president of the Chicago Stake. He was the only man I knew during my studies who was both an outstanding lawyer and an exemplary Latter-day Saint. (I had no lawyers in my family and hardly any among my acquaintances as I was growing up.)

President Edmunds had a powerful influence over my spiritual development. (See my tribute to him in *Church News,* 11 March 1978, 2.) The period of graduate education is an unsettling time when personal values and beliefs are challenged. This was especially true for me in my first two years at the University of Chicago Law School when I was the only Mormon in the law school. This was also my first experience outside the small towns of Utah and Idaho where I had grown up. I was surrounded by philosophies and influences quite alien to anything I had ever experienced.

President Edmunds was instrumental in helping me gain the spiritual nourishment and eternal perspective I needed to handle these strains. He had a powerful testimony of the Lord Jesus Christ and of the Prophet Joseph Smith. He stressed the fundamentals: faith, repentance, love, tithing, and the reality of a living prophet. Except in occasional interviews, I rarely had personal conversations with him. But as I sat in stake conferences and in priesthood leadership meetings, I always felt that he was speaking directly to me.

He always impressed and inspired me with his use of the scriptures, his spirituality, and the power of his example. Under his influence I was able to keep my life in balance—spiritual, intellectual, and practical. As to the latter, I saw him adjust his professional life to serve the Lord in his calling—a model I would later follow in my own life.

After graduation and a year clerking in Washington, D.C., I returned to Chicago to practice law with a large law firm in a highly competitive atmosphere. This was a time for further decisions on the relative priorities of family, Church, and profession. Soon, at a time when I was handling a heavy load of cases and working four evenings a week, President Edmunds called me as a stake missionary. He told me this calling would require about 40 hours of missionary time each month, which meant three to four evenings per week. I couldn't see how I could accept this calling and still keep up with my law practice. Yet I could not say no to a calling that I knew to be from the Lord, especially when that calling came through a servant of the Lord who had wielded such a powerful influence in my life. Gathering all my faith, I accepted the call.

That decision was a turning point in my life. I reduced the time spent in my law practice, almost entirely omitting night work, and devoted that time to missionary activity. Yet I observed no reduction in my performance or advancement in the profession. I was seeking first to build up the kingdom of God, and all those other things were added to me (see Matt. 6:33; JST Matt. 6:38). This altered pattern also prepared me to receive and accept an offer to become a professor of law at the University of Chicago. This proved to be a crucial decision in my life.

Here I feel to mention something else I learned by watching President Edmunds. This has influenced my Church work and may be useful to you also. In his administration of the Chicago Stake, President Edmunds gave special emphasis to a limited number of things. The ones I remember to this day as being repeated again and again in every meeting were tithe-paying and the principle of priesthood leadership expressed in section 121 of the Doctrine and Covenants beginning at verse 34:

> Behold, there are many called, but few are chosen. And why are they not
> chosen?
>
> Because their hearts are set so much upon the things of this world, and
> aspire to the honors of men, that they do not learn this one lesson—
>
> That the rights of the priesthood are inseparably connected with the
> powers of heaven, and that the powers of heaven cannot be controlled nor
> handled only upon the principles of righteousness. [D&C 121:34–36]

And so forth. I can still hear his voice speaking those words and sending
them right into my heart as an inspiration and a challenge.

From his example I learned that if Church leaders single out a small
number of key principles and emphasize them again and again, these few
fundamentals have the capacity to raise individual performance on a multitude of other subjects rarely mentioned. This is more effective than trying to push everything equally, like the proverbial river a mile wide and an
inch deep that never achieves the concentration necessary to erode a mark
on the landscape. Leadership requires selective concentration.

Knowing that I am speaking to many who have important positions
of leadership in the Church, I voice the prayer and challenge that you
are doing for your impressionable young people what my inspiring stake
president did for me.

3. Chief Justice Earl Warren

All of us know something about my third father in the law, Chief
Justice Earl Warren. I served as one of his three law clerks for 1957–58. My
law school sponsored and recommended me to another justice, but I was
not chosen. I decided independently to apply to the chief justice. The law
school had no connections with him and offered me no encouragement.
I contacted President Ernest L. Wilkinson of BYU, who put me in touch
with his law partner, Carl Hawkins, who had clerked for Warren's prede-
cessor and still had a contact in that office. Hawkins also secured a recommendation from Senator Arthur V. Watkins of Utah. In March, after
I had given up hope for a clerkship, we were all surprised when the chief
justice phoned Dean Levi to ask if I was a likely enough prospect to invite
to Washington for an interview. Levi gave me such a recommendation that
the chief justice told him to tell me I had the job without an interview.

My year clerking for the chief justice was challenging, satisfying,
and far-reaching. Beyond the obvious opening of doors for professional
advancement, it was a remarkable educational experience. I was allowed
to see and participate in the work of the nation's highest court and to
work side by side with lawyers who were the present and future leaders
of the bench, the bar, and the nation. Among the special guests our 18 law
clerks invited to our weekly two-hour luncheon interchanges were Dean
Acheson, the most impressive advocate I saw argue a case that year, and

John F. Kennedy, a young junior senator from Massachusetts who was to be elected president less than three years later.

Chief Justice Earl Warren was an unlikely mentor and boss for a conservative lawyer like me. As you know, he and others on the so-called "Warren Court" are the authors of many opinions that represent and set the direction for what is now known as judicial activism. In my view this judicial activism has worked far-reaching mischief in the law. Whether one agrees or disagrees with the outcome of these activist decisions, they are unfortunate precedents because they are matters that should be decided by elected lawmakers, not life-tenured federal judges.

For this and other reasons my confidential personal year-end tally shows that I disagreed with the chief justice's votes on 40 percent of the cases decided on the merits that year. The 60 percent in which I agreed with him were obviously more comfortable for me, especially in cases where he was writing the opinion for the Court. Many of these were very satisfying to me personally.

Those cases in which I disagreed with the votes of the chief justice allowed me to learn a good lesson in professionalism. Regardless of your opinion of your client's choices, it is your professional duty to serve your client to the best of your ability—subject, of course, to the constraints of legality and legal ethics.

In contrast to my disagreements with his votes on some cases, I adored the chief justice as a person, and I admired him as an administrator of the Court and as a wise and considerate employer. On his part, the Chief (as we always called him) frequently praised my work, we got along well in every circumstance, and after about nine months he asked me to stay another year. But, typical of his consideration for his clerks, he told me I should feel free to decline if I felt this was best for me and my family. I therefore acted on my urge to get back to Chicago to practice law.

I loved how the Chief treated those who came to his office. He always came from behind his desk, shook hands, and ushered the visitor to a seat. He often did this even for his law clerks, who were in and out of his office on a daily basis. He told me he adopted this practice as a public official in California. He said it was his way of showing his feeling that each person was important and his official position did not put him above anyone. Here I recall the prophet Nephi's statement that "all are alike unto God" (2 Ne. 26:33) and Jacob's teaching that "the one being is as precious in [God's] sight as the other" (Jacob 2:21). In my lifetime I have observed that some people, like the Chief, have the quality of treating everyone like a child of God even though they lack the doctrinal understanding that requires this. Others who have the doctrine sometimes fail to act on it.

The Chief also taught me about professional confidences. He shared everything with his clerks, and in return advised us that he expected absolute confidentiality about the work of the Court, forever. We should never talk or write about the confidential matters we had observed at the Court, since this was, as he said, "destructive of the free exchange of ideas among court members and of public confidence in the Court." Since I was schooled in that way, you can imagine my disgust at some of the disclosures made by former confidants of public figures who get wealthy by betraying their confidences in so-called "kiss and tell" autobiographies.

The chief justice was faithful to his wife and his family in every sense of that word. We talked about family things many times. He had me bring my wife and our three young children to meet him, and he spent considerable time with them. His interest was genuine. In all of this I was learning how a man of the law—even the chief justice of the United States—assigned the highest priority to his family.

He shared one example I have never forgotten. I only wish I had applied it as effectively in my professional life as he did in his. He told me that when he was attorney general and governor of California he would never allow any state papers to be delivered to his home. That was his home, the place where he devoted himself to his family, he explained, and he didn't want any outside intrusions there. Once one of his staff phoned to say he had some papers of the utmost importance he needed to get to the governor right away. Could he bring them over to the house? Warren said he told him no, not to the home, but if the matter was that important the governor would change his clothes and come to the office and receive them there. The Chief said that when this became known, it reduced drastically the amount of interruptions he had at home without cutting off the avenue to deal with true emergencies—at the office.

The chief justice had a great respect for our Church and its leaders. He often spoke of his fondness for President Heber J. Grant. This gave me freedom to speak with him about Church matters, and that led to a funny experience. The Chief took me along when he dedicated the new University of Chicago Law School building during the year of my service. After dinner that evening Dean Levi had the honored guests to his house for after-dinner drinks. When Earl Warren declined a drink, indicating that he seldom drank after dinner, I told Dean Levi in the presence of the chief justice "that I had the Chief living the Word of Wisdom." Both seemed to enjoy that claim, but candor compels me to admit that if the Chief was living the Word of Wisdom after dinner, he was not a teetotaler before. He partook, but very moderately.

The chief justice gave his three law clerks a farewell luncheon on July 3, 1958. I recorded these thoughts in my personal journal:

> I felt a keen loss at leaving him. Though these pages scold him severely . . . in regard to what I consider his faulty notion of how a judge should reach decisions, I have developed a profound affection and respect for him. I believe he is completely honest, sincere, and utterly without guile. He has wonderfully

mature judgment about many matters, and he is the most kind and considerate employer one could ask for. I will miss him.

The Chief continued his interest in all his clerks. He urged me not to practice law in Chicago, which he considered a "crooked" place, but he later rejoiced when I told him I was leaving the practice to teach.

"Oh, that's great," he said. "You'll be able to influence these young lawyers. That's a wonderful thing to do" (from my personal journal, quoted in Ed Cray, *Chief Justice*, 355 [1997]).

When the chief justice resigned in 1969, while still in good health at age 78, I wrote him a letter recognizing his resignation as a fulfillment of his intention—frequently voiced to his law clerks—to resign while still at the peak of his powers and effectiveness.

"I believe you have done that," I wrote, then expressed my belief that this was "the right and proper course." I continued, "That is what I would have wanted for you if you had been my father, and I feel the same way about you as one of a small group of men who are in a very real sense my fathers in the law."

4. Lewis F. Powell

The fourth of my fathers in the law is Lewis F. Powell. You will remember him as a highly respected justice of the United States Supreme Court. But that came later. His impact on me was in the year 1970–71, when he was a practicing lawyer in Richmond, Virginia, and I was a professor of law at the University of Chicago. Although Powell's contribution to my education came 13 years after I graduated from law school, I consider him one of my fathers in the law because his tutelage was vital in preparing me for important things I needed to do as president of Brigham Young University and in other important responsibilities that followed.

A highly respected former president of the American Bar Association, Powell was serving as chairman of the board of the American Bar Foundation, the research arm of the American Bar Association. ABF, as we called it, was located next door to the University of Chicago Law School. In the summer of 1970 Powell arranged for me to have 75 percent released time from the law school to serve as the executive director of ABF. I was responsible to work with the board of directors and to direct the professional staff—the same task as the president of a corporation or the president of a university. I had never served on a board or worked under the direction of a board, so this was an entirely new experience.

I could not have had a better teacher than Lewis Powell. He was an expert at defining the respective responsibilities of a board and a professional staff. He was also brilliant at analyzing how to present matters to a board to obtain fruitful discussions and clear decisions to guide the staff. Powell was very wise in organizational principles, he knew the concerns of the entities, and he knew the people who had to make and implement the decisions. All of these skills were needed because I was appointed to manage ABF at a time when its board was so dissatisfied with the work of the staff that its continued funding was in doubt. Differences had to be resolved, new policies had to be formulated, and confidence had to be restored.

I described the results in my personal history:

> One of the most valuable experiences was watching Lewis Powell arrange and preside over ABF board meetings, skillfully resolving hot issues by deft phrasing and skillful compromise, all with the purpose of preserving harmony and keeping the organization moving forward within the limits of consensus and cheerful support.

Less than a month after this tutorial ended, I was meeting with the Board of Trustees of Brigham Young University, which then included the First Presidency and members of the Quorum of the Twelve, including five future presidents of the Church. What I learned from Lewis Powell was vital to my responsibility to help the board make the policies that would move the university forward. These included the foundation policies for the new J. Reuben Clark Law School.

Many times I have thanked a loving Heavenly Father for what I was privileged to learn from Lewis Powell. His teachings have been crucial in my subsequent and frequent service on boards, including particularly my five years as chairman of the board of the Public Broadcasting Service and my eight years as chairman of the board of the Polynesian Cultural Center.

My last meeting with Lewis Powell concerned Brigham Young University. When President Harold B. Lee, First Counselor in the First Presidency, advised me that I had been chosen as president of BYU, I told him that when I was made head of the American Bar Foundation just a year earlier, I had committed to Lewis Powell that I would serve for at least five years.

"Go see him," President Lee directed, "and ask if he will release you from that commitment."

I flew to Richmond and met my friend and teacher in his law office. I told him what had happened and asked him what I should do. I remember his words as if they had been uttered yesterday:

"I have been offered the presidency of several universities during my professional life," he said, "and I have never seriously considered leaving the practice of law for that occupation. But I know enough about you and enough about Brigham Young University to know that yours is a perfect fit. We give you an honorable release from your commitment. You go with our blessing."

A few years later Justice Lewis F. Powell came to BYU for the ceremony dedicating the new Law School, and we awarded him an honorary degree.

I have spoken of four men whom I call my fathers in the law, reviewing some of the things they taught me in my formative years in the legal profession. Each of you has had or is having mentors who teach you and help you fix your ethical and practical course in the profession. I hope you have been as blessed through your mentors as I have been through mine.

II. The End of a Lawyer

Now I speak of the conclusion of the professional journey. In time, each of us will come to the end of our formal work in the legal profession. It may be by planned retirement, by serious illness, by death, or by a switch in occupations—planned or otherwise. Mine was the latter.

In 1984, while happily serving on the Utah Supreme Court, I went to the University of Arizona to judge a moot court. There, on Friday evening, April 6, I received a telephone call from President Hinckley of the First Presidency that changed my life. I enjoyed serving as an appellate judge more than anything else I had done in my 30 years in the legal profession, and now it was over, and I was to leave the active practice of the law. Suddenly I saw my work in the legal profession in a new light, as a means of preparing me for something else to follow. Since that transition will come to all of us, it is wise to ask now: What will remain when we reach the end of our formal work in the legal profession? What will we have besides the property we must also leave behind, eventually?

Most of us will conclude our formal activity in the legal profession before we die. But the skills and ways of thinking we have acquired as lawyers will remain—for better or for worse. And when properly applied, those skills and ways will still be a source of blessing to many.

For example, I am conscious every day that my approach to gathering facts, analyzing problems, and proposing action is a product of my legal training. So is my idea of justice. (The law has been less influential in teaching me about mercy.) If one makes proper use of opportunities, the study of law disciplines the mind and the practice of law strengthens the character.

My participation in litigation wars has stamped my soul with an imperative to avoid the uncertainties and ambiguities that foster controversy. It has also given me a bias to resolve differences, where possible, by private settlement rather than by adversary litigation, causing me to believe that sometimes even a poor settlement is better than a good lawsuit.

I have also seen the gospel ideal of service to others being nobly expressed by the uncompensated and even the compensated service of members of the legal profession.

And, finally, I rejoice in the fact that the profession of the law is clearly the best preparation for the role of Advocate, a role and title our Savior designated for Himself (e.g., D&C 29:5, 110:4; 1 John 2:1; Moro. 7:28).

So what will remain when a lawyer comes to the end? Each of us will have our record of service to our clients, our profession, our communities, and our God. There will remain what we have become by that service. We will also have the eternal family relationships we treasure, as defined by the terms of our covenants and promised blessings and our fulfillment of the conditions on which they are based. All of this we can take with us as we have our last appearance before a judge. As we know from sacred writ, we "must all stand before the judgment-seat of Christ" (Morm. 3:20), who "will judge all men according to their works, according to the desire of their hearts" (D&C 137:9). That appearance will provide the ultimate definition of what remains at the end of a lawyer.

My dear brothers and sisters, our lives are patterned by our faith in the Lord Jesus Christ. I testify to you that that faith is sound and justified and that the promises we receive from keeping the commandments of our Lord are sure. The gospel of Jesus Christ is a safe anchor, and we are led by a prophet as we walk the path designated by that gospel. I testify to you of the truth of these things and pray the Lord's blessings upon you as you serve your families, your communities, your profession, and our God, in the name of Jesus Christ, amen.

This satellite fireside address was given to the J. Reuben Clark Law Society at the Conference Center in Salt Lake City on February 11, 2005. Reprinted from the Clark Memorandum, *spring 2005, 2–11.*

Dallin H. Oaks received his JD from the University of Chicago in 1957 and clerked for Chief Justice Earl Warren of the U.S. Supreme Court 1957–58. He served as president of Brigham Young University 1971–1980 and as a justice on the Utah Supreme Court 1980–84. He is currently a member of the Quorum of the Twelve Apostles.

On the Shoulders of Giants

Boyd K. Packer

In my hand is a two-pound English coin. Around the edge are inscribed the words "Stood on the shoulders of giants." Sir Isaac Newton invented calculus and the reflective telescope, defined the laws of motion, and did an astonishing list of other things. Asked how he was able to do it all, he answered: "I stood on the shoulders of giants."[1] We stand on the shoulders of a giant: President J. Reuben Clark.

Less than a month after my 37th birthday, I was sustained as a General Authority. On October 6, 1961, I was set apart in the council room by the First Presidency, and later that same day I received word, "President Clark just passed away." His ministry closed the same day that mine began.

The mention of his name polishes the windows of my memory. I see clearly and feel deeply the memory of this great man. Now you must not assume that I suppose that I compare in stature with him. I am, with you, one of many who stood on his shoulders.

My close personal contacts with President Clark were very few. I heard him speak many times. I stood in awe of him.

I was in his office once and remember very clearly how he looked and what he said. I sat next to him at the dinner when he gave his address entitled "Reflective Speculation."[2] And there were other times.

The Question

Now I have a question for you of the J. Reuben Clark Law Society. I quote President George Albert Smith, the second of the three Presidents to whom J. Reuben Clark served as a counselor.

President Smith said:

> A number of years ago I was seriously ill; in fact, I think everyone gave me up but my wife. With my family I went to St. George, Utah, to see if it would

225

improve my health. We went as far as we could by train, and then continued the journey in a wagon, in the bottom of which a bed had been made for me.

In St. George we arranged for a tent for my health and comfort, with a built-in floor raised about a foot above the ground, and we could roll up the south side of the tent to make the sunshine and fresh air available. I became so weak as to be scarcely able to move. It was a slow and exhausting effort for me even to turn over in bed.

One day, under these conditions, I lost consciousness of my surroundings and thought I had passed to the Other Side. I found myself standing with my back to a large and beautiful lake, facing a great forest of trees. There was no one in sight, and there was no boat upon the lake or any other visible means to indicate how I might have arrived there. I realized, or seemed to realize, that I had finished my work in mortality and had gone home. I began to look around, to see if I could not find someone. There was no evidence of anyone living there, just those great, beautiful trees in front of me and the wonderful lake behind me.

I began to explore, and soon I found a trail through the woods which seemed to have been used very little, and which was almost obscured by grass. I followed this trail, and after I had walked for some time and had traveled a considerable distance through the forest, I saw a man coming towards me. I became aware that he was a very large man, and I hurried my steps to reach him, because I recognized him as my grandfather. In mortality he weighed over three hundred pounds, so you may know he was a large man. I remember how happy I was to see him coming. I had been given his name [George Albert Smith] and had always been proud of it.

When Grandfather came within a few feet of me, he stopped. His stopping was an invitation for me to stop. Then . . . he looked at me very earnestly and said:

"I would like to know what you have done with my name?"

Everything I had ever done passed before me as though it were a flying picture on a screen—everything I had done. Quickly this vivid retrospect came down to the very time I was standing there. My whole life had passed before me. I smiled and looked at my grandfather and said:

"I have never done anything with your name of which you need be ashamed."

He stepped forward and took me in his arms, and as he did so, I became conscious again of my earthly surroundings. My pillow was as wet as though water had been poured on it—wet with tears of gratitude that I could answer unashamed.[3]

The question is: What are you doing with the name of President J. Reuben Clark?

President J. Reuben Clark

President Clark's service was divided into two equal parts: twenty-eight years in law and government and twenty-eight years as counselor in the First Presidency.

President Clark grew up as a farm boy in tiny Grantsville. At age eleven he could plow with a team of horses. If the weather was too cold for others to go, he would walk to the evening sacrament meeting alone.

In a large family he learned to work. He had a father and a mother of pioneer virtue and integrity. His father wrote in his journal, "I went down between the barley and wheat in the old ditch, and knelt down and prayed and dedicated the grain that we have sown and asked the blessings of the Lord upon it; this I do every year with everything that I plant."[4]

Another local boy, Heber J. Grant, knew him well. These two farm boys would meet again.

With an elementary school education and at the urging of his father, President Clark moved to Salt Lake City to go to college. Dr. James E. Talmage was his mentor. When he went east to school, Dr. Talmage said, "He possessed the brightest mind ever to leave Utah."[5]

He married Luacine Savage. They became parents of three daughters and one son. From 1898 to 1903 he was teacher and administrator in Heber and in Cedar City.

Before leaving to study law, he called on President Joseph F. Smith. President Smith cautioned him about the field of law and set him apart on a mission to be an exemplary Latter-day Saint.

Years earlier another young man wanted to go east to study law. James Henry Moyle, father of President Henry D. Moyle, met with President John Taylor. President Taylor said he was "opposed to any of our young men going away to study law. It is a dangerous profession."

His counselor George Q. Cannon persuaded President Taylor that "Brother Joseph had to engage lawyers. So [did] Brother Brigham."

President Taylor agreed then that it would be all right for Brother Moyle to go, and then he spoke of "the pitfalls into which the young man might slip unless he [was] careful." He gave him a blessing, from which I quote:

> As thou hast had in thine heart a desire to go forth to study law . . . , we say unto thee that this is a dangerous profession, one that leads many people down to destruction; . . . abstain from corruption and bribery and covetousness, and from arguing falsely and on false principles, maintaining only the things that can be honorably sustained by honorable men; . . .
>
> We set thee apart . . . to go forth as thou hast desired to study and become acquainted with all the principles of law and equity; [then there is a big "if" in the blessing] if thou wilt abstain from chicanery and from fraud and from covetousness, and [another "if"] if thou wilt cleave to the truth, God will bless thee.

He was promised by President Taylor that if he would do these things, he would "grow up in virtue, in intelligence, power and wisdom, and stand as a mighty man among the House of Israel, and be a defender of the rights and liberties and immunities of the people of God."

And this promise: "But if thou doest not these things, thou wilt go down and wither away."[6]

In 1903 President Clark took his family to New York City to attend the Columbia University School of Law. In 1906 he graduated head of his class with an LLB degree. Shortly after he was appointed as Department of State Assistant Solicitor, and he published his classic "Memorandum on the Right to Protect Citizens in Foreign Countries by Landing Forces." (Does that not sound familiar today?)

While living in Washington, D.C., he was appointed as an assistant professor of law at George Washington University.

He opened law offices in Washington, D.C., in New York City, and in Salt Lake City, where he specialized in international and municipal law.

A staunch Republican, he became influential in both Utah and national politics.

They tried more than once to draft him to run for the United States Senate. There was also an effort made to draft him as a candidate for the presidency of the United States until he firmly refused.

During World War I President Clark served as a major on duty with the U.S. Attorney General's office. He helped prepare the original Selective Service regulations. He was awarded the Distinguished Service Medal.

President Calvin Coolidge appointed him as Under Secretary of State in 1928. He then published his "Memorandum on the Monroe Doctrine." Even his critics praised it as a "monument of erudition," a "masterly treatise."[7]

The title of your society's semiannual publication is *The Clark Memorandum*.

Call to the First Presidency

In 1930 J. Reuben Clark was named as U.S. ambassador to Mexico. Two and a half years later he was called by letter as second counselor to President Heber J. Grant.

General conference had come and gone, and a vacancy in the First Presidency was not filled. A senior Apostle told me that two members of the Twelve waited upon President Grant and said, "We see you did not fill the vacancy in the Presidency."

President Grant replied, "I know the man the Lord wants me to have, and he is not ready yet." Pointing his cane at each of them, he said, "I know that feeling when it comes. I had it when I called you! And I had it when I called you!"

"When that cane pointed at me," one of them told me, "I felt as if I had been electrocuted."

It was nearly a year before President Clark was able to come to Church headquarters. During the first fifteen months he was away for five months in Washington, D.C., or abroad on-call for the President of the United States.

In October 1933 J. Reuben Clark Jr. was honored at a dinner in Beverly Hills, California. Telegrams of tribute arrived—also one letter from Will Rogers, philosopher and humorist, perhaps the best-known American of his time. Will Rogers apologized for the letter but said, "I have more to say than I am able to pay for [in a telegram]."

John Nance Garner, the vice president of the United States, was there, of whom Rogers said in his letter, "He . . . deserves [better work] than he's got."

Rogers then spoke in admiration of J. Reuben Clark and closed, "So, God Bless Reuben Clark, and make him a Democrat, or Republican as necessity demands! [signed] Will."[8]

President Clark came to the First Presidency virtually unknown in the Church. He had held no administrative positions, even on the local level.

He kept things very plain and simple. The president of Equitable Life once sent him a speech. President Clark replied, "A lot of it was over my head [trying to understand it], but I sort of held my breath and struggled to the top. . . . I accept your conclusions whether or not I fully understand the reasons, and I congratulate you on another fine speech."[9]

I can imagine President Clark in his library with words scattered about on his desk. I see him discarding the longer ones and then picking up a word and fitting it into a sentence and then replacing it with one easier to understand. From words he made sentences, often very long ones, fastening them together into paragraphs and bundling them together into his inspired sermons.

His Reverence for the Lord

One way or another his writing and his speaking had a common theme. It was there when he first spoke in church at age eleven. Like Nephi, "[he talked] of Christ, [he rejoiced] in Christ, [he preached] of Christ, [he prophesied] of Christ, and [he wrote] according to our prophecies, that our children may know to what source they may look for a remission of their sins" (2 Nephi 25:26).

His classic books *Our Lord of the Gospels*[10] and *Behold the Lamb of God*[11] are examples.

His "The Charted Course of the Church in Education,"[12] prepared by assignment from the First Presidency, is an enduring classic akin to scripture.

I give you two examples from his sermons. To the priesthood he spoke of the burden of debt:

Interest never sleeps nor sickens nor dies; it never goes to the hospital; it works on Sundays and holidays; it never takes a vacation; it never visits nor travels; it takes no pleasure; it is never laid off work nor discharged from employment; it never works on reduced hours. . . . Once in debt, interest is your companion every minute of the day and night; you cannot shun it or slip away from it; you cannot dismiss it; it yields neither to entreaties, demands, or orders; and whenever you get in its way or cross its course or fail to meet its demands, it crushes you.[13]

From his classic address "They of the Last Wagon" given in 1947, the centennial of the arrival of the pioneers:

Morning came when from out [of] that last wagon floated the la-la of the newborn babe, and mother love made a shrine, and Father bowed in reverence before it. But the train must move on. So out into the dust and dirt the last wagon moved again, swaying and jolting, while Mother eased as best she could each pain-giving jolt so no harm might be done her, that she might be strong to feed the little one, bone of her bone, flesh of her flesh. Who will dare to say that angels did not cluster round and guard her and ease her rude bed, for she had given another choice spirit its mortal body that it might work out its God-given destiny?[14]

President Clark's mother was one of those so born in 1848.

Criticism

To President Clark criticism seemed to be an inescapable accompaniment of the doing of righteousness. He once wrote:

It seems sometimes as if the darkness that surrounds us is all but impenetrable. I can see on all sides the signs of one great evil master mind working for the overturning of our civilization, the destruction of religion, the reduction of men to the status of animals. This mind is working here and there and everywhere.[15]

President Clark spoke of the pioneer leaders and in so doing described himself:

Upright men they were, and fearless, unmindful of what men thought or said of them, if they were in their line of duty. Calumny, slander, derision, scorn left them unmoved, if they were treading the straight and narrow way. Uncaring they were of men's blame and censure, if the Lord approved them. Unswayed they were by the praise of men, to wander from the path of truth. Endowed by the spirit of discernment, they [knew] when kind words were mere courtesy, and when they betokened honest interest. They moved neither to the right nor to the left from the path of truth to court the good favor of men.[16]

Intellectual Vision

President Harold B. Lee said of President Clark:

In the universal sweep of his great intellectual vision he had few equals and perhaps no superiors. He once said of his grandfather on his maternal line, Bishop Edwin D. Woolley: "He was so eloquent in political discourse that even his enemies came out to hear him." So it has been with this grandson of Bishop Woolley [referring to President Clark]. Even those who violently disagree with his views [and there were many] are intrigued by his eloquence, his forthrightness, pure logic, and penetrating insight into the center and core of whatever subjects he undertakes to expound.[17]

It was said of Bishop Woolley that if he should drown in a river, they would look upstream for the body.

President Spencer Woolley Kimball was a cousin of President Clark. When President Kimball would be very resolute (a kinder word than *stubborn*), one of the Brethren would say, "Well, he's a Woolley."

A young university student of political science once spoke to Elder Lee about the student's vigorous disagreement with President Clark's lecture "Our Dwindling Sovereignty" at the University of Utah. Elder Lee's response was, "Yes, I suppose it would be difficult for a pigmy to get the viewpoint of a giant. When I go to hear [a] world authority . . . , I go to learn and not to criticize."[18]

Other Giants

There are other giants of the law upon whose shoulders I have stood—Presidents Marion G. Romney, Henry D. Moyle, Howard W. Hunter, and James E. Faust.

The saintly Abraham Lincoln said that "lawyers should discourage litigation. Persuade [your] clients to compromise. The lawyer who is a peacemaker can become a good man. There will be business enough. . . . Never stir up litigation. If you do, a worse man can scarcely be found."[19]

John K. Edmunds had a distinguished legal career. He served as a stake president in Chicago. David M. Kennedy, later secretary of the treasury, was his counselor. Brother Edmunds later served as president of the Salt Lake Temple.

He told me that a widow once came to him for help on a property matter. When he completed the papers and gave them to her, she asked, "How much do I owe you?"

He looked at her and said, "Why don't you pay me what you think it's worth."

Relieved, she got out her coin purse and produced a quarter and put it in his hand.

He told me, "I looked at the quarter and looked at her. Then I got out my coin purse and gave her ten cents change."

Only a wicked lawyer would take advantage of a widow or orphans or anyone else.

In Liberty Jail, Erastus Snow, who probably could not afford legal counsel, asked Joseph Smith what he should do:

> Brother Joseph told him to plead his own case.
>
> "But," said Brother Snow, "I do not understand the law."
>
> Brother Joseph asked him if he did not understand justice; he thought he did.
>
> "Well," said Brother Joseph, "go and plead for justice as hard as you can, and quote Blackstone and other authors now and then, and they will take it all for law.[20]

A Charge

Those giants I named, like you, had something that I do not have—a degree in law. With this credential comes obligation.

You who hold the priesthood must be exemplars above reproach.

And I charge each of you lawyers and judges and put you on alert: These are days of great spiritual danger for this people. The world is spiraling downward at an ever-quickening pace. I am sorry to tell you that it will not get better.

I know of nothing in the history of the Church or in the history of the world to compare with our present circumstances. Nothing happened in Sodom and Gomorrah which exceeds the wickedness and depravity which surrounds us now.

Satan uses every intrigue to disrupt the family. The sacred relationship between man and woman, husband and wife, through which mortal bodies are conceived and life is passed from one generation to the next generation, is being showered with filth.

Profanity, vulgarity, blasphemy, and pornography are broadcast into the homes and minds of the innocent. Unspeakable wickedness, perversion, and abuse—not even exempting little children—once hidden in dark places, now seeks protection from courts and judges.

The Lord needs you who are trained in the law. You can do for this people what others cannot do. We should not need to go beyond the members of the Church to find superior legal counsel.

A Caution

Now I caution you, as President John Taylor warned James Moyle and as Joseph Smith warned Stephen A. Douglas at the pinnacle of his political triumph, "If ever you turn your hand against . . . the Latter-day Saints, you will feel the weight of the hand of Almighty upon you."[21]

We must look to you for legal counsel. You have, or should have, the spirit of discernment. It was given you when you had conferred upon you the gift of the Holy Ghost.

You must locate where the snares are hidden and help guide our footsteps around them.

Morally Mixed-Up World

You face a much different world than did President Clark. The sins of Sodom and Gomorrah were localized. They are now spread across the world, wherever the Church is. The first line of defense—the home—is crumbling. Surely you can see what the adversary is about.

The Prophets Have Warned

We are now exactly where the prophets warned we would be.

Paul prophesied word by word and phrase by phrase, describing things exactly as they are now. I will quote from Paul's prophecy and check the words that fit our society:

> This know also, that in the last days perilous times shall come.
> For men shall be lovers of their own selves—Check!
> covetous—Check!
> boasters—Check!
> proud—Check!
> blasphemers—Check!
> disobedient to parents—Check! Check!
> unthankful—Check!
> unholy—Check!
> Without natural affection—Check! Check!
> trucebreakers—Check!
> false accusers—Check!
> incontinent—Check!
> fierce—Check!
> despisers of those that are good—Check!
> Traitors—Check!
> heady—Check!
> highminded—Check!
> lovers of pleasures more than lovers of God—Check! Check!
> Having a form of godliness, but denying the power thereof: from such turn away.
> For of this sort are they which creep into houses, and lead captive silly women laden with sins, led away with divers lusts,
> Ever learning, and never able to come to the knowledge of the truth.
> [See 2 Timothy 3:1–7]

Recently Judge Robert H. Bork said:

> Judicial invention of new and previously unheard-of rights accelerated over the past half-century and has now reached warp speed. It is not just Grutter's permission to discriminate against white males and Lawrence's

creation of a right to homosexual sodomy. The Court has created rights to televised sexual acts and computer-simulated child pornography and, in direct contradiction of the historical evidence, has continued its almost frenzied hostility to religion. . . .

In these and other judgments, the Court is shrinking the area of self-government without any legitimate authority to do so, in the Constitution or elsewhere. In the process it is revising the moral and cultural life of the nation.[22]

Once, with other members of a city council, we met in the office of the city attorney. He pointed to a wall with law books and said, "Gentlemen, they are just like a violin. I can play any tune on them you are willing to pay for." I thought there was something not right about that.

The Lord Himself, strongly condemning the lawyers, scribes, and Pharisees, said: "Woe unto you also, ye lawyers! for ye lade men with burdens grievous to be borne, and ye yourselves touch not the burdens with one of your fingers" (Luke 11:46).

From the writings of the Prophet Alma:

These lawyers were learned in all the arts and cunning of the people; . . .

[The lawyers] began to question Amulek, that thereby they might make him cross his words, or contradict the words which he should speak. . . .

They knew not that Amulek could know of their designs. . . . He perceived their thoughts, and he said unto them: O ye wicked and perverse generation, ye lawyers and hypocrites, for ye are laying the foundations of the devil; for ye are laying traps and snares to catch the holy ones of God. . . .

And now behold, I say unto you, that the foundation of the destruction of this people is beginning to be laid by the unrighteousness of your lawyers and your judges. [Alma 10:15–17, 27]

Nephi, son of Helaman, described what happened when the Gadiantons took over the lawyers and the judges: "Condemning the righteous because of their righteousness; letting the guilty and the wicked go unpunished because of their money" (Helaman 7:5).

You have heard of the courageous lawyer who, having been fined fifty dollars for contempt of court, replied, "It is an honest debt, Your Honor, and I shall gladly pay it."

Lawyers and judges and even the sacred institution of the jury are being tarnished. When one considers some of the high-profile verdicts, one could believe this conversation:

Judge: "Ladies and gentlemen of the jury, have you reached your verdict?"

Jury: "We have, Your Honor. We find the defendant innocent by reason of insanity."

Judge: "What? All twelve of you?"

When Moroni was translating the twenty-four gold plates, he interrupted his narrative to speak directly to us in our day. He told of the Gadiantons and their bands (in our day we would call them *gangs):*

> Wherefore, O ye Gentiles [that is us], it is wisdom in God that these things should be shown unto you, that thereby ye may repent of your sins, and suffer not that these murderous combinations shall get above you, . . .
>
> [He then warned us in unmistakable plainness]: Wherefore, the Lord commandeth you, when ye shall see these things come among you that ye shall awake to a sense of your awful situation, because of this secret combination which shall be among you; . . .
>
> Wherefore, I, Moroni, am commanded to write these things that evil may be done away, and that the time may come that Satan may have no power upon the hearts of the children of men, but that they may be persuaded to do good continually, that they may come unto the fountain of all righteousness and be saved. [Ether 8:23–24, 26]

When the Saints in Missouri were suffering great persecutions, the Lord said that the Constitution of the United States was given

> that every man may act in doctrine and principle pertaining to futurity, according to the moral agency which I have given unto him. [Notice that it does not say *free agency,* it says *moral agency.* The agency we have is a moral agency.] . . .
>
> For this purpose have I established the Constitution of this land, by the hands of wise men whom I raised up unto this very purpose, and redeemed the land by the shedding of blood. [D&C 101:78, 80]

The present major political debate centers on values and morals and the Constitution.

There occurs from time to time reference to the Constitution hanging by a thread. President Brigham Young said:

> The general Constitution of our country is good, and a wholesome government could be framed upon it; for it was dictated by the invisible operations of the Almighty. . . .
>
> Will the Constitution be destroyed? No. It will be held inviolate by this people; and as Joseph Smith said "the time will come when the destiny of this nation will hang upon a single thread, and at this critical juncture, this people will step forth and save it from the threatened destruction." It will be so.[23]

I do not know when that day will come or how it will come to pass. I feel sure that when it does come to pass, among those who will step forward from among this people will be men who hold the Holy Priesthood and who carry as credentials a bachelor or doctor of law degree. And women, also, of honor. And there will be judges as well.

Others from the world outside the Church will come, as Colonel Thomas Kane did, and bring with them their knowledge of the law to protect this people.

We may one day stand alone, but we will not change or lower our standards or change our course.

What Will You Do with His Name?

Near the end of his life, President Clark spoke at a dinner at Brigham Young University. I sat next to him. We steadied him as he made his way slowly and laboriously down the steps to his car and drove away into the night. That was the last time I saw him.

The funeral of President J. Reuben Clark Jr. was the first General Authority funeral I attended. South Temple was blocked off between State Street and West Temple. The General Authorities assembled in front of the Church Administration Building. There were thirty-eight of us then. With measured steps, we followed the hearse down the center of the street.

The solemn procession moved through the south gate of Temple Square and around to the northwest door of the Tabernacle. There we formed an honor guard, half on each side of the door, and stood at attention while the Clark family and President Clark's casket passed between us.

I ask you who belong to the J. Reuben Clark Law Society, What *will* you do with his name? It is very certain that one day you will be accountable to President Clark.

And it is equally certain that you members of The Church of Jesus Christ of Latter-day Saints will be accountable for what you have done with the Lord's name.

I wonder if you who are now lawyers or you who are students of the law know how much you are needed as defenders of the faith. Be willing to give of your time and of your means and your expertise to the building up of the Church and the kingdom of God and the establishment of Zion, which we are under covenant to do—not just to the Church as an institution, but to members and ordinary people who need your professional protection.

Another Testimonial Dinner

I told you about the dinner honoring J. Reuben Clark in Beverly Hills, California. There was another dinner held at the Waldorf-Astoria in New York City. It was a tribute to President J. Reuben Clark on his retirement from the board of the Equitable Life Assurance Society. Elder Harold B. Lee was there to succeed him on the board.

Elder Lee told me that prior to the event President Clark called him to his hotel room. He found President Clark sitting, leaning on his cane, pensive and unusually nervous. He wanted to inspect Brother Lee's formal dress to see that his cummerbund was just right.

Imagine those assembled, the great men of the world—cabinet ministers, leaders in business and government—all of different faiths. President Clark and Elder Lee were the only two members of the Church present.

President Clark began his valedictory by addressing them as "my brethren." He taught them about the Lord Jesus Christ and concluded with his fervent testimony.

I conclude with my fervent testimony and invoke a blessing upon you who are lawyers and judges and who have great power to defend this people.

I invoke the blessings of our Heavenly Father upon you in your studies, in your practice, and more particularly in your home and in your family, that the Spirit of the Lord and the spirit of righteousness will be with you.

I pray that you can take justice and mercy and find a balance in them and fix them firmly with absolute integrity, in the name of Jesus Christ, amen.

This satellite fireside address was given to the J. Reuben Clark Law Society at the Conference Center in Salt Lake City on February 28, 2004. Reprinted from the Clark Memorandum, *fall 2004, 2–11.*

Boyd K. Packer received his EDD from Brigham Young University in 1962. He has served as a General Authority since 1961 and as a member of the Quorum of Twelve Apostles since 1970 and was acting president of the Quorum of Twelve Apostles 1994–2008. He is currently president of the Quorum of the Twelve Apostles.

Notes

1. Sir Isaac Newton, letter to Robert Hooke, Feb. 1676.

2. J. Reuben Clark Jr., "Reflective Speculation," address given at Seminary and Institute Teachers Summer Session, 21 June 1954.

3. *Sharing the Gospel with Others,* Preston Nibley, comp. [Salt Lake City: Deseret Book Co., 1948], 110–12.

4. Journal of Joshua Clark, vol. 12, 25 Mar. 1886.

5. Harold B. Lee, "President J. Reuben Clark, Jr.: An Appreciation on His Ninetieth Birthday," *Improvement Era,* Sept. 1961, 632.

6. Gordon B. Hinckley, *James Henry Moyle: The Story of a Distinguished American and an Honored Churchman* [Salt Lake City: Deseret Book Co., 1951], 130–33.

7. David H. Yarn Jr., "Biographical Sketch of J. Reuben Clark, Jr.," *BYU Studies,* 13 (spring 1973), 240.

8. Will Rogers to "Mr. Toastmaster," 13 Oct. 1933.

9. J. Reuben Clark Jr. to Thomas I. Parkinson, 11 July 1947, fd 16, box 376, J. Reuben Clark Papers.

10. J. Reuben Clark Jr., *Our Lord of the Gospels: A Harmony of the Gospels* [Salt Lake City: Deseret Book Co., 1954].

11. J. Reuben Clark Jr., *Behold the Lamb of God,* [Salt Lake City: Deseret Book Company, 1991].

12. *The Charted Course of the Church in Education,* rev. ed. [pamphlet, 1994; item 32709].

13. J. Reuben Clark Jr. in *Conference Report,* Apr. 1938:103.

14. J. Reuben Clark Jr., "They of the Last Wagon," *Improvement Era,* Nov. 1947, 705.

15. J. Reuben Clark Jr. in *Conference Report,* Oct. 1935, 92.

16. J. Reuben Clark Jr., "They of the Last Wagon," *Improvement Era,* Nov. 1947, 747–48.

17. Harold B. Lee, "President J. Reuben Clark, Jr.: An Appreciation on His Ninetieth Birthday," *Improvement Era,* Sept. 1961, 632.

18. *Ibid.*

19. Abraham Lincoln, notes for a law lecture, 1 July 1850.

20. *History of the Church,* 3:258.

21. *History of the Church,* 5:394.

22. "Has the Supreme Court Gone Too Far?" *Commentary,* vol. 116, no. 3 [Oct. 2003], 25–48.

23. Brigham Young in *Journal History,* 4 July 1854.

Acquired by Character,
Not by Money

Kenneth W. Starr

This afternoon, on this special day in the lives of the Class of 1990, I would like to pause with you for just a few minutes and look into the future, to examine the profession to which you are being called as members.

The graduates here today would no doubt agree that pausing and reflecting while in law school is an important thing to do. They might even give some friendly advice to that effect, to the incoming law students who will soon be the Class of 1993 here at this great institution. Back when I was worried about LSATs and law school applications, I was working in Washington, D.C., for the State Department. I had just abandoned graduate school in political science and had made a basic turn in the career road—a turn toward the law.

During that year, I had the good fortune to work with a fellow who was spending the summer in Washington, D.C., between his first and second years of law school at Yale. As was appropriate for a greenhorn wondering about the mysteries of law and law school, I asked this ersatz big brother what advice he would share with me, a fledgling, would-be law school rookie. He thought for a minute and said: "If I had that first year to do over, I would study less." My spirits rose, as you can well imagine, because I had heard the usual horror stories about that first year of law school. "I would study less," he went on, "and think more."

For the record, I think that's sound advice, not only for law school, but—more relevantly for today's graduates—sound advice for one's entire legal career. Unfortunately, in law, as in life, there is little need to think in order just to get by. But, as Aristotle wisely opined that the unexamined life is not worth living, so too one's life in the profession that our graduates are today entering should remain—in a constructive, positive spirit—under the gentle watch of a careful eye. Like Nora in Ibsen's enduring play *A Doll's House,* we have an obligation to come to know ourselves for what we really are.

The legal profession is at a crossroads. We in the profession are called upon in a fundamental sense to choose what it is that we are all about. I have a gnawing fear that we are gradually, but inexorably, choosing the wrong road.

Several months ago, at the midwinter meeting of the American Bar Association in Los Angeles, the American Bar Foundation took note of the career and contributions of two outstanding individuals. One is a household name in the law, one of our century's towering figures—Justice Thurgood Marshall.

That was a splendid event. In hearing Justice Marshall, I had a vivid sense of listening to history. There, standing before those many members of the organized bar, was the individual who stood at the podium of the Supreme Court almost 40 years ago (as the president of this great university has done with such distinction so often), and called upon the Court to do the right thing in vindicating the rights of all persons—including schoolchildren—to be free from line drawing because of race.

Counting by race, the Court held, was wrong. It is not only morally repugnant but goes against our basic constitutional values.

For all too long, of course, the Court had turned a blind eye to the constitutional and moral evil of a race-based society Yet, the Court—and the country—labored under the harsh, corrupt regime of *Plessy* v. *Ferguson* for over a half century; what is more, the process of dismantling *Plessy's* quasi-apartheid system was destined to require many more years.

But ultimately the moral vision of basic human dignity and basic human rights assured by our Constitution was translated into law, through the forceful advocacy of Thurgood Marshall and his colleagues, who at the time included my former chief judge on the D.C. Circuit, Judge Spottswood Robinson III.

The leadership of Thurgood Marshall and his colleagues is an integral part of a noble and enduring tradition in our profession. Not long ago I had the privilege of addressing the nation's oldest organized bar, the Philadelphia Bar Association. That bar has many traditions, but one of the proudest is to give to the leader of the bar, upon his or her retirement as chancellor of the bar, a small gold box. The box is a replica of one given two and a half centuries ago to the greatest of Philadelphia lawyers, Andrew Hamilton. It was given to Mr. Hamilton for his remarkable defense of freedom of the press in the immortal trial of John Peter Zenger. The little gold box, used in bygone years as a snuff box, bears a wonderful inscription which captures that which is highest and noblest in our profession—"acquired not by money, but by character."

A generation after that great trial in Philadelphia, 55 delegates gathered in that very city to establish a proposed framework of government. They were great men at the convention, and some of the greatest were not lawyers.

But when one examines the records of that convention, one quickly discovers that the intellectual leaders—the true shapers of our government—were lawyers. From Madison and Randolph of Virginia, to Wilson of Pennsylvania, Elsworth of Connecticut, and Paterson of New Jersey, these were individuals who had been called to the bar.

Tocqueville, that astute observer of American democracy, took note in his magnificent work, *Democracy in America,* of the extraordinary role that the law—and thus lawyers—plays in the governance of the American republic. The landed aristocracy, the merchant class of New England and the Mid-Atlantic states, and the great pioneers of the West failed in the main to rise to the pinnacles of power in our representative democracy. To be sure, the country on occasion looked, as do many nations, to its heroes in war to take the helm, but its leaders and representatives have been primarily those called to the legal profession. For every Washington, Jackson, Grant, and Eisenhower, there are several Adamses, Jeffersons, Madisons, Monroes, Lincolns, and Roosevelts— those called to the law.

Indeed, the importance of law—and thus of those who practice, enforce, and interpret law—was abundantly evident to those sages who had not had the good fortune to read the law and to apprentice themselves to a wise lawyer of ability and integrity. It was in his first term of office that our first president, our military-hero, nonlawyer president, George Washington, wrote to the Supreme Court as follows:

> I have always been persuaded that the stability and success of the National Government, and consequently the happiness of the American people, would depend in a considerable degree on the interpretation and execution of its laws.

That statement was written two hundred years ago this month—in the early part of April 1790. And the force of the statement resonates across the many generations and stands as a tribute to the function of the bar, of the bench, and of others entrusted with the care and custody of the law. The task was admirably stated by former Attorney General Griffin Bell, in the title of his wonderful memoir, "Taking Care of the Law."

That, ultimately, is the duty you will soon take on as members of the profession—to take care of the law. That, of course, is the duty imposed by the Constitution upon the president of the United States, who takes an oath of office prescribed by the Constitution, to take care that the laws be faithfully executed. It is a duty that rests upon all members of the executive branch (including your own Professor Lynn Wardle, laboring with us so ably at the Justice Department).

But each person in our profession is called upon to take part in that process that President Washington described. Each is to do his or her part in assuring the rule of law and fidelity to law.

It's time now to come back to the crossroads that I mentioned before.

In oral argument (as I'm sure President Lee would agree), one of the most important aspects of advocacy is to have thought the case through—to have a well-developed theory of the case. Obviously, one must know one's case. But the good lawyer must also have a well-conceived theory of the case. It will not do when the hard hypothetical comes from the bench to say in lame response: "But, Judge (or Justice), that's not this case!"

Here, then, is my theory (or, more precisely, my proposition)—the great tradition of public service of which our profession can justly be proud is in danger. The tradition of Andrew Hamilton, the tradition of the Framers, and the tradition of Thurgood Marshall is increasingly in jeopardy. That tradition is in danger by virtue of our losing our way, losing our sights as to what the profession should be all about. The profession should be a way, either through public service or though private practice, to be of service to the public and ultimately to the cause of justice. Justice—that which Sir Thomas More described so admirably as the great idea of God and the great ideal of mankind. Regrettably, the profession is being seen less as a way of serving the cause of justice and more as a way to make a handsome living, perhaps to become rich, and maybe even a little famous.

We are seeing this process at work in my office. We are very fortunate in the Office of Solicitor General to be blessed with some of the finest legal talent in the country. Our 23 lawyers have credentials that we would be pleased, in a nonarrogant way, to put up against any law firm, public or private, anywhere in the country.

But as the years have gone by, it has become increasingly difficult to *keep* these splendid lawyers in public service. They may be with us today, but they will likely be gone tomorrow. Rare is the person who, at the outset, commits himself or herself to public service and then stays there. Indeed, if the person has done well in law school, the person may never enter public service. Success in the profession becomes translated into partnership and high income levels. Success means prosperity. The successful firm is the prosperous firm. Increasingly, the theme of our profession is "acquired by money, not by character."

Now there are severe opportunity costs, as the economists would say, occasioned by the law-as-business environment in which the profession finds itself. Most directly, one can see a direct correlation between increases in earned income and decreases in professional satisfaction (and basic human happiness). It wasn't so many light years ago that I entered this profession and with one of the nation's leading law firms. The emphasis at the time was on the quality of one's work. Make it good. No, do better than that. Do the very best. Be the very best.

And that emphasis did not translate so overwhelmingly into the green-eyeshades folks examining with exacting scrutiny the total number of billable and collectible hours. Oh, to be sure, that factor was highly relevant; it was important. But its place in the relative scheme of things was seen in the bottom-line fact that billing around 1,700 hours or 1,800 hours was right on target. And that left time—time to think, time to refresh oneself mentally, time to become involved in the community, in the church, and to be truly engaged in the family.

Something else is being lost—something very important to the well being of the profession. And that is the ancient sense in the profession that one owes something to one's country, to one's community, and to one's profession. That was, of course, the spirit at the founding of the American republic. To their great moral credit, our forebearers who devoted themselves to public service impoverished themselves in the process. In his later years, Jefferson had to sell his much beloved books to the Library of Congress to avoid acute financial embarrassment. He had not been back home at Monticello building a financial empire; he had been living life greatly, remembering and paying attention to what T. S. Eliot was destined so wisely to call "the permanent things." And he died a poor man.

"Acquired by character, not by money." It was, of course, the Apostle Paul who warned about the corrupting power of money or, more precisely, the love of money. Lord Acton, centuries later, was also right about the corrosive, corrupting nature of power. That is precisely why our system of government is adorned with the elaborate set of checks and counterweights, to prevent the accumulation of power in the hands of a single person or branch of government.

Where is the check against the corrosive power of the desire for money? As a believer in the Jeffersonian tradition of limited government, and as a subscriber to Lord Acton's maxims, the answer does not, in my opinion, lie in the all-too easy solution in this century—to call upon government to solve the problem. Anyone who believes that government is mystically endowed with magical answers would do well to recall Bismarck's maxim, that one should never see either laws or sausages made. To believe that Washington has all the answers is, in my humble judgment, woefully misguided.

That is to say, it would be misguided, and incompatible with our traditions, to embark on a zealous regulatory mission to regulate lawyers and law firms and law fees. Let's leave that to the marketplace and the profession itself.

But we lawyers are making ourselves too costly, especially in a time when we are increasingly concerned about American competitiveness. Whether we are unduly litigious as a society, (as I think we are), or whether litigation serves entirely benign purposes in an astonishingly pluralistic society in which we take every person's rights seriously (as part of our cultural heritage of rugged individualism and, put more felicitously, the dignity of each human being), lawyers simply charge too much for their services. We should live comfortably, but we should not be so pricey that honest, hardworking Americans can't afford to talk to us.

Proposing a restructuring of the delivery of legal services in the 1990s goes wildly beyond what I can hope to accomplish in this brief set of reflections on this happy occasion. What I do think, however, is that the law-as-business movement is of such increasing force that public service is likely to provide an important and attractive career alternative in the 1990s. And I encourage thoughtful, prayerful consideration of that very alternative—even if only for a while—as the future now stands before you with its promise and hope.

That is, with a good solid dose of humility, with a firm, good old American common-sense notion that by entering public service I am emphatically not going to save the world, public service—even if only for a brief while—provides a modest way of restoring, in each individual's own way, the original moral vision of our profession.

Everyone needs heroes. At a minimum, one needs fine examples. I cannot think of a better standard bearer, a finer example, a more splendid hero than that of your own president of this great university, a remarkable individual who has served his country so ably in the highest traditions of our profession.

It was Holmes who said, wisely and correctly, that one can live greatly in the law as elsewhere. Public service, I venture to predict, will make a real comeback in the 1990s, even with the inevitable—and I think not inappropriate—compensation gap between the private and public sectors. Despite one's politics—whether they are on the left or the right on the political spectrum, or somewhere in between—the call of public service represents that which is best and noblest in our tradition as a profession.

Jefferson, trained in the law in beautiful Williamsburg, left his heirs precious little by way of the world's possessions. But he left the country and the entire human family a record of astonishing accomplishment and contribution. He left the world poor, but he left the world itself immeasurably enriched by what he was and what he did.

He was imperfect, of course, falling short in countless ways, naturally, as do we all. It was, again, the Apostle Paul who wrote that "we all sin and fall short of the glory of God." But his was an ennobling life, a lawyer dedicated to the higher, loftier things, to service of his country, and to the permanent things of life, that which can be acquired not by money, but by character.

This w convocation address was given at the Provo Tabernacle on April 27, 1990. Reprinted from the Clark Memorandum, *fall 1990, 8–11.*

Kenneth W. Starr received his JD *from Duke University in 1973, clerked for David W. Dyer of the* U.S. *Court of Appeals for the Fifth Circuit 1973–74, and clerked for Chief Justice Warren E. Burger of the* U.S. *Supreme Court 1975–77. He served as counselor to* U.S. *Attorney General William French Smith 1981– 83, judge for the* U.S. *Court of Appeals for the* D.C. *Circuit 1983–89, solicitor general of the United States 1989–93, and independent counsel 1994–99. He is the author of* First Among Equals: The Supreme Court in American Life *(2002). He is currently of counsel at Kirkland & Ellis in Los Angeles and the Duane and Kelly Roberts Dean and Professor of Law at Pepperdine University School of Law in Malibu, California.*

J. REUBEN CLARK LAW SCHOOL

Why the J. Reuben Clark Law School? Dedicatory Address and Prayer of the J. Reuben Clark Law Building (September 5, 1975)

Marion G. Romney

As I approach this task of saying a few words in the presence of this august gathering, realizing that this school is named after President J. Reuben Clark, I'm reminded of a question that he once put to me. I was at the time manager of the Welfare Office as assistant managing director of the program. In that capacity I had frequent contact with him because he was the member of the Presidency responsible for that particular work. I used to write letters to the Presidency on problems and sometimes they didn't answer very promptly. I remember once when I had a problem that I wrote to the Presidency, saying, "I think these are the facts and I think the decision should be this. If I don't hear from you shortly, I will so proceed." When he received my note, President Clark called me on the phone and said: "Kid, who do you think you are, writing to the Presidency like that?" "Well," I said, "I've got to move and I can't get answers." He said: "When we don't respond, you have your answer."

As I attempt to participate on this program in the presence of all the wisdom we've heard from President Kimball, President Tanner, President Oaks, the chief justice of the Supreme Court of the United States, and Justice Powell, I'm asking myself that question, "Who do you think you are?"

It has been suggested, nevertheless, that I might comment on the reasons for the establishment of J. Reuben Clark Law School. I cannot say with certainty what was in the minds of those who made the final decision to establish the school. I can, however, tell you why I used such influence as I had to get it established. To begin with, I have long felt that no branch of learning is more important to an individual or to society than law. I further felt that the educational base at Brigham Young University—the flagship of our Church educational system—would be and should be broadened by the establishment of a law school. I likewise felt that the atmosphere of honor, integrity, patriotism, and benevolence prevailing at Brigham Young University would be a good influence upon a law school and its student body. I also desired to have perpetuated on this campus the memory and influence of President J. Reuben Clark Jr.—a great lawyer, patriot, statesman, and church leader. It's my hope that all faculty and student body members will familiarize themselves with and emulate his virtues and accomplishments.

President Clark believed in law, both human and divine. He accepted as truth the modern scripture which declares that there is a

> light [which] proceedeth forth from the presence of God to fill the immensity of space—
> ... which [light] is the law by which all things are governed. ...
> And [that] there are many kingdoms; ...
> And unto every kingdom is given a law; ...
> And [that God] hath given a law unto all things, by which they move in their times and their seasons;
> And their courses are fixed, even the courses of the heavens and the earth, which comprehend the earth and all the planets. ...
> The earth rolls upon her wings [saith the Lord], and the sun giveth his light by day, and the moon giveth her light by night, and the stars also give their light, as they roll upon their wings in their glory, in the midst of the power of God. ...
> ... and any man who hath seen any or the least of these hath seen God moving in his majesty and power.[1]

President Clark also believed, as do all Latter-day Saints, that the law which "proceedeth forth from the presence of God" is binding upon this earth and its inhabitants. He believed as do we, that

> [t]here is a law, irrevocably decreed in heaven before the foundations of this world, upon which all blessings are predicated—
> And when we obtain any blessing from God, it is by obedience to that law upon which it is predicated.[2]

Laws on which a peaceful, progressive, prosperous, and happy society must be built are prescribed in the Ten Commandments and the Sermon on the Mount. Our knowledge that the origin, scope, and universality of law is thus revealed in the scriptures enhances rather than demeans or diminishes our appreciation and respect for the law of the land.

> We believe that governments were instituted of God for the benefit of man; and that he holds men accountable for their acts in relation to them, both in making laws and administering them, for the good and safety of society.[3]

As a matter of fact, we believe that the Almighty was instrumental in setting up the constitutional government of the United States. He himself so declared. In the early days of the Church (1833), the Lord admonished the Saints to importune for redress:

> According to the laws and constitution of the people, which I have suffered to be established, and [which] should be maintained for the rights and protection of all flesh, according to just and holy principles;
> That every man may act in doctrine and principles pertaining to futurity, according to the moral agency which I have given unto him, that every man may be accountable for his own sins in the day of judgment. . . .
> And for this purpose have I established the Constitution of this land, by the hands of wise men whom I raised up unto this very purpose.[4]

The Lord also said that the

> law of the land which is constitutional, supporting that principle of freedom in maintaining rights and privileges, belongs to all mankind. . . .
> I, the Lord God, make you free, . . . and the law also maketh you free.
> Wherefore, honest men and wise men should be sought for diligently, and good men and wise men ye should observe to uphold.[5]

The Prophet Joseph Smith Jr., who under divine direction organized The Church of Jesus Christ of Latter-day Saints, said:

> The Constitution of the United States is a glorious standard; it is founded in the wisdom of God. It is a heavenly banner; it is to all those who are privileged with the sweets of its liberty, like the cooling shades and refreshing waters of a great rock in a thirsty and weary land. It is like a great tree under whose branches men from every clime can be shielded from the burning rays of the sun.[6]

What has been said about law, as revealed in the scriptures, does not in any way conflict with the law of the land. To the contrary, the divine author of our modern scriptures says, and I quote:

> Let no man break the laws of the land, for he that keepeth the laws of God hath no need to break the laws of the land. . . .
> Behold, the laws which ye have received from my hand are the laws of the church, and in this light ye shall hold them forth.[7]

Our background increases our love for the Constitution, deepens our respect for the bar and the judiciary, and urges us, individually, to be law-abiding. President Clark expressed our point of view well when, speaking to the Los Angeles County Bar Association, he said:

> I am . . . mindful that in speaking to you, I am speaking to a distinguished group of that great body of our citizenry, who, because of their training and experience, must take an important place in the future of this country, whether we shall go left or go right. You who are elevated to the Bench are

the dispensers of justice and equity to the people, the guardians of the peace and the order of our society. You who are of the Bar man the watchtowers of the nation that give view far and near. Your eyes must be the first to see and you the first to make ready to meet the oncoming of tyranny. Upon the Bench and the Bar of the country rests the great responsibility of seeing that our liberties and free institutions are preserved. Legislators may be incompetent, executives may be dishonest, but if the Bench and Bar be honest and filled with integrity, then under the Constitution, the people are secure, and the free institutions will still live with us. But security and liberty both take flight where the [Bar and/or] the judiciary [are] corrupt.[8]

In establishing this J. Reuben Clark School of Law, we hoped to attract a student body capable of being trained and to assemble a faculty competent to teach, train, and inspire such students to be topflight lawyers and superior judges—men who in their private and professional lives will, by precept and example, implement the high ideals and standards which we have been talking about.

Although we have been in operation but two years, operating in makeshift quarters, we feel that we have made creditable progress. With this new building, we shall move rapidly toward our goals.

Now if you will join with me in a prayer, we shall dedicate this magnificent edifice.

Dedicatory Prayer

Our beloved Father in heaven, reverently we approach thee on this memorable occasion in earnest prayer. We thank thee for the vision of the importance of education, legal and otherwise, with which thou hast inspired the leaders of thy people from the time of the Prophet Joseph Smith Jr. until today. We express our appreciation for this splendid building; we thank thee for the material prosperity which has enabled us to erect it, including the generous contributions made by liberal friends and supporters.

We are grateful for the life and example of the late President J. Reuben Clark Jr., in whose honor this building is named. And now, in the authority of the holy priesthood, we dedicate this magnificent edifice unto thee to house the J. Reuben Clark Law School. We dedicate the building, its furnishings, the library, and every other thing appertaining thereto, including the land on which it stands. We pray that thou wilt preserve it and protect it from the ravages of nature and the molestation of evil men.

We invoke thy blessings upon the administrators, faculty members, and students who shall function therein. We pray, Father, that the students trained in this building will rise to the challenge of Josiah Gilbert Holland's stirring lines:

God give us men. A time like this demands
Strong minds, great hearts, true faith, and ready hands! . . .
Men whom the spoils of office cannot buy;
Men who possess opinions and a will;
Men who have honor; Men who will not lie;
Men who can stand before a demagogue
And damn his treacherous flatteries without winking.
Tall men, sun-crowned, who live above the fog,
In public duty and in private thinking.
For while the rabble, with their thumb-worn creeds,
Their large professions and their little deeds,
Mingle in selfish strife—lo! Freedom weeps;
Wrong rules the land, and waiting Justice sleeps.

And Father, help the lawyers trained in this law school to remember that they are to be the guardians of the law Isaiah spoke of three thousand years ago, when he said: "Out of Zion shall go forth the law, and the word of the Lord from Jerusalem."⁹ These thanks we give, Father, these blessings we plead for, and this dedication we make in the worthy name of Jesus Christ, our Redeemer, amen.

This dedicatory address and prayer was given at BYU Law School on September 5, 1975. Reprinted from Dedication: To Justice, To Excellence, To Responsibility: Proceedings at the Convocation and Dedication of the J. Reuben Clark College of Law, Brigham Young University, Provo, Utah, September 5, 1975 *(Provo, Utah: BYU Printing Service, 1975), 43–48.*

Marion G. Romney (1897–1988) received his LL.B. *from the University of Utah in 1932 and an honorary Doctor of Laws from Brigham Young University in 1975. He served as a General Authority 1941–88, member of the Quorum of Twelve Apostles 1951–88, counselor in the First Presidency 1972–85, and president of the Quorum of Twelve Apostles 1985–88.*

Notes

1. D&C 88:12–13, 37–38, 42–43, 45, 47.
2. D&C 130:20–21.
3. D&C 134:1.
4. D&C 101:77–78, 80.
5. D&C 98:5, 8, 10.
6. *History of the Church*, 3:304.
7. D&C 58:21, 23.
8. J. REUBEN CLARK JR., *Some Factors in the Proposed Post-War International Pattern, in* SELECTED PAPERS ON INTERNATIONAL AFFAIRS 407, 407–8 (David H. Yarn Jr. ed., 1987) (address at the Los Angeles Bar Association, Feb. 24, 1944).
9. Isaiah 2:3.

Dedicatory Remarks and Prayer of the Howard W. Hunter Law Library (March 21, 1997)

Gordon B. Hinckley

I am delighted to be here on this great and significant occasion, my brothers and sisters and friends. I thank each of you for being here. This is a day of great appreciation and thanks and respect. I am grateful that Sister Inis Hunter is here with her family.

What a wonderful thing it is to be here on this significant occasion. What a glorious thing it is that we live in a nation that functions under the rule of law. When you see all the anarchy in the world, when you see all the trouble, when you see the civil wars and the strife and the difficulty among people, what a reassuring and wonderful thing it is to know that we live under law and that it becomes the safeguard of our liberties, of our security, of our peace. How thankful I feel to be a citizen of the United States of America living under a glorious Constitution, which brings with it tremendous privileges and opportunities and blessings. How thankful I am for the great provisions of the First Amendment and the Bill of Rights, which extend to each of us so many safeguards and blessings. How thankful we ought to be. You do not have to travel very far in this world to have a great increase in your love for this land of which each of us is a part.

I am thankful, and I express my thanks in behalf of the Board of Trustees, for this beautiful and serviceable building which will aid every scholar of the law who studies here. It is a remarkable and wonderful facility, and how grateful we are to have it, and how grateful we are to all who have made it possible. Our very deep thanks to each one of you: the Huntsmans, who out of their great love for their neighbor and friend,

President Hunter, have given so generously, and to the many others who have given generously, to Jack Wheatley and Alan Ashton, who are here, and to scores and scores of others including the starving student who may have given his mite to the construction of this great facility.

I just want to say a word about President J. Reuben Clark Jr., whose name is carried in this school. A generation is almost gone since he died. There are not very many people now who remember him well. I think I knew President Clark rather well. He was a true and good friend to me, I was almost a boy at that time. He was a man remarkable in so many respects: deliberate, careful, and thoughtful of what he said. He was a great student. His regular regimen was to go home each day after a day at the office and take a little nap. Then at 6:30 p.m. he would have a little supper. Then he would sit up and study and write until about midnight when he would go to bed and get up in time to be at the office at 8:00 a.m. We owe so much to this wonderful man who came out of a life of poverty, a farm boy really, who rose to the highest levels in his profession and in his service to this nation. How proper in every way that this great law school should carry his name. Thanks be to J. Reuben Clark Jr., who was loved by everybody who knew him, certainly respected by everybody who ever came up against him. I am grateful for his life. I am grateful for the fact that his name is memorialized in this school.

Now, just a word about Brother Hunter—Howard William Hunter. I sat next to him for 20 years in the Council of the Twelve. I was on his left hand as we went around the circle. That circle is a rather sacred thing in the Council of the Twelve and very carefully observed. What a great soul he was: a student, yes; a scholar, yes; a hard worker, yes. But above all, he was a man of great kindness and love and respect and care and thoughtfulness and consideration. It was not his brilliance in the law that came through as you knew him. It was his love for humanity which made the big difference in his life. He was a man who loved and respected people. He did a great deal of *pro bono* work as a lawyer, a vast amount of *pro bono* work to help those in need and in distress, the poor and the struggling among us who needed help. He observed the great dictum of the Master that we go about doing good.

I am so grateful for my acquaintance with him and for what he did for me, for the contribution which he made to my life of being careful of what you do, what you say, how you do it, nothing that was not deliberate and careful and proper. God bless his memory to our great good, each of us.

I just want to say a word about this marvelous facility. I do not know whether there is a better law library anywhere in the world than this. There are great libraries, of course, huge libraries of various kinds. Not long ago I was at the great Vatican Library in Rome, and it was a most inspirational experience to see those old illuminated texts, hundreds and hundreds of years old, that had been preserved for the blessing of mankind.

I once studied in the British Museum, the great national library of Britain, in great tall stacks of books, hundreds and hundreds and hundreds of thousands of them.

I love libraries. I love books. There is something wonderful about a book. You can pick it up. You can heft it. You can read it. You can set it down. You can think of what you have read. It does something for you. You can share great minds and great actions and great undertakings in the pages of a book. I would not get far with this kind of law book over here I am afraid, but they are the stuff of which the study of law is basic and fundamental. What a marvelous thing that we have this tremendous facility—400,000 volumes here. That is a great library to which will be added many more through all the years to come.

I just want to again express my profound gratitude for this great facility. Thanks to all who made it possible, and my congratulations, my warm and hearty compliments, to every student of this great law school who will become the beneficiary of what has been done here. You have been blessed; you and those who come after you have been immeasurably blessed by the creation of this marvelous and wonderful facility. The carrels in which you will study, we wish everybody on this campus had such a carrel. Thanks and my blessing I leave with you and my appreciation and my very deep respect on this sacred and significant occasion.

Now I invite each of you to bow your heads and close your eyes and join in a prayer of dedication.

Dedicatory Prayer

Our Beloved Father in Heaven, Our Father and Our God, with thankful hearts we bow before Thee. We are grateful for Thy wonderful blessings so bounteously bestowed. We thank Thee for this great institution of learning, for its distinguished faculty, for its great body of students.

We thank Thee for this J. Reuben Clark School of Law, for its stature among its peers, and for the confidence that it will continue to grow in stature.

We thank Thee for this new and spacious library. We thank Thee for the generosity of those who have made it possible, for their gifts freely given to provide the means to build it.

We thank Thee for the architect, the contractor, and all who have worked to bring it to completion.

We thank Thee for our friend and associate President Howard W. Hunter, whose name it bears. His life was guided by principles of equity and justice. He loved the law. It was his profession before he was called to a high and holy responsibility in Thy church and kingdom. Out of love and respect for him it carries his good name.

We are grateful that his widow is here, that members of his family are here. We thank Thee for the great tradition which they are carrying on.

Now, in behalf of the Board of Trustees, and in behalf of the officers and faculty of the university, as friends of President Hunter and as friends of the Law School, we are met here today to dedicate this useful and attractive addition to the Law School building.

Acting in the authority of the Holy Priesthood and in behalf of the Board of Trustees, I dedicate the Howard W. Hunter Law Library Addition for the purposes for which it has been designed and created.

With its hundreds of thousands of volumes and other materials and facilities, we pray that it will be a wonderful resource to both faculty and students. It is here to be used, and we pray that it may be a great treasure house of knowledge to the scholars who will partake of its offerings. We pray that its unique facilities may provide a place of quiet where the pursuit of knowledge may be experienced in a personal and individual way.

May these very facilities become an inspiration to all who will use them.

May those who have given generously to make this structure possible have satisfaction in the knowledge that it will fill a need, and that it will add immeasurably to the stature of this school.

May it contribute to the strength of scholarship and the attitude of those who are graduating from this institution. May they go forth into the world of work as defenders of the law and of the precious Constitution of this nation. May the plaque which adorns the hall of this library, and which contains words on the law and government from the Doctrine and Covenants, prove an inspiration to all who shall pause to read it.[1]

May the graduates of this institution bring dignity and integrity to the profession of which they will become a part.

Bless this Brigham Young University and all of its schools and departments. Increase its stature among its sister institutions throughout the world. May it be blessed in its great mission to nurture faith in Thee, in Thy Beloved Son, and in Thy divine purposes, as it serves also as a teacher of secular truth.

Bless Thy church, which is the sponsoring institution of this great university that its work may roll forth to fill the earth. This law school is one bright facet of a tremendous program designed to bless Thy children everywhere who will accept and live by its teachings.

And now, at this hour of dedication, we rededicate ourselves to good citizenship in the nation and to the on-rolling of Thy great cause and kingdom.

Accept of our thanks, of our love, of our prayer and our labors, we humbly ask in the name of Thy Beloved Son, even the Lord Jesus Christ, amen.

This dedicatory address and prayer was given at the Howard W. Hunter Law Library at Brigham Young University on March 21, 1997.

Gordon B. Hinckley (1910–2008) received his BA *in English from the University of Utah in 1932, was awarded 10 honorary degrees, and given a Presidential Medal of Freedom, the United States' highest civil award, in 2004. He served as a General Authority 1958–2008, member of the Quorum of Twelve Apostles 1961–1981, counselor in the First Presidency 1981–1995, and 15th president of The Church of Jesus Christ of Latter-day Saints 1995–2008.*

Notes

1. *See* Doctrine and Covenants 134.

The House that Rex Built

Dee V. Benson

Every story has its beginning, and in my opinion the story of BYU Law School began when a telephone rang in a law office in Phoenix, Arizona, in 1971. The law office belonged to Rex Lee. He told me this story himself, so I'm sure it's true. He said he had a secretary who was a veteran of the law firm and not easily impressed, and all of a sudden she yelled out from the outer office, "Hey, there is some guy named Harold Lee on the phone from Salt Lake City. Do you want to talk to him?" Rex said it took a minute to digest—"Harold Lee, do I know a Harold Lee?"

When it occurred to him it was Harold B. Lee, the president of the Church, he took the call. That was the conversation in which President Harold B. Lee asked Rex Lee if he would serve on the committee searching for a dean for the new law school that the Church was planning for Brigham Young University.

Coincidentally, my genesis with the legal system began at that same time. I was on a mission in Sweden, dutifully tracting and trying to convert people to the gospel. I was planning to do a split with another pair of missionaries in the southern Swedish town of Malmo. We went to the other elders' apartment, and when we got there my companion and I found them in a heated exchange with their landlord. The landlord claimed they hadn't paid their rent; the missionaries said they had. There was a strong smell of alcohol in the air, and I was pretty sure it wasn't coming from the elders. Their landlord was really drunk and really mad, and so I tried my first-ever attempt at mediation. I intervened, and all it did was cause the landlord to grab a very big butcher knife with a blade of about eight inches. The landlord came around the table after me, saying he was going to slice my throat. We elders went running down the road with him chasing us and yelling Swedish obscenities all the way.

The next thing I knew, courtesy of the state of Sweden, I was on a train headed back to Malmo to attend the trial against the landlord. I was the state's chief witness; it was a great little diversion from tracting. I took the witness stand, the prosecutor asked me what happened, and I told him. It was quite uneventful. Then the defense lawyer stood up. I still remember what he looked like: He was this very heavyset Swedish man, middle-aged, wearing a three-piece suit. He had a book on the counsel table. He stood up, looked at me, and said, "So, you're a missionary?"

I said, "Yes."

He picked up the book, and it was the Bible. Then he said, "So, do you believe in the Bible?"

I said, "Yes." I didn't think that this was the time to do the "as far as it is translated correctly" thing.

So, then he said, "Have you read it?"

This is when I was glad that the mission president wasn't there, because I was under oath. I said, "Parts of it."

He said, "Have you read the New Testament?"

I said, "Yes." Then he opened it up and with great drama said, "Are you familiar with the scripture that says: 'I was an hungred, and ye gave me meat: I was thirsty, and ye gave me drink. . . . Inasmuch as ye have done it unto one of the least of these my brethren, ye have done it unto me'?"

I said, "I'm generally familiar with that scripture."

And he said, "Do you believe it?"

I said, "Yes."

He leaned into me and said, "Do you live it?"

I said, "I try to."

He stomped away and with dramatic flourish said, "I think not!" And he sat down. That was the whole thing!

We had an intermission shortly after that, and I asked the prosecutor what he thought, and he said, "Thank you. You did fine. We'll let you know how it turns out."

I then pointed to the defense lawyer, who was huddling up with the landlord, and I said, "So, what was that all about?" and he said in Swedish, "Jag har ingen aning," which means, "I have no idea."

I finished my mission without getting killed and returned to my studies at BYU, as a PE major. I didn't think a whole lot of this incident until I heard President Oaks announce at a devotional assembly—which, I want noted, I attended—that a law school would be formed at BYU. Somehow it got my mind working in that direction, and I took the LSAT. So, there I was in the charter class at the first class that was ever held, with Rex Lee teaching. The search committee had found as its first dean one of the searchers. It was such an interesting experience: all of us brand-new law students and listening to Rex. I remember he emphasized two things: One, he said, "We're not going to teach you law so much as we're going to teach you to think like a lawyer." As soon as he'd emphasized that, he started teaching us some law. He told us about the common law of England, emphasizing the difference between questions of fact, which go to juries, and questions of law, which go to the court. Just when I thought I was grasping the distinction, it would leave my brain. I think I was seated next to Bruce Whiting, and when we had an intermission, he turned to me and said, "What was that all about?"

I said, "I have no idea."

About a month later, I remember, Professor Bruce Hafen, who was my torts professor, saw me after class and said, "So, Mr. Benson, are you learning to think like a lawyer yet?"

I said, "Well, if it means going through life in a state of perpetual confusion, I am getting it down."

He laughed and said, "It will get there; you'll get there."

So, here it is 30-plus years later, and I would like to happily announce that I have finally learned to think like a lawyer. I do it all the time. I am no fun anymore, but I have learned how to think like a lawyer, and I thought I'd employ that skill for you here tonight—try to say something really erudite, really profound. Perhaps I could explain how BYU Law School in its brief 30 years has taken Constitutional law to new heights and shown the world what it really means. But I couldn't come up with anything that sounded sufficiently brilliant. Not even to me. Then it hit me, after 12 to 14 hours of watching nonstop ESPN, what I would do. They have this series of programs about the best this and the best reasons for that, which I have become quite fond of, and I thought, that's it! I'll use that same approach to tonight's talk. I will focus briefly on the many accomplishments our law school has achieved during the past 30 years and sort through all the reasons why. Then, in the end I will tell you the number one reason the Law School has been such a success. I will try to tell you why we have these lofty numbers, like being currently ranked the 34th best law school in the country by U.S. News & World Report. Only 14 law schools in the nation have had more Supreme Court law clerks in the last 30 years than BYU— we have had 12. We have seen 65 of our graduates appointed as state court judges. We have had three presidentially appointed federal judges, two district judges—Mike Mosman in Oregon and me here in Utah—and we have one judge in the ninth circuit court of appeals. We've had five U.S. attorneys; we've had three members of Congress. We have had a senior partner or junior partner in most of the major law firms in America. We have what is reputed to be the best law library west of the Mississippi, if you don't count Stanford. We have distinguished faculty members with accomplishments too numerous to mention.

I could go on and on. But the main reason for all of this success comes down to one man. The indisputable number one reason why BYU Law School has been such a smashing success is because of one man: Rex

Edwin Lee. After Rex was named the founding dean, he became to our law school what George Washington was to the original colonies. They say Yankee Stadium was the house that Ruth built; well, the J. Reuben Clark Law School is the house that Rex Lee built. I wish you could have seen him in those early years. I wish you could have been there when Rex taught classes in the J. Reuben Clark Law School when we sat in that old Catholic elementary school. As gifted as he later proved himself to be as an appellate advocate, there he employed those same tools as a classroom teacher. He did so much for the Law School; his contributions were so vast. I've never seen any man and a job come together better than it did for Rex Lee and that founding deanship. Rex had a manner about him and an enthusiasm and a salesmanship that brought together all of the separate parts that made up the early Law School. He taught classes, he even picked the façade of the new building. He was the one who got them not to put the tan brick that is seen on most of the buildings on campus. He did everything. We thought he was near deity then, because being number one in your class at the University of Chicago Law School and clerking for Justice Byron White on the Supreme Court and being a member of a law firm and actually having passed a bar was a pretty good thing in our eyes. But in fairness, viewing his credentials now with a more experienced eye, he didn't come to the job with unusually high qualifications. When he received that telephone call from President Harold B. Lee, Rex Lee was only 36 years old. Beyond any résumé credentials, what Rex happened to bring to the job was himself. And he had an unbridled enthusiasm for the project. I think the most important thing he did for us in the early years was to imbue the Law School with a sense of importance. He made us feel as if we were in the middle of the best project on earth. He called the room that we took classes in "The Great Hall." It was nothing more than an old auditorium in that elementary school, but as far as we were concerned, it may as well have been in Cambridge or Oxford. He made it feel that important.

Rex was the man who managed to get Carl Hawkins to leave Michigan. Carl was a legend even then in torts professor law circles. Rex knew the Law School needed a nationally known faculty member, someone wise and with a bit of gray hair. Rex asked him three times, and Carl turned him down twice. Finally he came. Ed Kimball quickly followed. Rex enticed Woody Deem out of California—I don't know how he did that. Woody was the most celebrated district attorney in California. People would stop doing what they were doing on their lunch hours just to go listen to the great Woody Deem give a closing argument. Rex got him to leave that and come to Provo. He talked Keith Rooker into leaving private practice and coming to teach at the Law School. Keith was the first in his class at the University of Chicago and one of the most brilliant men I ever met—I never understood a single thing he said, but he was brilliant. That first nine-member faculty was an outstanding faculty, and it was all the work of the new dean.

I have classmates who were accepted to Harvard and Stanford and Virginia and other leading law schools in the country, but they all came to BYU because of one man. Bruce Duffield is an example. He, like so many others, will readily say that the one thing that turned him around was Rex Lee. By the time people left Rex's office, they were willing to come to a new law school in Provo working out of a converted elementary school on Ninth East, a law school that hadn't been given ABA accreditation yet, rather than accept offers from some of the country's best universities. He sold the Law School so well that he almost caused me not to go there. I was accepted to the University of Colorado in Boulder, and I almost went there because I didn't think I would get into BYU. That's why I'm a good candidate to be here tonight, because I wasn't one of those people, like Lew Cramer, who was highly recruited. I think Rex Lee probably personally recruited at least half of my class, maybe two thirds. He talked Carolyn Stewart into coming down from the University of Utah and being his administrative assistant, and if I were to list the top 10 reasons the Law School has been a success, she would be one of them.

I've never had membership in a group that I've cherished more than that in the charter class of this law school.

It was inevitable, I think, that Rex wouldn't stay in Provo. He was gifted and talented, and everyone that worked with him knew it. He took a leave of absence from the Law School to serve as chief of the civil division in the Department of Justice in the Ford administration and then returned to resume his position as dean. And then when Ronald Reagan was elected president, he selected Rex Lee to be the nation's highest lawyer: the solicitor general of the United States.

I got to know him during those solicitor general years. The first day I saw Rex in Washington was when a friend of mine, Stan Parrish, who worked with me on the staff of Senator Orrin Hatch, asked if I'd like to go for a run with him during the lunch hour. He said that he was going to join a couple of his running buddies along the way. So there at Ninth and Constitution, right across from the Department of Justice, was my old law school dean, Rex Lee. I was suddenly nervous. I thought I'd say something stupid, which came with regularity during law school, and I didn't see why this would be any different, and I remember wondering if the position of solicitor general had gone to my former dean's head. Well, he greeted me so warmly that my nervousness was immediately gone. Then, just as we all started jogging along the National Mall, we were stopped, interestingly enough, by a park policeman. He said we had all run a red light. He gathered the four of us around and was giving us a lecture on running safety, and I'm sure he didn't know he was talking to the solicitor general of the United States. As he was talking, Rex, who was being very friendly about it, said, "If you're going to give us a citation, will you please make mine for speeding, because that would really impress my wife." So there went my concern about this important job going to his head. I became, I admit, a bit of a Rex Lee groupie after that. I don't know—we must have gone on hundreds of runs together during the next three or four years, and in spite of 13 years' difference in age, we became not only running buddies but also very good friends. It is one of the great friendships of my life. I became addicted to Rex's arguments in the U.S. Supreme Court, which were terrific to see. I soaked up all his many comments about law. And he talked about everything, especially BYU football. He was on the short list for the Supreme Court in those days and he knew it, the one job he would have loved as much as being dean.

My favorite memory of Rex in the Supreme Court came when he was arguing a case involving paying private religious school teachers to provide remedial educational instruction to needy children after regular school hours. Rex was arguing that that did not violate the establishment clause of the First Amendment, and the plaintiffs who had brought the case were arguing that it did. He had a deputy attorney general who was arguing almost an identical issue in a case that preceded Rex's on the court's docket that morning. All of the nine justices were there, of course, and they were asking Rex various questions. Just a few days before that Rex had told me that one thing you never do is try to be funny in court. It will always backfire. If you actually happen to say something funny, that's okay, he said, but don't try to be. So, the chief justice asked a question at the very end of this argument. He said, "So, General Lee, what if we rule against your deputy in the previous case? It's a very similar issue; the facts were different slightly. What then should we do with yours?" Rex told me later that he felt like somebody hanging from a cliff with his climbing partner below him on the rope, "Do I cut him off, or do we both fall to our deaths?" As he was trying to think of the answer, there was a silence, and it was a longer pause than usual, and finally he said, "Mr. Chief Justice, in that event, I would only hope that the court would not err twice." The room erupted in laughter much louder than yours, but you had to be there. Fortunately for Rex, it seemed like no one laughed harder than Justice Rehnquist. Later he won the case, and so did his deputy.

One of Rex's most remarkable qualities for such an intellectually gifted man was his wit. Among my best memories of that wit and Rex's sense of humor is one that involves Dale Kimball, who joined the faculty during our second year. Dale is now on the district bench with me, and he is still given to bouts of immaturity. On the day Harold B. Lee passed away and Spencer W. Kimball was installed as the new prophet, Dale, who was a very distant relative of Spencer W. Kimball's, called Rex on the phone and said just one thing, "The Lees are out, the Kimballs are in," and hung up. Eleven years later Rex called me and said, "President Kimball passed away, and Ezra Taft Benson is the new prophet. I want you to call Dale Kimball in Salt Lake. When he answers the telephone, I want you to say just this and nothing more: 'The Kimballs are out, the Bensons are in.'" So I did—delivered it just like he told me—and before I could hang up, Dale said, "Benson, Rex put you up to this." Judge Kimball later told me I wasn't smart enough to think of this on my own. But he wasn't smart enough to find somebody named Hunter a few years later.

When Rex was leaving the solicitor general's office, we must have devoted 12 runs to nothing but fielding his job offers. It was a vicarious thrill for me. They were some of the best law firms in the country. And a seat on the Tenth Circuit Court of Appeals was offered as well, which he turned down, because, he said, he wanted to make some money for a change. He wanted to buy Thomas Muffins instead of the generic brand at the Giant grocery store in McLean, Virginia. But the one thing he insisted upon most of all, no matter what job he took, was that he be allowed to continue teaching at the Law School and move back to Provo. That arrangement was fine by the law firm of Sidley and Austin, and Rex became, by anyone's measure, the foremost Supreme Court advocate in the United States. And through it all, he taught classes at the Law School.

Then cancer came calling. I watched Rex go through an enormously difficult battle with a rapidly progressing form of cancer in his lymph system. He and Janet came back to Washington, where Rex was treated at the National Institutes of Health, and I watched her nurse him along. I'll never forget the day we went to the King's Dominion theme park; it was their daughter Kristy's birthday. Janet was being a good mother but, at the same time, constantly thinking of that hospital bed where Rex was lying. I know funeral plans were going through her mind. The chemotherapy was stopped, the radiation was stopped, and it looked hopeless. Then, the cancer went into remission. It was as close as I've ever been to a miracle. The medical doctors started sounding like lawyers. When asked how this happened, all they could say was, "I have no idea." But God did, and he preserved Rex Lee for another decade on this earth. He went back to Provo and continued his work as an appellate advocate. Then the Church came calling, asking him to be the president of Brigham Young University. He and Janet served through that period until another bout of illness caught up with him, and he was gone from us much too young at the age of 61.

Rex did a lot of things through the period between that phone call in 1971 and his death in 1996. Who knows why he was taken so early? I have a theory on that. You know how they have this 10-run rule in Little League baseball, and after the fourth inning, if you're 10 runs ahead they call the game? Well, I think if you accomplish the things that 10 really successful people could do in a lifetime, then God needs you on the other side and He takes you over. That is the only way I can explain why Rex Lee left us so early. From the age of 36 through 61, he did so many remarkable things, and nothing was more remarkable than assisting our law school and making it the nationally known school that it is today. Before Thomas Jefferson died, someone asked him what he wanted to be remembered for. Remember, this was a man who had been president of the United States and ambassador to France, and he built Monticello and had a very long list of other remarkable accomplishments. But Jefferson said he would like to be remembered for just two things: "I'd like to be remembered for writing the Declaration of Independence and for founding the University of Virginia," he said. I think I know Rex Lee well enough to say that I think he'd like to be known for being the foremost appellate advocate of his generation and the founding dean of BYU Law School. Next to family and church, he always said that BYU Law School was his great love.

I know tonight I've used a lot of hyperbole and a lot of superlatives in trying to describe just a little bit about why Rex Lee was the number one reason the Law School has been so successful. For those of us who were involved with J. Reuben Clark Law School, Rex Lee's memory should never be forgotten, not because he deserves it, but because he lends us so much. Winston Churchill said at the end of World War II that the future is unknowable but the past should give us hope. Rex Lee was our past, and he should give us hope. I would think that for this law school—from Dean Kevin Worthen, who is a product of Rex Lee; to Reese Hansen, who is certainly a product of Rex Lee; to the entire current faculty—there is a thread running back to him. It would be good to stop and ask ourselves, "I wonder if Rex would've done it this way?"

This Founders Day address was given to the J. Reuben Clark Law Society at Little America Hotel in Salt Lake City on September 14, 2006. Reprinted from the Clark Memorandum, *spring 2007, 22–28.*

Dee V. Benson received his JD from J. Reuben Clark Law School in 1976, served as legal counsel to the U.S. Senate Judiciary Committee 1984–86, and was U.S. attorney for the District of Utah 1989–91. He is currently a judge for the U.S. District Court for the District of Utah in Salt Lake City.

A Walk by Faith:
Founding Stories of the Law School

Bruce C. Hafen

My main qualification to talk tonight is that I was present at the law school's founding. In 1971, when I was four years out of law school, the new president of BYU, Dallin Oaks, hired me as his assistant—primarily to help get the law school started. I accepted that job because I hoped to be on the school's faculty.

I've been encouraged to tell some of the Law School's founding stories. Why would those stories interest us after so many years? Because there is power in stories. Even the scriptures are primarily a collection of personal stories. In His desire to give us guidance about life, God could have given us a large rule book, a series of essays, or perhaps a Gilbert's outline with the title "Life, in Black Letter Law." But He didn't. He gave us scriptural stories about people like ourselves. We can identify with these stories, and then we learn from them. Think of it as case law—real cases about real people who are often in perplexing circumstances. What these people discover teaches us about principles derived from real-life experience. Sometimes the scriptures tell us a story and then say, "And thus we see . . ." Some of the Law School's founding stories are like that.

The person who first proposed the J. Reuben Clark Law School was Ernest L. Wilkinson during his final years as president of BYU. President Wilkinson had done more than anyone to create the magnificent BYU campus we see today, and I am grateful to him that he proposed a law school. However, his vision of legal education carried some political overtones that some of the Church's leaders did not share. Moreover, his proposal ran counter to BYU's basic mission as an undergraduate university. So Ernest's motion might have died for want of a second. But somehow the law school idea caught the First Presidency's imagination enough that they chose to pursue it in their own way.

They talked with many leading LDS lawyers and law professors. None of the three lawyers who ended up as the Law School's first leaders—Dallin Oaks, Rex Lee, and Carl Hawkins—at first thought the Law School's creation was a very good idea, and they all expressed that view to Church leaders. They saw no need to train more LDS lawyers, and they worried that the school might become someone's political captive.

In spite of that candid advice, and even though they chose not to adopt President Wilkinson's politically flavored model, the Brethren decided to create the Law School anyway. They had felt a clear spiritual nudge, and they knew from experience that the reasons for that nudge would eventually become more clear. The process of acting on an inspired premise and then discovering a supporting rationale by hindsight is not unusual. That is what happened with the Law School's founding, and it happens in other ways when we walk by faith.

Dallin Oaks was a full professor at the University of Chicago Law School and a stake presidency member in Chicago during the discussions about two concurrent events—appointing someone to replace Ernest Wilkinson and creating the Law School. When the Brethren talked with him about becoming BYU's president, they knew his reservations about starting a law school. They said they only wanted a school that met very high professional standards, and they were willing to fund it. Then they asked, if he were president, would he see it as his duty to carry out their vision for the school? President Oaks accepted their counsel and superbly carried out their mandate. Thus we see that giving counsel to Church authorities means two things: give your best honest advice; and, when they make a decision, don't oppose it—advocate it.

Here's how I learned firsthand about the nonpolitical attitude of the Brethren toward the Law School. President Marion G. Romney was the First Presidency's representative for Law School matters. He had chaired the committee that recommended Dallin Oaks to be BYU's president. That same committee later selected Rex Lee to be the founding dean. President Romney also conducted a personal interview with each prospective law faculty member.

During his interview with me, President Romney said, "Now, let's talk about your politics." That got my attention. He said, "Are you either a Socialist or a John Bircher?" I said, "Some people think those are the only two choices." He said, "I know. That's why I'm asking. Are you a Socialist or a Bircher?" I said, "No, I'm neither." He said, "Then you're alright. Let's talk about something else." Later on, when I shared that experience with President Oaks, he said, "Tell that story—widely and often."

One of the best role models for the Law School's commitment to political diversity is President James E. Faust. He was once president of the Utah State Bar, and he served in the Utah legislature as an active Democrat. While in the First Presidency, he once said, "Both locally and nationally, the interests of the Church and its members are [best] served when we have . . . good men or women running [from both parties], and then no matter who is elected, we win."

I once heard President Faust say that his most satisfying experiences as a lawyer came not in representing big corporations but in representing those he called "the little people," meaning people who are disadvantaged in some way, perhaps including their ability to afford legal advice. As a lawyer, he was a humane servant and a spiritual healer.

Is it inconsistent to be both a healer and an advocate? The Master Healer often referred to Himself as our "advocate with the Father." I will forever be grateful that Christ, the greatest Advocate, is willing not only to represent the guilty but also to heal them. The story of the Savior's life and mission is the most significant story embedded in the deepest foundations of the Law School.

Let me return to 1971 and 25 years of working closely with Rex Lee. Rex was one of the most talented and colorful characters ever to walk among us. He came from a tiny town in Arizona to BYU in 1953 as a wide-eyed freshman who dreamed of someday becoming one of the greatest lawyers in America.

Rex's first great victory as an advocate came in his BYU student days, when he persuaded Janet Griffin to marry him. With her grace, refinement, and deep spiritual instincts, she made that Arizona diamond in the rough really sparkle. Early in their dating, Rex once heard that Janet had been out with somebody else. His way of communicating his feelings was to call her on the phone, and without identifying themselves, Rex and his cousin played their guitars and sang to her with pure Arizona honky-tonk pathos: "Your cheatin' heart will tell on you. . . ."

Rex never lost his rural Arizona sense of humor. Once when he was telling jokes at a BYU fund-raising dinner, a non-LDS visitor at our table said, "Who is that guy? Listen to his sense of timing! He could make a fortune as a stand-up comedian." I still remember one of Rex's favorite stories—maybe he told it that night: A very frugal man dies. His widow, honoring his frugality, calls the local paper and asks, "What is the cheapest obituary I can buy?" The paper agent says, "We're having a special today—you can get six words for the price of three—just 15 dollars." She says, "Is that your cheapest obituary?" He says, "Yes." "Alright," says the widow, "let's try 'Fred died Wednesday.'" "Okay," he says, "you get three more words—it's all included in the 15 dollars." "Oh," she says, "'Fred died Wednesday. Toyota for sale.'"

Rex and I served in the same BYU student stake for a few years; he was on the high council and I was in the stake presidency. Once he told me why he liked being on the high council so much. He said, "That calling has the best ratio between work and glory of any job in the Church." We didn't know whether to increase his work or decrease his glory. Another time we sat together in a sacrament meeting on a warm afternoon. Rex had dozed off. I nudged him and whispered, in jest, "Rex, you're supposed to get up and give the closing prayer." He opened one eye and said, "The First Amendment to the Constitution of the United States protects the right of religious freedom. You worship your way, and I'll worship mine." Then he went back to sleep.

In a more serious vein, may I share what I heard Rex say more than once to graduating law students. With that look he flashed when he was feeling what he called "deadly serious," he would say,

> If you forget everything I've taught you about constitutional law, please remember one thing about me. I wasn't there on that spring day in 1820 when Joseph Smith saw the Father and the Son; but I know as surely as if I had been there that Joseph was God's prophet and that Jesus is the Christ.

When I heard these words from Rex's heart, I sensed that J. Reuben Clark, whose massive old desk was in Rex's law school office, would have felt glad about the school that bears his name.

In late 1971, after interviewing a number of people, including some with considerable experience as law teachers, President Romney's committee selected 36-year-old Rex Lee as our founding dean. At the time, this seemed like a very risky, even audacious, decision. The Law School wasn't accredited; it had no faculty, no building, no library, and no students; and everything rode on the academic reputation of the dean and the faculty. Rex was a young practitioner from Phoenix who had never been a full-time law teacher and had never published a law journal article as a faculty member, though he had taught a part-time class or two. He had graduated at the top of his class at Chicago and had clerked for Justice Byron White; but his was a career of potential, not accomplished fact. Only later would Rex go on to be assistant U.S. attorney general, then solicitor general, and then a star Supreme Court advocate.

Because other LDS candidates considered for dean had far more experience in legal education, I was frankly a bit astonished when Rex was chosen. Yet just before I learned of his selection I had a strong premonition that Rex would be the dean. I once had a chance to ask President Romney why his committee chose Rex. He said in his matter-of-fact way,

> Well, I told the Brethren that I didn't know anything about how to pick a law school dean. But I did know how to pick a stake president, because I'd done that many times. They said I could do this the same way. So that's all we did: we interviewed carefully, searched their hearts, and prayed for direction. All I know is, Rex was the man the Lord wanted, and I couldn't tell you why.

Now, with over 30 years of hindsight, it was a brilliant decision, for all of the reasons Judge Dee Benson cited last year about Rex's charismatic leadership and his eventual national reputation in the U.S. Justice Department and beyond. But no one could have foreseen that with certainty in 1971. Rex was simply a young man of promise. The decision to appoint him was an act of faith based on a clear prompting to the Lord's anointed servants. Thus we walk by faith, not always knowing beforehand the things we should do.

As important as choosing the dean—in some ways even more important—was the selection of the first faculty. The whole idea of trying to build a genuinely religious law school that would be nationally recognized seemed pretty far-fetched in 1971. A new law school can't be accredited until after the first class graduates. So how do you persuade talented new law students to risk their future careers on an unknown school? The ABA's accrediting team was already very skeptical about mixing religion with legal education. And how about the very secular law firms who would need to hire the graduates? Most important, because so much else hinged on it, how do you persuade experienced LDS law teachers to leave secure positions for an unproven venture? Yet if the Law School couldn't establish strong credibility right at the beginning, it might have been impossible to claim it later on.

A few months after Rex's appointment, we were getting a little frantic. None of the experienced LDS law teachers had committed to come. Rex and others had made personal visits to each person on this very short list, but they were all waiting to see what one man—Carl Hawkins—did. Carl was a senior professor at the University of Michigan, one of the nation's top law schools. He was the stake president in Ann Arbor, was the coauthor of a well-known torts casebook, and was respected in the world of legal education for both his intellect and his integrity. Carl wasn't about to leave all of that to take a chance on BYU. Indeed, he believed he could help the Church more by staying at Michigan, because that vantage point gave him a more objective supporting voice.

In an act of desperation, Rex recommended to President Romney that the First Presidency call Carl on a mission to the Law School. President Romney said, "We don't do things that way." Ever the creative advocate, Rex said, "But President Romney, remember when Joseph Smith and Oliver Cowdery received the Aaronic Priesthood, and Joseph had to baptize Oliver before Oliver had baptized him? Sometimes when we're just starting out, we have to do things a little differently." But it was no use. We could do nothing but pray.

Then one day Rex and I were in President Oaks' office with BYU's academic vice president Robert Thomas. President Oaks' secretary called to say that Carl Hawkins was on the line. Dallin took the call and talked softly with Carl out of our hearing. When he hung up he looked out the window of his office at Mount Timpanogos, and I saw tears in his eyes. Then he smiled and said to us, "The Lord must really want this Law School. And He wants it to be a good one. Carl is coming!" We whooped and hollered as if Lancelot were coming to Camelot. From then on, the other positive dominoes fell into place, and Carl became our senior statesman and expert witness, attesting to all comers that this law school met the highest standards of professional quality.

Some people have attributed Carl Hawkins' decision to the formidable persuasive powers of Dallin Oaks and Rex Lee, and it is true that their presence at BYU was a positive factor for him. But Carl is a very private person who doesn't say much about his most personal feelings. Only years later did he tell me the real reason why he came. I share this now with his permission.

He knew his decision was pivotal for other people, but he honestly felt he should stay at Michigan. He "could not imagine a more satisfactory professional position" than the one he held. An unusually rational and orderly thinker, he made a list of the reasons for staying and for leaving. He talked with friends and family. But as the practical deadline drew near, he decided to fast and pray. The day he chose to fast turned out to be an exasperating day at school, leaving him no time for personal reflection. So he went to his evening stake presidency meeting, where he planned to discuss his question with his counselors. But pressing stake business took more than their available time. Finally Carl arrived home after his wife, Nelma, was asleep. He was tired and frustrated that his desire for prayerful meditation that day had gone unfulfilled.

Nonetheless, as he began praying in his bedroom, he reviewed his list of factors for and against going to BYU. Carl later wrote in his personal history:

> As I reviewed the list, I drifted into a state that I cannot adequately describe, involving something more than cognitive processes or rational evaluation. Each consideration was attended by a composite of feelings that could not be expressed in words but still communicated something more true and more sure than rational thought. Every consideration that I had listed in favor of going to BYU was validated by a calm, overwhelming sense of assurance. Each consideration I had listed for not going to BYU was diminished to the point where it no longer mattered.
>
> [For example,] I had been deeply concerned whether my valued colleagues at Michigan would be able to understand my reasons for leaving. Now that concern melted away or evaporated into the night mists. . . . If some did not [understand], that would be their problem, and it would not diminish me. I fell asleep, content that I had finally made the right decision.

Soon afterward Carl made that phone call to President Oaks.

The detailed interaction between reasoning and revelation in Carl's experience illustrates the Lord's words: "I will tell you in your mind and in your heart, by the Holy Ghost, which shall come upon you. . . . Now, behold, this is the spirit of revelation" (D&C 8:2–3).

"In your mind and in your heart"—so was the Law School founded on spiritual processes or rational ones? That question would have made no sense to President Romney, because he believed that you need to use your head, even when you end up following your heart. Of course spiritual processes are more important, but, to him, as to his great mentor, J. Reuben Clark, intellectual excellence was simply part of abundant spiritual excellence, and religious devotion was no excuse for professional mediocrity.

At the same time, the stories I've told show that the process of revelation played a bigger part in founding the Law School than some people might realize. I bear witness of the divine source and significance of that inspiration in the decisions to create the school, to appoint the first dean, and to bring together the first faculty.

I also saw the crucial role of reason, homework, and professional credibility in those same decisions and in the later fruits of the early decisions. Someone once said that the most important factor in solving human problems is the character and the competence of the people trying to solve the problems. When I remember those founding fathers—President Romney, President Oaks, Rex Lee, and Carl Hawkins—I am grateful not only for their faithfulness but also for their competence.

In the 35 years since that founding era, I have marveled time after time at incidents that confirm to me the value and purpose of having this Law School. I'd love to know all the stories of graduates and faculty whose personal life experiences together provide that confirmation. For now, I offer examples from just two legal fields.

First, Marie and I have just returned from four years in the Europe Central Area Presidency, where the process of obtaining legal recognition for the Church in some countries is still unfolding. I saw firsthand in countries like Slovakia, Moldova, and Serbia the fruits of Professor Cole Durham's decades-long effort to establish his professional credibility as an expert on international religious freedom. I also saw his work greatly augmented by Law School graduates who had developed the necessary skill and relationships to help make a difference.

I have reason to think that Cole's initial steps into the field of religious liberty came in answer to his own prayers as a young faculty member about how his scholarly work could someday bless the Church. The quality of his work over many years won the respect of other scholars on international human rights long before he knew that new governments in Eastern Europe and beyond would someday need and welcome the expertise he developed on religious liberty. I recently saw the power of his influence as missionaries who had earlier been asked to leave certain countries could now go back.

When the First Presidency first felt that spiritual nudge to create the Law School, how could they have known that within 20 years the Berlin Wall would fall and that Professor Durham's stature and capacity would help open the doors of many new nations to the Church?

The second example is family law. When I was a law student, family law was among the most boring topics in the curriculum. But since those days family law has become a raging battleground for some of the most significant legal and social issues of our time—issues in which the values of the restored gospel are very much at stake.

Just as the Brethren in 1970 couldn't have foreseen the fall of Communism, they also couldn't have known that family life would come under the relentless—often legally based—attacks we see today.

One way to answer those attacks is to take prophetic statements, such as the Proclamation on the Family, as the premises for our reasoning, then to look for the evidence and develop the rationale to support the premises—something anyone with legal training can do.

For instance, we are living through a revolution in the way people think about marriage. Traditionally the law strictly limited the terms on which people could either start or end a marriage, primarily because the law saw marriage as our culture's primary social institution. But in the 1960s both our courts and our culture began to see marriage more as a private choice than as a social institution. That opened the door to no-fault divorce, which helped make America the world's most divorce-prone society. That trend has led to what some call "the remarkable collapse of marriage," creating many unstable families and damaging America's children. Damaged children create a damaged society, and when enough families are dysfunctional, society itself is dysfunctional.

President Hinckley has said that the number of people hurt by crumbling families today is an international problem of urgent concern. In his words, "I think it is my most serious concern."

We are also now in the midst of a national debate about same-gender marriage. The First Presidency has taken a public position against such marriages, but once more they haven't provided a complete rationale. Yet those with legal training can articulate the developing rationale as it is needed. For example, we can see that the gay marriage movement is based on the same individualistic legal concept that created no-fault divorce in the late 1960s. When the law upholds an individual's right to *end* a marriage, regardless of social consequences (as happened with no-fault divorce), that same legal principle can be used to justify the individual's right to *start* a marriage, regardless of social consequences (as happens with same-gender marriage).

So what is the rationale for the principle that our marriage laws should be highly concerned with social consequences? And what evidence supports the proposition that same-gender marriage is harmful to society? In general, the rationale for both of these principles is in the overwhelming empirical evidence that children do far better by every measure of child well-being when they live with both biological parents.

This isn't the time to develop those comments further, but I'll share an image from family law that reflects a larger point. I remember a Japanese family law professor who came to BYU a few years ago after reading some of our faculty's scholarly work. He was troubled about the devastating effect of individualistic American law on Japan's traditional, family-oriented culture, but he had seen a much more encouraging approach coming from the work at our law school. He said, "The Americans beat us in the Second World War; why do they also have to inflict on us their movies and their laws?" After he had been on the campus in Provo a few days, he said, "This place is an island of hope in the land of the Apocalypse." He was especially curious about the students he had met. Speaking of them he asked, "What is it about these wonderfully bright and wholesome young people? Please tell me the secret behind all the shining eyes."

In an important sense, each student and graduate of this Law School has a duty to articulate wisely the secrets behind his or her shining eyes, whether in religious liberty, family life, or any other topic laden with gospel values. These are not mere political issues. In so doing, you will illustrate in your own way the inspiration in the founding of the Law School.

You will also demonstrate that inspiration by living lives of consecrated Christian discipleship. Whether in your family, your ward, your office, or your daily walk in life, the influence of your personal example of faithfulness combined with uncompromising competence will do as much as anything else to fulfill the Law School's original purpose. I've heard people from all across the country—senior partners in law firms, judges, political leaders, Church leaders, and others—speak with admiration about the students from this school. I've heard them over and over, and when I do, I think, "There's another example of why the creation of the Law School was an inspired idea."

Tonight's theme about acting by faith and understanding by hindsight is fundamental doctrine. When Nephi first began to build his ship of curious workmanship, the Lord told him,

> And I will also be your light in the wilderness; and I will prepare the way before you, [and] inasmuch as ye shall keep my commandments ye shall be led towards the promised land; and ye shall know that it is by me that ye are led.
>
> . . . After ye have arrived in the promised land, ye shall know that I, the Lord, . . . did deliver you from destruction; yea, that I did bring you out of the land of Jerusalem. [1 Nephi 17:13–14]

These words apply fully to our Law School of curious workmanship as we look back now and know that "it is by me that ye [were] led."

I hope we might draw on this doctrine in the very personal process of following the counsel of the Lord and His prophet, even when we don't always fully understand the reasons why they give us that counsel. The Law School's founding is a type and shadow of other moments when the Lord may give us a strong prompting or the First Presidency may give us a clear conclusion without supplying a fully developed rationale. Experience shows that in such cases, the rationale will become more clear with time.

That happened in founding the Law School, and it happens in our experience as members of a Church that is blessed by prophetic guidance. Sometimes in seeking spiritual help for our personal decisions, we simply cannot know everything that would fully explain why a particular path is the right one. So we must often walk by faith, without demanding a complete explanation before we will proceed. Thus, as Paul wrote,

> Cast not away therefore your confidence, . . .
> . . . that, after ye have done the will of God, ye might receive the promise.
>
> . . .
>
> Now the just shall live by faith: but if any man draw back, my soul shall have no pleasure in him.
> But we are not of them who draw back. [Hebrews 10:35–36, 38–39]

I am grateful that the Law School founders were not "of them who draw back." They were willing both to work and to wait to see the fulfillment of the Lord's promises about the value of having the school.

One implication of this theme is that as we gain experience in following the Lord and His servants, we will increasingly see reasons for the hope that is in us. Your legal training will bless you to see those reasons unfold after you have committed yourself to walk by faith in some demanding situation. As you see the emerging rationale and evidence, you can help others by articulating to them what you see. That is what good advocates do. As Peter wrote, "But sanctify the Lord God in your hearts: and be ready always to give an answer to every man that asketh you a reason of the hope that is in you with meekness and fear" (1 Peter 3:15).

I thank the Lord for the hope that is in me, above all for my hope in Christ. I testify that He lives and that He directs the work of His servants and answers the prayers of His people, at times communicating with them through "something more true and more sure than rational thought," even to very rational people, even law professors. I not only believe this, I know it. I know it both by a spiritual witness and because of what Helaman calls "the greatness of the evidences" (Helaman 5:50) the Lord has shown me—in my life and in the lives of many others, including our collective experience with J. Reuben Clark Law School. In the name of Jesus Christ, amen.

This Founders Day address was given to the J. Reuben Clark Law Society at Little America Hotel in Salt Lake City on August 30, 2007. Reprinted from the Clark Memorandum, *spring 2008, 20–26.*

Bruce C. Hafen received his JD from the University of Utah in 1967. He served as a law professor at J. Reuben Clark Law School 1973–1996, president of Ricks College (now BYU–Idaho) 1978–1985, dean of J. Reuben Clark Law School 1985–89, and provost of Brigham Young University 1989–1995. He is currently a member of the First Quorum of the Seventy.

The Essence of Lawyering in an Atmosphere of Faith

Kevin J Worthen

This is your first formal meeting as law students. It is my first formal greeting as a dean. All of us may be wondering exactly where we are, where we are headed, and how we got here.

It reminds me somewhat of the fellow who found himself in front of the Pearly Gates. As he started to go in, Peter stopped him and explained that it's not that easy to get into heaven. "You have to have done something good."

"Like what?" the man responded.

"For example," Peter asked, "were you religious in your life? Did you attend church?"

"No," said the man.

"Well," Peter asked, "were you generous with your money? Did you give some to the poor?"

"No."

"Were you a good neighbor? Did you help them?"

"Not really."

Peter, now a little exasperated, said, "Look, I'd like to help, but you've got to work with me. Surely, sometime in your life you did something good for someone. Now think!"

After a moment the man said, "There was this one time when I helped an old lady. I came out of a store and found her surrounded by a dozen Hell's Angels. They had taken her purse and were shoving her around, taunting and abusing her. I got so mad I threw my bags down, fought through the crowd, and got her purse back. I helped her to her feet and then went up to the biggest, baddest biker and told him how despicable, cowardly, and mean he was and spat in his face."

"Wow," said Peter, "that really is impressive. When did this happen?"

"Oh, about two minutes ago," replied the man.[1]

Things really can change quickly for us.

As I have tried to learn a little about the role of a dean this summer, I discovered that the first dean in a U.S. university was John Collins Warren, who was appointed dean of the Harvard medical school in 1816.[2] "His primary charge," you will be pleased to know, was "to be friendly and charitable to students."[3] Although the duties of a dean have expanded considerably since that time, I think that initial charge is still in place, and it is as a friend that I want to visit with you today, a friend who can hopefully provide some helpful perspective as we begin these new phases of our lives together.

You are a remarkably diverse group with a wide variety of experiences and backgrounds, as Dean Pullins has indicated. We appreciate the diversity each of you brings to the Law School. That diversity will enrich your law school experience more than you likely anticipate at this point. I wish to focus, however, not on your differences but on the two features that you all have in common: 1) You have all chosen to study law, and 2) you have all chosen to study law at J. Reuben Clark Law School.

There is more to these seemingly obvious common features than may initially appear. Let me start with the first. You have all chosen to study law. But what does it mean to study law? Some of you may anticipate that the study of law will involve a massive mind meld, that in the course of the next three years the faculty will, through some mysterious process, convey to you all the statutes, cases, and other legal rules you need to instantaneously answer any question a client might put to you. While you will certainly memorize a number of legal principles during the next three years, a brief tour of the library should quickly convince you that you are not going to have time to internalize all that material.

Some may believe that the study of law is principally a research exercise, that it consists of learning how to find the information you need in that massive library. Although research instruction will be part of your legal education, it is only part. And, while important, it is not the central part.

Many if not most of you are ahead of me on this point and already anticipate that sooner or later I will trot out the shopworn phrase commonly invoked on occasions such as this and inform you that the study of law ultimately consists of teaching you to "think like a lawyer." That comes closer to the truth, but that phrase involves more than may first appear. Moreover, even a more in-depth understanding of that concept does not completely capture the fullness of the study of law.

But let me start with that concept. What does it mean to think like a lawyer? First, let me clarify a couple of things it does not mean. Contrary to the impression given by the behavior of some lawyers, "[t]hinking like a lawyer does not mean being argumentative and contentious."[4] As one lawyer noted, "You don't need three years of law school to learn how to annoy and irritate others."[5] At the outset, therefore, I implore you not to confuse the untoward actions of some lawyers with the essence of lawyering. While there are times when you need to be zealous in your advocacy, being argumentative and contentious no more makes you a lawyer than shaving your head and wearing Nikes makes you Michael Jordan.

Nor does thinking like a lawyer consist of the ability to use clever rhetoric to take advantage of others. The story is told of a lawyer whose neighbor approached him and asked him how much he charged for his advice. "I charge $200 for answering three questions," the lawyer responded.

"That's awfully steep, isn't it?" the neighbor replied.

"Yes it is," said the lawyer. "Now what's your third question?"

A good joke, perhaps, but not good lawyering. Again, don't mistake the outward trappings for the essence of the matter. Thinking like a lawyer involves much more than merely being clever.

So, just what does thinking like a lawyer involve? The fact that there is no consensus as to the precise meaning of the term despite its constant use in describing what the study of law is all about[6] is telling in and of itself because it indicates how deep and multifaceted the concept is. However, I believe it is possible to provide a good insight into what is at the heart of thinking like a lawyer at this point and that such a glimpse will be helpful as you start the process of studying law.

As the words in the phrase suggest, thinking like a lawyer is primarily—though not exclusively—a mental skill, a way of thinking about things that is different from the ways you may have thought about things in the past. It is an analytical method of thinking that requires keen observation, logical reasoning, and a willingness to study matters in depth. It also involves an ability to explain conclusions and reasoning in a logical way.

At the ceremony celebrating the opening of this law school in 1973, then President Dallin Oaks, described part of the analytical and communicative skills that thinking like a lawyer involves. A person who thinks like a lawyer, he said,

> is a student of meaningful differences among apparently similar situations, and meaningful similarities among situations of no apparent connection. A person who is keen at spotting differences or similarities, discarding the unimportant ones, fastening upon the important ones, and being prepared to explain the reasons for their importance, is well along toward thinking like a lawyer.[7]

Because it involves a relatively new way of viewing things, thinking like a lawyer can be a challenge. You will be asked to forget some of the habits you have developed and to develop new ones. As one scholar observed, you will be "expected to learn a new language, a new way of looking at the world, and a new and distinct way of expressing [your] understanding."[8] That is quite a task— one that can be painful at times. But the results can be exhilarating. Karl Llewellyn expressed the process lyrically with the classic poem "The Bramble Bush."

> There was a man in our town
>   and he was wondrous wise;
> he jumped into a bramble bush
>   and scratched out both his eyes—
> and when he saw that he was blind,
>   with all his might and main
> he jumped into another one
>   and scratched them in again.[9]

Elder Oaks was a little more direct when he explained:

> Learning to think like a lawyer is rigorous and frustrating. But the objective is worth the effort. The study of law has few equals in disciplining the intellect. Properly conceived and executed, there is nothing mechanical or repetitious about it. It teaches its students a new way to think, and that skill is serviceable beyond the limits of the practice of law.[10]

While learning to think like a lawyer is the core component of the study of law, particularly the first year of study, the true study of law requires development of characteristics other than analytical and communicative skills. It requires an ability to understand and deeply care about the human condition. True legal education involves more than abstract analytical thinking because, at the end of the day, law has an impact well beyond its abstract conception. Law matters in the real world. In fact, law matters a lot in the real world, at both a macro and an individual level. Because law matters a lot, its study cannot be limited to mere mental abstract exercises.

At a macro level, law matters because it ultimately provides the framework for determining and protecting basic rights and obligations in a society. The status and destiny of nations is shaped by how law is created and implemented. It is, in my opinion, not a coincidence that in the founding of the most stable and productive democracy in the world, "[t]wenty-five of the thirty-six signers of the Declaration of Independence, thirty-one of the fifty-five members of the Constitutional Convention, and thirteen of the first sixteen presidents [of the United States] were lawyers."[11] The political structure on which we depend in the United States is largely attributable to the efforts of lawyers who not only thought deeply about the law but also understood its impact on the human condition.

The impact of law at a macro level extends well beyond political rights. A study by the Inter-American Development Bank in 2000 determined that of the more than $10,000 gap between the per capita income of developed countries and that of Latin American countries, approximately $6,000 was attributable not to demographic differences (such as the age of the population) or geographic differences (such as access to transportation and world markets) but to the fact that the public institutions in Latin America—the institutions in which the law plays itself out—were "less effective, predictable and transparent" than those in the developing countries.[12] In other words, if the legal system in Latin America operated differently, each person in those countries could potentially be $6,000 richer.[13] Law truly matters at a macro level.

Perhaps more important, however, law matters a great deal at an individual level. Because of the ubiquity and complex nature of law in our society, people are required to trust lawyers with their hopes, their dreams, their fortunes, their rights, and sometimes even their lives. How lawyers deal with those precious commodities is of extreme importance to those people. And, as lawyers really learn how to think like lawyers, how important it is that they learn to really care enough about the human condition that they will refine and use those skills to improve others' lives.

Because law matters a lot, it matters a lot that you have chosen to study law. At the dedication of the Law School building in 1975, President Marion G. Romney, who was not noted for hyperbole, stated that one of the reasons he worked to have a law school established here was that he had "long felt that no branch of learning is more important to an individual or society than law." Given the eternal perspective of its author, that statement is worth considerable contemplation. I repeat: "No branch of learning is more important to an individual or society than law."

Because the study of law matters a lot, it also matters a lot how you choose to study it. What you learn here in the next three years—not just the rules of law, not just research skills, and not just how to think like a lawyer, but the entire spectrum of law in both its intellectual and human aspects—will matter a lot to a lot of people. Thus, I urge you to study law with full intensity.

I urge you to study law the way that Domingo Catricura did. Domingo was a student in an Indian law class I team-taught at the University of Chile Law School a decade ago. Domingo was in his mid-50s at the time and was one of about 25 non–law students who, along with 30 law students, attended the class. The non–law students were invited to attend the course because they were leaders in various Mapuche communities, the Mapuches being the largest indigenous group in Chile. The course primarily covered the history of Spanish and Chilean interaction with the indigenous peoples of Chile and the first comprehensive Chilean Indian law, which had been enacted the year before. I provided a comparative perspective, contrasting the Chilean experience with that of the United States. As is typical of law classes in a civil law system, the course was highly abstract and theoretical.

Although not a law student and therefore without any hope of obtaining a law degree, Domingo attended the three-hour once-a-week class every week, occasionally making a 9- to 10-hour bus ride from his small native village of Chiuimpilli in southern Chile in order to attend. He was anxious to learn everything he could about law, even that which I attempted to convey about u.s. law in my somewhat rusty Spanish. Although of limited economic means, he purchased a small tape recorder to make sure that he thoroughly understood and remembered everything covered in the class. He also took copious notes, which he frequently reviewed with his two teenage children, who occasionally attended the class with him. He absorbed the information in class and wanted to discuss it after-hours.

For Domingo the theoretical aspects of the law were as important as the practical ones, because he sensed, early on, that in law the former drives the latter. And to him the latter mattered greatly, because he hoped it would help him maintain the cultural integrity of his native village. Thus, Domingo not only read the materials we covered, he reread them, contemplated them, and wrestled with them. Vivid in my memory is the image of Domingo with his tape recorder and notebooks in hand staying after a three-hour lecture in an unheated room in winter following a long day's travel in order to further discuss the day's subject.

Domingo, like you, chose to study law. He understood what that meant. I hope that you, like Domingo, soon discover that there is more to your choice to study law than you initially thought and that there is a lifetime of understanding and fulfillment ahead of you if you pursue it the right way.

Let me now turn to the second thing you have in common with one another: your decision to study law at this Law School. This fact may also be more significant than you originally thought—at least I hope it becomes more significant over the ensuing years. A little historical perspective may help initiate that developmental process.

The initial suggestion that law be part of the curriculum at a school sponsored by The Church of Jesus Christ of Latter-day Saints was first made in 1897 when Joseph Whitely, a teacher of civics and public law at the University of Utah, proposed a law course for the Provo branch of what was then the Brigham Young Academy.[14] The proposal went nowhere, because, in the words of former Dean Carl Hawkins, "the time was not propitious" for such an endeavor—in part because the school was in shaky financial condition.[15] I suspect, however, that part of the Church's reluctance to commit resources to the study of law had something to do with the suspicion that many early Church leaders shared about lawyers and the impact the study of law would have on those who undertook it.

When, in 1882, a young man named James Henry Moyle approached his stake president, Angus Cannon, and expressed his desire to go east to study law, President Cannon's reaction was quite telling. According to Moyle's biographer, President Cannon "brought his fist down on the counter of the office and said, 'You are going to hell!'"[16] Fortunately for Moyle, Angus' brother George, who was a member of the First Presidency, did not have the same misgivings, and he arranged for Moyle to meet with John Taylor, who was then president of the Church. When Moyle informed President Taylor of his desire, President Taylor replied that he too was "opposed to any of our young men going away to study law." It was, he stated, "a dangerous profession."[17] When President Cannon pointed out that the Church would always have need to employ lawyers, President Taylor eventually relented and agreed that it might be "all right for Moyle to go," but only after warning him in a blessing that if he did not constantly seek divine guidance in the endeavor, he would "go down and wither away."[18] The experience made clear that at least some of the leaders of the Church at that time had severe misgivings about the study of law. They might tolerate it as a necessary evil for a few, but they were not anxious to promote it.

Given that history, the decision of the Church leaders to establish this law school at this university, as well as President Romney's observation about the importance of the study of law, may take on new significance. Clearly something had happened to change the Church leaders' views about the study of law in the years between their interchange with James Moyle and the establishment of this school. While there were undoubtedly a number of things that contributed to that change, I believe one of the most significant was their close association with J. Reuben Clark Jr., the international lawyer and former member of the First Presidency for whom the Law School is named. Indeed, when explaining why he championed the cause to establish a law school at this university, President Romney (who was also a lawyer) indicated that one of his main motivations was "to have perpetuated on this campus the memory and influence" of President Clark.[19]

Thus, we owe more than we may think to J. Reuben Clark Jr. He not only provided a name for this law school, he also provided a model of the positive impact that the study of law could have on those with deep religious faith, and he did it in a way that I believe altered the view of many in the Church.

J. Reuben Clark was a man of enormous intellect. When he left Utah to study law at Columbia University in 1903, Reuben, stated Elder James E. Talmage, "possessed the brightest mind ever to leave Utah."[20] President Clark was also one who loved learning. "The eighth grade was the highest level [of schooling] available in [his hometown of] Grantsville, so after he finished it once, he repeated [it] two more years because he wanted" so much to learn.[21] He also understood that intellectual curiosity achieved its maximum impact when accompanied by hard work. "I have learned," he said in later years, "that work, more work, and more work is the only way in which one may acquire knowledge."[22] The result of this combination was evident in his law school years. In the words of one of his biographers:

> When given an assignment, [Reuben] did far more than brief a case or two in the customary fashion; he hounded the errant problem back into its past, rooting through precedents, commentaries, ancillary discussions, and anything else he could find. Then, amid a chaos of notes, citations, and open books piled high, he observed step by step how the matter came into being.[23]

In other words, J. Reuben Clark pursued the study of law with the same enthusiasm and energy that Domingo Catricura did. Thus, it is not surprising that President Clark excelled in law school to such an extent that upon graduation he was offered a position as assistant solicitor in the State Department in Washington D.C., thus commencing an illustrious career of public service that culminated in his work as U.S. ambassador to Mexico some 25 years later. J. Reuben Clark personified the qualities of intellect, love of learning, and hard work that make for a successful law student and lawyer.

Yet, I suspect it is not just the combination of these qualities but the presence of others not commonly associated with lawyers that most impress those who so fondly remember President Clark. One incident from his life provides an example. Many members of the Church are familiar with President Clark's statement "In the service of the Lord, it is not where you serve but how." Fewer, however, are familiar with the circumstances under which he made that statement.

From 1934 to 1951, President Clark was the First Counselor in the First Presidency of the Church, serving both Heber J. Grant and George Albert Smith. In 1951 when President Smith passed away, President David O. McKay became President of the Church, and, as was his right, chose his counselors. Many were surprised when he selected Elder Steven L. Richards as First Counselor and President Clark as Second Counselor. While they fully supported the decision, even some of the members of the Quorum of the Twelve were caught somewhat off-guard. President Spencer W. Kimball, then a member of the Quorum of the Twelve, wrote in his journal that he was "stunned" when he first heard the news.[24] Given his prominence in both the world and the Church, it may have been possible for President Clark to have been upset at what some perceived to be a "demotion." Instead, he himself presented the names of the counselors for a sustaining vote, and then, in his subsequent remarks, set forth his famous statement that "in the service of the Lord, it is not where you serve but how."[25] President Kimball recorded in his journal his view of that particular conference session: "[T]he congregation was breathless . . . [and] there were many tears throughout the congre-gation. . . . No one could tell if Pres. Clark carried any scars or injuries. . . . No complaint, no self-pity neither in act nor attitude."[26] President Kimball then added that J. Reuben Clark's "perfect reactions . . . did more . . . to establish in the minds of this people the true spirit of subjection of the individual to the good of the work . . . than could be done in thousands of sermons."[27]

Among other things, J. Reuben Clark was, for those who established this law school, living proof that the study and practice of law at the highest levels does not necessarily lead to arrogance and pride, nor to a weakening of faith or character.

At the dedication of this building in 1975, President Romney expressed a desire that "all faculty and student body members . . . familiarize themselves with and emulate [the] virtues and accomplishments" of J. Reuben Clark.[28] This and other charges given by Elder Oaks and President Romney at the establishment of the Law School and the dedication of this building provide a helpful perspective on the significance of your decision to study law at this law school. I commend those and other "foundational documents" for your reading and discussion in the coming year.

As important as was the impact of the life of J. Reuben Clark on the establishment and direction of this law school, I am convinced that the decision of the leaders of the Church to start this school and to continue to support it so generously did not rest solely on the view that it is okay, or maybe even desirable, for members of the Church to study law at a good law school. Having now become more familiar with the budget figures and the generous subsidy we receive from the Church, I can assure you that if the Church leaders' only goal was to provide a good legal education to 150 students of faith every year, they would have been money ahead simply to provide generous scholarships to deserving individuals, who could then attend one of many outstanding law schools that exist throughout the country. What the founders had in mind, as President Romney stated at the opening ceremony, was the establishment of "an institution"—"an institution in which [students could] . . . 'obtain a knowledge of . . . [the] laws of . . . man' in the light of the 'laws of God.'"[29] What they saw—or at least what I envision now—is not just a group of individuals studying law but a community of scholar saints—or to particularize it somewhat more and to put my individual spin on it—an intellectually and spiritually invigorating community in which the law can be studied and lawyers and leaders of diverse backgrounds can be shaped in an atmosphere of faith.

Let me briefly tell you what I mean by this. I envision—and ask you to help create—a community that is both intellectually and spiritually invigorating. On the intellectual level, I envision—and ask you to contribute to—a place where the classrooms, carrels, and hallways are filled with lively discussion about important topics, involving a wide variety of informed viewpoints. That will require that you fully prepare for class everyday, a task that will become more difficult as the months and years roll on. It will require that you attend and participate in academic symposia that occur at the Law School. It will require that you seek out and respect the views of others who disagree with you. It will also require that you be willing to not assume that you already know everything. For some that may be a real challenge. However, experience has shown that you are more likely to advance in knowledge if you approach topics with a good deal of humility. Justice Byron White, for whom I had the opportunity to clerk, noted on more than one occasion that the law clerks were "rarely in doubt and often in error," while the justices were "often in doubt and rarely in error." There is a great deal of wisdom in that observation, wisdom that can hold the key to a truly invigorating intellectual climate.

On the spiritual level, I envision—and invite each of you to contribute to—a community in which we can help one another work through and consider fully the very real spiritual challenges that the study and practice of law bring to the surface, a community in which we can help one another discover the soul-satisfying aspects of the study and practice of law, aspects whose absence in the modern bar causes so much disillusionment among lawyers today. More specifically, I invite you to take part in the professional seminar courses that are offered, the Spirit of the Law discussions that take place here, and the devotionals sponsored by the university. I also urge you to find ways to be of real service to others around you, both inside and outside the Law School and both inside and outside your faith. If you do that, not only will you improve spiritually, you will also help create a spiritually invigorating environment in which all can be edified.

Most of all, I envision—and ask you to contribute to—a community in which faith is an integral part of all we do. I have pondered much President Romney's charge that we create an environment in which the laws of man can be learned in light of the laws of God. Just how does the light of the laws of God help us as we study the laws of men? The full answer to that question will take years to discover, but I encourage you to begin that process now. Let me suggest two simple initial responses, by way of example of what President Romney may have had in mind.

First, the laws of God teach us that we are all children of heavenly parents and that each has divine potential within. That one truth ought to alter fundamentally the way in which you approach the study of law. It ought to provide more incentive to study earnestly so that you might be prepared to truly help those sons and daughters of God. It also ought to shape the way you interact with others both inside and outside the Law School as you engage in what is often a stressful process. As your patience wears thin at arguments that seem annoying or at actions that seem indifferent, the laws of God can remind us that, as C. S. Lewis has noted:

> It is a serious thing to live in a society of possible gods and goddesses, to remember that the dullest and most uninteresting person you can talk to may one day be a creature which, if you saw it now, you would be strongly tempted to worship. . . . There are no ordinary people. You have never talked to a mere mortal. . . . [I]t is immortals whom we joke with, work with . . . snub, and exploit.[30]

While the traditional study of law emphasizes the utilitarian importance of tolerating the views and differences of others, the laws of God require it as a manifestation of our love for God and His children.

Second, understanding the laws of God can help us see that the study of law is even more intellectually engaging and profoundly important than we might have ever imagined. Consider, for example, this provocative statement in Doctrine and Covenants, section 88, verse 34: "That which is governed by law is also preserved by law and perfected and sanctified by the same." I suggest that the unpacking of that statement could involve years of intellectual struggle and produce a plethora of soul-satisfying insights, a process, again, that I hope you begin at this school.

Operating in an atmosphere of faith also means that we create space to share spiritual feelings with one another from time to time. That will usually happen in private conversations. However, I want to follow the pattern set by Dean Hansen in his last public decanal pronouncement at graduation last spring and let you, my friends, know in my first public decanal pronouncement of my faith in our Heavenly Father. I believe with all my heart that He lives and loves each one of us with a love more profound than we can imagine. I believe with all my being that we are literally His sons and daughters, that he has placed us on earth to allow us to experience the things we need to experience in order to eventually enjoy the fullness of joy that He enjoys, and that because of the atoning sacrifice of His Son Jesus Christ, we can experience that joy despite our current imperfections. I also firmly believe that He has had a hand in the establishment of this Law School and that He cares about what each one of us does with the opportunity we have to study here.

What you do here in the next three years matters a lot. It matters to me. It matters to you. It matters to your families. It matters to countless others. It matters to God.

May we all be blessed as we go forward in this important and wonderfully joyous endeavor is my prayer in the name of Jesus Christ, amen.

This address was given to entering law students at BYU Law School on August 18, 2004. Reprinted from the Clark Memorandum, *fall 2004, 32–40.*

Kevin J Worthen received his JD from BYU Law School in 1982. He clerked for Judge Malcolm R. Wilkey of the U.S. Court of Appeals for the D.C. Circuit 1982–83 and for Justice Byron R. White of the U.S. Supreme Court 1983–84. He has served as a law professor since 1987 and was associate dean 1999–2004 and dean 2004–08 of J. Reuben Clark Law School. He is currently Hugh W. Colton Professor of Law and advancement vice president at Brigham Young University in Provo, Utah.

Notes

1. Thanks to Eldon Bott for relating this and numerous lawyer jokes to me.

2. Mimi Wolverton, Walter H. Gmelch, Joni Montez, Charles T. Nies, *The Changing Nature of Academic Deanship* 5 (2001) (citing Earl J. McGrath, *The Dean*, 70 J. OF HIGHER EDUC. 599, 600 (1999).

3. Wolverton, et al., *supra* note 1, at 5 (citing John S. Brubacher and Willis Rudy, *Higher Education in Transition* (1st ed. 1958).

4. Jack Chorowsky, *Thinking Like a Lawyer*, 80 U. DET. MERCY L. REV. 463–465 (2003).

5. *Id.*

6. David T. ButleRitchie, *Situating "Thinking Like a Lawyer" Within Legal Pedagogy*, 50 CLEV. ST. L. REV. 29, 32 (2003).

7. Dallin H. Oaks, [Opening Remarks], *Addresses at the Ceremony Opening the J. Reuben Clark Law School, August 27, 1973*, at 14 (1973).

8. ButleRitchie, *supra* note 6, at 33.

9. Karl N. Llewellyn, *The Bramble Bush* (1951).

10. Oaks, *supra* note 7, at 13–14.

11. Robert A. Ferguson, *Law and Letters in American Culture* 11 (1964).

12. Inter-American Development Bank, *Development Beyond Economics: Economic and Social Progress in Latin America*, at 26 (and Fig. 1.48).

13. *See* Kenneth H. (Buddy) MacKay Jr., *Corruption, Transparency and Rule of Law*, 13 FLA. J. INT'L L. 10, 12 (2000) (noting that "$6,000 a year is caused by the weakness in the rule of law and the prevalence of corruption").

14. Carl S. Hawkins, *The Founding of the J. Reuben Clark Law School*, BYU Studies 1 (1999).

15. *Id.*

16. Gordon B. Hinckley, *James Henry Moyle: The Story of a Distinguished American and Honored Churchman* 128 (1961).

17. *Id.*, at 130.

18. *Id.*, at 132.

19. Marion G. Romney, *Why the J. Reuben Clark Law School? Dedicatory Address and Prayer of the J. Reuben Clark Law Building* in DEDICATION: TO JUSTICE, TO EXCELLENCE, TO RESPONSIBILITY: PROCEEDINGS AT THE CONVOCATION AND DEDICATION OF THE J. REUBEN CLARK COLLEGE OF LAW 43–44 (1975).

20. Marion G. Romney, *Becoming J. Reuben Clark's Law School*, CLARK MEMORANDUM, Fall 1993 at 8.

21. David H. Yarn Jr., *J. Reuben Clark, Jr: A Role Model* 4 (1985) (address to Law School, March 28, 1985).

22. Frank W. Fox, *J. Reuben Clark: The Public Years* 35 (1980).

23. *Id.*, at 34.

24. D. Michael Quinn, *J. Reuben Clark: The Church Years* 122 (1983).

25. *Id.*, at 122–23.

26. *Id.*, at 124.

27. *Id.*

28. Romney, *supra* note 19, at 44.

29. Romney, *supra* note 20, at 7 (quoting D&C 93:53).

30. C. S. Lewis, *The Weight of Glory* 39–40, quoted in *C. S. Lewis: The Man and His Message* 150–51.

Lawyers and the Rule of Law

James D. Gordon III[1]

Welcome to J. Reuben Clark Law School. It is a privilege to study law, and it is a blessing to study it at Brigham Young University. The Law School's Mission and Goals state: "The mission of J. Reuben Clark Law School is to teach the laws of men in the light of the laws of God. The Law School strives to be worthy in all respects of the name it bears, and to provide an education that is spiritually strengthening, intellectually enlarging, and character building, thus leading to lifelong learning and service."[2]

One of the Law School's goals is to "[f]oster an enlightened devotion to the rule of law."[3] Respect for the rule of law makes a free society possible. Without it, society could devolve into tyranny on the one hand or anarchy on the other. Incidentally, my favorite bumper sticker says, "Anarchists for good government." Lawyers help the rule of law to function. It could not exist without them.

In 1972 five men broke into the Democratic National Committee Party headquarters in the Watergate Hotel in Washington, D.C. They were arrested. It turned out that they worked directly or indirectly for the Committee to Re-elect the President. The burglars were tried and convicted. As the result of the case, additional information came out. Eventually it appeared that President Nixon, some members of the White House staff, and the attorney general of the United States had attempted to cover up the break-in and to obstruct justice.

The U.S. Senate conducted an investigation. I remember as a young man watching part of the Watergate hearings on television. The Senate committee discovered that President Nixon had a tape recording system in the Oval Office. The special prosecutor and the Senate committee issued subpoenas for the tape recordings. President Nixon refused to provide the tapes, citing executive privilege. He released edited transcripts of some tapes, but he refused to release the actual tapes.

President Nixon asked that a federal district court judge quash the subpoena, but the judge ruled against the president.[4] The president appealed to the Supreme Court, which unanimously ordered President Nixon to produce the tapes.[5] Six days later President Nixon complied with the Supreme Court's order. Ten days after that he resigned the office of President of the United States. *Time* magazine called Watergate "the worst political scandal in u.s. history."[6]

The federal judge who presided over the trial of the Watergate burglars and who denied President Nixon's request to quash the subpoena was John J. Sirica. At the time he had a young law clerk named Todd. Many law students do a judicial clerkship, working for a judge for a year after graduation. Todd planned to take a job with a Washington, d.c., law firm after the end of his one-year clerkship. However, Judge Sirica telephoned the law firm and said, "I can't let Todd go. He is too valuable. He is the only person I can talk to."[7] So Todd stayed on longer as a clerk.

In April 2008, Todd—now Elder D. Todd Christofferson—was sustained as a member of the Quorum of the Twelve Apostles. When he was a law clerk, fresh out of law school, he helped the rule of law in our country to prevail.

In case you think that the rule of law is merely a jurisprudential abstraction, we might think about places in the world where the rule of law does not function well. In some countries, governmental corruption is common, and basic human rights are not protected. Some countries lack a stable legal system. Contracts are not enforced, commerce is underdeveloped, and people are not able to lift themselves out of poverty.

Lawyers help make the rule of law possible. They do so as law clerks, judges, legislators, and members of local governments. They do so by representing public entities and private parties, by enforcing the law, by defending against government overreaching, by resolving disputes, by solving problems, and by helping the civil and criminal justice systems to function. They counsel and help people to comply with the law, and they protect and vindicate people's rights. They are essential to a free society.

The Law School's goals mention "enlighted" devotion to the rule of law, suggesting that the law can be reformed and improved. Lawyers should work for legal reform and help to make a better society.

At the opening of J. Reuben Clark Law School, byu President Dallin H. Oaks said:

> The rule of law stands as a wall to protect civilization from the barbarians who would conduct public affairs and settle private disputes by power, position, or corruption, rather than by recourse to the impartiality of settled rules of law. Lawyers are the watchmen on that wall.[8]

President Oaks also said:

[A] lawyer's predominant professional loyalty should be to the principles of the law, not to the officials who administer them or to the person, organization, or other client in whose interest those principles are applied. A lawyer obviously owes a high duty of loyalty to his client, but the duty he owes to the Constitution and laws is higher still.[9]

Interestingly, President Oaks made those remarks in August 1973, during the same summer as the Senate Watergate hearings, when the rule of law was a topic of national focus.

Dallin Oaks himself had demonstrated that a lawyer's duty to the rule of law is greater than the duty to a client. As a young lawyer in Chicago, he was attending the deposition of an employee of one of his firm's clients. The witness began to lie under oath. Dallin Oaks got on the phone to the man's employer and said, "Either you get somebody down here who is going to tell the truth, or you get yourself another lawyer." Good lawyers have that kind of moral backbone.

The history of the Latter-day Saints illustrates the importance of the rule of law and of lawyers in upholding it. For example, on June 23, 1843, the Prophet Joseph Smith was arrested in Illinois by Sheriff Reynolds of Jackson County, Missouri, and another person. The charge was treason against the state of Missouri. Joseph Smith said:

[B]oth of them presented cocked pistols to my breast, without showing any writ or serving any process. Reynolds cried out, ". . . [I]f you stir I'll shoot. . . ." I answered, "I am not afraid of your shooting; I am not afraid to die." I then bared my breast and told them to shoot away. . . .

They then hurried me off, put me in a wagon without serving any process, and were for hurrying me off without letting me see or bid farewell to my family or friends. . . . I then said, "Gentlemen, if you have any legal process, I wish to obtain a writ of habeas corpus," and was answered,—". . . [Y]ou shan't have one." They still continued their punching me on both sides with their pistols.

. . . The officers held their pistols with muzzles jamming into my side for more than eight miles, and they only desisted on being reproached by [Stephen] Markham for their cowardice in so brutally ill-treating an unarmed, defenseless prisoner. On arriving at the house of Mr. McKennie, the tavern-keeper, I was thrust into a room and guarded there, without being allowed to see anybody. . . .

I again stated to Reynolds, "I wish to get counsel," when he answered. . . . ["Y]ou shan't have counsel: one word more, . . . and I'll shoot you." . . . I saw a person passing and shouted to him through the window, "I am falsely imprisoned here, and I want a lawyer."[10]

Ultimately, Joseph Smith was able to get a lawyer, and he obtained a writ of habeas corpus, which resulted in his freedom. One year and four days later he was murdered by a mob at Carthage Jail. If any people believe in due process of law, in protecting people's constitutional rights, and in the rule of law instead of mob rule, it should be the Latter-day Saints.

Lawyers have played a critical role in our country's history. Our nation could not have been founded without the efforts of lawyers like Thomas Jefferson, John Adams, James Madison, and others. Many of the signers of the Declaration of Independence and about one-half of the signers of the Constitution were lawyers. Lawyers serve in elected and appointed positions in federal, state, and local governments. In large measure, ours is a society led by lawyers.

Many lawyers serve ably and well; they are clear thinkers and speakers; they stand up for us and speak in our behalf. They also help resolve disputes, and good lawyers do this in a civil, peaceful, and noncontentious manner. The Savior said that "he that hath the spirit of contention is not of me."[11] He also said, "Blessed are all the peacemakers, for they shall be called the children of God."[12]

The study of law is important. Brigham Young said:

> If I could get my own feelings answered I would have law in our school books, and have our youth study law at school. Then lead their minds to study the decisions and counsels of the just and the wise, and not forever be studying how to get the advantage of their neighbor. This is wisdom.[13]

He also said, "[G]et up classes for the study of law."[14]

Law school is a great time of preparation for future service. I loved law school, and I would like to give you a few words of advice to help you enjoy it and to have a successful experience. I hope that in doing so I don't sound like Polonius to Laertes in Shakespeare's play *Hamlet*—especially when I remember what happened to Polonius. I'm not referring to the fact that he was killed behind the arras, but rather that over the centuries he has been portrayed by literally thousands of bad actors.

Polonius gave such sage advice as "[n]either a borrower nor a lender be."[15] I suppose that this is fine if you want to live in preindustrial England and build your own house out of mud and sticks. But if you don't care for a house made of wattle and daub, a mortgage is probably in your future—at least if we make it through the current mortgage crisis. And many of the people who will help resolve it will be lawyers. Since this is J. Reuben Clark's law school, I should add that although J. Reuben Clark himself borrowed money to attend law school, he paid the debt off as soon as he could.

First, you might recall a story about a person who was asked to build a house. He decided to cut corners, use cheap materials, and do a poor job. When he was done, the owner handed him the key, and said, "I'd like to give you this house as a gift." Attending law school is like that. You can work hard and do a good job. Or you can cut corners and do a poor job. Either way, you're the person who is going to live in the house for the rest of your life. Your legal education will enable you to serve others and to provide a living for you and your family. At the end of law school, we'll hand you the key. You will have created your own "house of learning."

Education is one of the few things for which people want to get less than they pay for. The reason is that, while tuition is one cost, an additional cost is the work required to learn. Some people love to learn. Others seem to think that they know enough already. It reminds me of the story of a man who was asked if he wanted to learn a foreign language. He replied, "If heaven intended us to learn a foreign language, then how come the Bible was originally written in English?"

If you decide not to work hard, not only will you cheat yourself, but also you will affect others who will depend on you, including your family and the people whom you will serve. I encourage you to work diligently, to learn a lot, and to prepare well for the future.

Second, keep up on class preparation, attendance, and outlining. There are people who have this philosophy: "The sooner you get behind, the more time you have to catch up. Do it today!" However, I recommend keeping up.

Third, have a study schedule. You could study all the time. I suggest that you have a time when you will study and a time when you will do other things. Decide on a schedule that works for you. Then try to stick to your schedule.

Fourth, break the sound barrier in class. Participate in the class discussion. You can improve your thinking and oral advocacy skills through practice. I used to be a slow thinker. Once I was attacked by a couple of snails. The police asked me about it, and I said, "I don't know; it all happened so fast." Then, in one law school class I had a professor who was a master of the Socratic method. Class discussion was exciting, and I decided that I wanted to get in on some of the fun. So one day I prepared extra well. I made a point in class. The professor didn't humiliate me. It wasn't so bad. The next time was a little easier. You can get better at thinking quickly. You can learn to respond when you're being challenged and a lot of people are looking at you.

Fifth, have things in your life other than law school. Take time for family, friends, outside activities, physical exercise, and recreation. It's also important to fulfill Church callings and to perform other service. These things are important for their own sake, they help you keep a broader perspective on things, and they help keep you balanced.

Sixth, take time to become friends with your classmates. These friendships can last throughout your whole life and can be one of the sweetest aspects of your law school experience. Your classmates are bright, good, and fascinating people. Take time to make friends.

Seventh, don't be afraid of failure. Perhaps you're the kind of person who looks in the mirror and says, "No success can compensate for being a total failure." Don't be afraid. Fear causes anxiety. All of you have the background and academic qualifications to succeed here. And you will succeed, if you do the work.

Eighth, remember that honest failure is better than dishonesty. How many of you have had a dream in which you're not prepared for an exam? You wake up, and you're so relieved to realize that it was only a dream. Well, now you're in law school, and the nightmare is real. If you get a failing grade, you can recover from that. You can take the class again. But if you cheat or plagiarize, and you get caught, you will be in serious trouble. You worked too hard to get here to jeopardize your future through dishonesty.

Even more important than the pragmatic reasons for being honest are the moral and spiritual reasons. You want to be a person of character. The pressures to be dishonest in law practice will be even stronger than they are in law school. Also, to do your best in law school, you need the assistance of the Holy Ghost, which means that you need to try to be honest. Try to avoid situations that create temptations for cheating or plagiarizing. One of those situations is procrastination. If you keep up and are prepared, you won't be as tempted to depart from your standards of honesty.

It's not a coincidence that two of the values I've emphasized are hard work and honesty. They are two hallmarks of the life of J. Reuben Clark, the member of the First Presidency after whom the Law School is named. They should also be hallmarks of the students and graduates of this law school.

Lastly, enjoy law school. It's exciting, fascinating, challenging, and fun. Sometimes law school has been compared to a besieged city: everybody outside wants in, and everybody inside wants out. But the secret to happiness is not to look forward to some future time when all your problems will be solved. The secret is to be happy today. There is joy in learning. Hopefully you will be lifelong learners.

In the Doctrine and Covenants, it says that "intelligence" is "light and truth."[16] It also says:

> Whatever principle of intelligence we attain unto in this life, it will rise with us in the resurrection.
>
> And if a person gains more knowledge and intelligence in this life through his diligence and obedience than another, he will have so much the advantage in the world to come.[17]

Note that it says that intelligence is obtained through diligence and obedience. That is an important principle. In the very next verses, it says:

> There is a law, irrevocably decreed in heaven before the foundations of this world, upon which all blessings are predicated—
>
> And when we obtain any blessing from God, it is by obedience to that law upon which it is predicated.[18]

If we do our best, God will strengthen us beyond our natural abilities and will bless us.

Law school is a wonderful time of preparation for the future. You have a mission in life. That mission has multiple dimensions. You have agency to choose your life's work and goals. Your legal education will help you to accomplish those goals and to fulfill your mission.

We're glad that you've decided to attend J. Reuben Clark Law School. I believe that being a student here is a position of trust. You will have certain responsibilities, and you will receive tremendous benefits. You will benefit from the contributions of faculty, staff, and tithe payers who make your legal education here possible. You will receive a heritage from students who have gone before you, and you will leave a legacy for the students who follow. Those contributions, that heritage, and that legacy are consecrated to an important and noble work. You are the most important part of that work. May the Lord bless you as you begin law school.

This address was given to entering law students at BYU Law School on August 20, 2008. Reprinted from the Clark Memorandum, *spring 2009, 2–7.*

James D. Gordon III received his JD from the University of California, Berkeley, in 1980 and clerked for Judge Monroe G. McKay of the U.S. Court of Appeals for the Tenth Circuit 1980–81. He served as associate academic vice president for faculty at Brigham Young University 1996–2000 and as interim dean of J. Reuben Clark Law School 2008–09. He is currently Marion B. and Rulon A. Earl Professor of Law at J. Reuben Clark Law School in Provo, Utah.

Notes

1. Apologies and thanks to Johnny Carson, Cliff Fleming, Doug Gordon, Elder Bruce C. Hafen, Gary Hooper, Steve Nelson, and Toby Threet.

2. BYU Law School, Mission and Goals of the J. Reuben Clark Law School (*quoting The Aims of a BYU Education*) <http://www.law2.byu.edu/mission_goals_learning_outcomes/missionandgoals.php> (accessed Dec. 19, 2008).

3. BYU Law School, Mission and Goals of the J. Reuben Clark Law School <http://www.law2.byu.edu/mission_goals_learning_outcomes/missionandgoals.php> (accessed Dec. 19, 2008).

4. U.S. v. Mitchell, 377 F. Supp. 1326 (D.D.C. 1974), *aff'd sub nom.* U.S. v. Nixon, 418 U.S. 683 (1974).

5. U.S. v. Nixon, 418 U.S. 683 (1974).

6. *Judge John J. Sirica: Standing Firm for the Primacy of Law,* Time, Jan. 7, 1974 <http://www.time.com/time/magazine/article/0,9171,910949-1,00.html> (accessed December 19, 2008). The facts regarding the Watergate scandal cited in my remarks come from Wikipedia, *Watergate scandal* <http://en.wikipedia.org/wiki/Watergate_scandal> (accessed Dec. 19, 2008).

7. Quentin L. Cook, *Elder D. Todd Christofferson: Prepared to Serve the Lord,* Ensign, Aug. 2008, at 10, 14.

8. Dallin H. Oaks, *Address,* in Addresses at the Opening Ceremony of the J. Reuben Clark Law School (Aug. 27, 1973).

9. *Id.*

10. Joseph Smith, 5 *History of the Church of Jesus Christ of Latter-day Saints* 440-42 (1964 ed.).

11. 3 Nephi 11:29.

12. 3 Nephi 12:9.

13. Brigham Young, 16 *Journal of Discourses* 9 (1967 ed.).

14. Brigham Young, 12 *Journal of Discourses* 32 (1967 ed.).

15. William Shakespeare, *Hamlet,* Act 1, Scene 3, 75 (1603).

16. D&C 93:36.

17. D&C 130:18–19.

18. D&C 130:20–21.

Index

Abraham, faithfulness of, 210
accountability, 162, 208
Acton, Lord, on power, 243
Adams, Abigail, influence of, 205
Adams, John
    on U.S. Constitution, 209
    supported America's founding, 205
adversary system, purpose and advantage of, 87, 103
advertising, by doctors, 132
agency, 124–125, 206–209, 235, 301
    and judgment, 25, 208, 251
    expression of God's love, 26, 72
Albania, law on religious freedom, 72
Albanian leader, on lining up for bread or to worship, 72
Alma
    and good seeds, 112, 164
    and obedience, 157, 164
    and power of word, 98
    asks questions, 159
    confronts stubborn issues, 124–125, 157
America
    founding of, 32–34, 203, 250–251
    liberty only lost by internal forces, 196
    promised land, 69
    sins of, atonement for, 202
American Bar Association, site visit, report on J. Reuben Clark Law School, 48
American Bar Foundation, 221–222, 240
American dream, 153–154, 188
American Inns of Court, 152
American Medical Association Council on Continuing Medical Education, 131
Ammon, a missionary, 73
Amulek, on lawyer unrighteousness, 234
Anacharsis, on the tongue, 97
angel
    brings gospel of peace, 104
    teaches King Benjamin, 84
anger, 43, 103–104, 108
Apollo 13, 95–96
Aristotle, on unexamined life, 239

army
    care for those who serve in, 199
    professionalism in, 177–178
    service motivation of, 176–178
Arnold, Thurman Wesley, on physicians, 132
arrogance, 75, 103–104, 137–140, 144–145, 177–178, 234
Article of Faith 8, 262
Article of Faith 11, 65
Ashton, Alan C., 256
assumption, 135–144
    definition of, 136, 145
athletes, 96–97, 135
Atkin, William F., 83
Atkins v. Virginia (2002), aftermath of, 28–29
Atonement, 6–7, 10–13, 25–26, 66, 93–94, 106, 163–164, 178, 202, 229, 271, 291
attorneys. *See* lawyers
avoidance behavior, 168
Azerbaijan, conference on religious freedom, 73

balance
    between work and home, 105–106, 130–131, 170–171, 219–220, 299
    in life, 88, 115, 168–169, 217
Bangerter, W. Grant, 4
baptism, 115
Barkan, Steve, on Jesuit law schools, 48
basketball, player, language of, 95–97
Bell, Derrick, on importance of conscience as lawyer, 50
Bell, Griffin, on duty of lawyers towards the law, 241
Berlin, Isaiah, quotes Immanuel Kant on man's imperfections, 138
Berman, Harold, on religion's importance in legal education, 49
Berra, Yogi, on humility, 86
Bismarck, Otto von, maxim on laws and sausages, 243
blessing, on James Henry Moyle to attend law school, 227–228
Bob Jones University v. United States (1983), 124